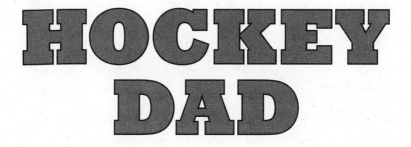

HOCKEY DAD

True Confessions Of
A (Crazy?) Hockey Parent

Bob McKenzie

WILEY

John Wiley & Sons Canada, Ltd.

Library and Archives Canada Cataloguing in Publication
McKenzie, Bob
       Hockey dad : true confessions of a (crazy?) hockey parent / Bob McKenzie.

ISBN 978-0-470-15939-2

     1. McKenzie, Bob. 2. Fathers—Canada—Biography.
3. Minor league Hockey—Canada. 4. Hockey—Humor. I. Title.

GV848.6.C45M34 2009   796.962092   C2009-901891-8

Production Credits
Cover design, interior design: Adrian So
Typesetting: Pat Loi
Author photos on jacket: Lorella Zanetti
Printer: Friesens

John Wiley & Sons Canada, Ltd.
6045 Freemont Blvd.
Mississauga, Ontario
L5R 4J3

Printed in Canada

1 2 3 4 5 FP 13 12 11 10 09

To Cindy, Mike and Shawn,
the best family a man could have.

To Mom and Dad,
I think you would have liked this.

To Graham Snyder and Hockey Dads who have
experienced the most painful loss imaginable,
bless you and your families always.

TABLE OF CONTENTS

PROLOGUE

IT WAS MY COLLEAGUE and good friend Gord Miller from The Sports Network (TSN) who first started it. The Crazy Hockey Dad thing, that is.

Through a good part of the 1990s and into the new millennium, Gord and I spent an ungodly amount of time together covering junior, pro and international hockey events all over North America and Europe. You spend that much time with someone—on planes, trains, automobiles and buses; in hotels, bars and restaurants; in arenas and TV studios—and you get to know that person really well. Maybe too well, much to my chagrin.

So as the proud father of two boys—Mike, an '86 (that's minor hockey slang for being born in 1986), and Shawn, an '89 (there you go, you've already got a big part of the lingo figured out)—Gord heard countless stories of the McKenzie boys' hockey-playing exploits, to say nothing of my foibles and follies as both a minor hockey parent and coach.

Armed with all that inside knowledge and dirt on the so-called Hockey Insider, Gord took great delight in inserting the needle. He and I would be in conversation with someone and at some point the fact that I had two boys playing minor hockey would come up.

When it did, Gord would raise one hand with the back of it facing me and, with the index finger of his other hand, repeatedly point towards me into the palm of his raised hand and say to our guest in a mocking tone with exaggerated enunciation as he rolled his eyes: "Cra-zee Hoc-kee Dad."

I would chuckle along with Gord and our guest—self-deprecation is one of my great strengths, though in the McKenzie household it's more a survival skill—and not wanting to be guilty of "he doth protest too much," I would put up only token resistance.

"I'm not really crazy," I would say. "Well, not too crazy."

On cue, like clockwork, Gord would keep it going: "What about the time you called the stick measurement?"

The guest's response was invariably the same. "You called a stick measurement in a kids' hockey game?" (Insert level of incredulity here.)

"Twice..." Gord would quickly add, smirking at me triumphantly and then pausing for effect, "...in the same game."

"Yeah, but..." I would say. Yeah, but...indeed. That was it, game, set and match. Thanks for coming.

I would vainly try to tell our guests the same thing I will try to tell you now: I am not a Crazy Hockey Dad. Well, not too crazy. Yeah, sure, there was that stick measurement game in Barrie when I was an assistant coach in Mike's atom year and, yes, it was two stick measurements in the same game, but only because the head coach of our team wouldn't give me the green light to call a third—damn you, Stu. But you can't possibly judge me and what I did that day until you have all the facts, the context and, most important of all, the knowledge it was payback for something really horrible the other team's coach did to our team a couple of years before that.

Why do I feel like I'm getting myself in deeper here?

For most people who see my face on television, they see Bob McKenzie, the Hockey Insider. That's fair. It's what I do. I go on TSN and radio stations across Canada and talk hockey, or I write about it on the internet. I have been doing this broadcasting thing, to varying degrees, for more than twenty years. I started in the newspaper business thirty years ago.

It's a great job—if you can call it a job—and I would say I'm passionate about it because I'm passionate about the game of hockey. It was that way when I was a kid, it was that way when I graduated in journalism from Ryerson Polytechnic Institute to my first full-time job, covering junior hockey for the Sault *Star* in Sault Ste. Marie, Ont.; it was that way in my nine years as Editor-in-Chief of *The Hockey News*, my six years as hockey columnist at the Toronto *Star*, another three years as Associate Editor of *THN*; and now that I've been wholeheartedly immersed in broadcasting as the Hockey Insider on TSN since the year 2000, it's been the same. I don't expect that will ever change.

But I will make one small distinction. Hockey Insider is what I do, not necessarily who I am.

The truth is, I see myself more as a Hockey Dad.

Crazy? Perhaps, though even on my worst days I would plead temporary insanity.

Yes, Hockey Dad is what I am. As passionate as I am about my job, as passionate as I am about hockey, I am even more passionate about my family. I have two fine sons who have grown up to be terrific young men and who share my obsession for all things hockey.

For as long as I have had kids, I have been leading this double life. My job is more or less all-encompassing. So, too, though, is being a Hockey Dad. But if you promise not to tell anyone, especially the good folks at TSN, I will let you in on a little secret—I've devoted at least as much time and energy (probably more) to being a Hockey Dad over the past twenty-plus years as I have to being a Hockey Insider.

Truth be told, it's a poorly kept secret, especially at TSN, where they have been unbelievably supportive in allowing me to do both.

Being a Hockey Dad hardly makes me unique. Hockey Dads are everywhere, all over the world, bless them. Most of them anyway. A lot of them get a bad rap. Hockey Dad has come to have sort of an ugly connotation to it, for all the obvious reasons for anyone who has followed some of the ridiculous things that have happened and continue to happen in hockey arenas across Canada and the United States.

So, why write a book on being a Hockey Dad?

Good question. Four answers come to mind.

One, to my knowledge, there has never really been a book written on this particular subject. (Maybe there's a message there.)

Two, to provide a public service for fellow Hockey Dads, and Moms, who perhaps can learn a thing or two from my mistakes before they make the same errors themselves (although scientific research suggests Hockey Dads truly are slow learners, if not incorrigible), as well as offer some broader insights on the good, the bad and the ugly of minor hockey.

Three, to celebrate—yes, celebrate, for the most part—a way of life, a Canadian way of life, an all-too-expensive way of life, where the game of hockey becomes the social and cultural epicenter for many families who can somehow wade through all the nonsense to find what is right and great about the game and its place in their hearts and their communities and their lives.

Four, therapy. Writing this book will be like a confessional and I suppose I'm looking for some form of absolution. It should be nothing if not a cathartic exercise. I look forward to cleansing my soul.

This story of Hockey Insider being Hockey Dad is primarily my story, and I am not going to lie, it's a deeply personal memoir. I would estimate almost all of the writing I've ever done in my professional career does not contain in it the word "I." It's never been my style to put myself in the story. This time, however, that is just not possible. This is a first-person account and there's no avoiding that. I have to tell you, though, it's not always easy to take a hard look at yourself in the mirror and spill it back out, good and bad, for all to see. And in order for me to tell my story properly, I cannot help but tell some of the story of my family—Mike, the '86, Shawn, the '89, and my wife, Cindy, the...well, the birth-date identification is really only for the kids.

Cindy is one of those people who prefers to keep a low profile and not make a spectacle of herself in any way, which isn't quite how I always conduct myself. Cindy is the mom of two boys who played hockey but not necessarily a Hockey Mom, if you know what I mean. It's not going to be possible for me to keep Cindy entirely out of the story but most of the time, when Cindy does appear, it will be as the voice of reason, level-headedness and sanity. And heaven knows it was often needed, though not always heeded.

Seriously, though, to accurately portray this Hockey Dad story, I must tell Mike's story and Shawn's story, too. In their own special ways, their respective minor hockey experiences are well worth telling. Mike has beaten the odds and experienced some highs and lows and navigated a long and winding road to become an NCAA Division One scholarship student-athlete at St. Lawrence University in Canton, N.Y. Shawn, meanwhile, has experienced more trials and tribulations—yes, even heartbreak—in minor hockey than any kid should have to deal with. But as much as the boys are talked about, ultimately the story being told here is *my* story and how I handled *their* experiences.

I desperately tried not to make this like a six-hour McKenzie home movie or a three-hundred-page family photo album, because there is nothing worse than having to sit through someone else's family history for hours on end. I like to think there are enough anecdotes, stories, insights, opinions and views that will strike a chord and resonate with so many who have lived the Hockey Parent experience for themselves or are perhaps just embarking on the journey now. In many cases, the personal experience of the McKenzies is nothing more than a jumping-off point for a much broader discussion of the issues affecting this level of the game.

Much of what you are about to read is culled and retold from memories—mine and many others'—because it's not like I was taking detailed notes in the rinks all those days and nights. And let's be honest, the mind and memory sometimes have a funny way of playing tricks on you, so if there are any discrepancies or factual errors in the retelling in any of what follows, they are my errors and mine alone. But the goal here is to strive for a true and honest picture. Trust me, there will be a lot of laughs, because what is minor hockey if not a good time, but believe me when I tell you there will also be tears and heartache, too, because not all minor hockey stories are destined to have a happy ending.

Throughout it all, perhaps I can even provide a compelling argument for my pal Gord that proves once and for all I am not a Crazy Hockey Dad. There are, after all, perfectly rational explanations for that time the police escorted me out of the rink at Mike's game or the time I camped out in an arena lobby for forty-eight hours to get Shawn registered for house league, to say nothing of that stick measurement...or two. No, really, there are.

Hockey Insider? Yes.

Hockey Dad? Absolutely.

Crazy? You will be the judge.

Mostly, though, I hope you enjoy reading this and take as much from it as I did from writing it and living it.

Bob McKenzie
May 29, 2009

IT WAS ALWAYS IN THE (HOCKEY) CARDS

WHAT YOU HAVE TO UNDERSTAND is there was never any doubt. None whatsoever, at least not in my mind. When my wife, Cindy, and I found out we were going to be parents for the first time, I just knew we were going to have a boy. A boy who would love hockey. A boy who would play hockey. It wasn't so much wishful thinking as it was a rock-solid assumption.

Now, I know how that sounds. I mean, I do get it. Any time a child is born there's a fifty-fifty chance it's going to be a boy. Or a girl. It could go either way and it's not something you can actually control. Besides, at the end of that glorious day when he or she does arrive, the only thing that ultimately matters is that the baby and mother are healthy.

So, yes, I will admit it was possible we could have been the proud parents of a baby girl and had that happened it would have been no less a day of joy and wonder for us and we would have loved that little girl to pieces. Hey, some of my best friends have daughters.

But it wasn't happening, not to us, and I just knew it. We were going to have a boy. And we did. He was going to love hockey. And he did. He was going to play hockey. And he did.

Michael Robert Thomas McKenzie, or Mike as we like to call him, was born in Toronto on April 29, 1986, so if one were trying to pinpoint exactly where and when I became a Hockey Dad, I suppose that would be the day.

I know what you're thinking. Just because a newborn baby is a boy is no guarantee he will grow up to like or play hockey and, yes, I get that too. I understand a boy could grow up to love baseball or playing the piano or solving math problems more than hockey.

That is, if, in my case, he were adopted.

I like to believe that if Mike had grown up to not like or to not play hockey I would have been okay with it, that I would have embraced whatever interests he pursued. That's what I like to think anyway. But just as I knew we were going to have a boy, I just knew we were going to have a boy who liked hockey. I was not disappointed.

Far greater minds than mine have insight as to what degree we are products of our environment versus inherited traits versus free will, but I can only tell you this: If a child's surroundings are indeed a great influence on how he or she turns out, Mike had no chance to be anything but hockey crazy, just like I was as a kid.

One of the first truly traumatic events of my life, at least that I can recall, was when, as a five-year-old, I went to my kindergarten class one day at Bendale Public School in Scarborough, Ont., with my complete set of O-Pee-Chee hockey cards (1961–62 series) only to forget them at school when I went home. When I went back the next day to get them, they were gone, never to be found again. Now, getting a complete set of hockey cards was no easy feat. On his way home from work each night, my dad would stop at the variety store down the street from our house and, without fail, pick up five packs of O-Pee-Chee hockey cards, at five cents per pack (which was no small expenditure in our household). I would greet my dad at the door. Every night. I can still smell and taste the pink stick of gum, see that white powder all over the cards as I looked through to see whether each card was a "got 'em" or a "need 'em" and what trades I might make the next day at school to get the complete set. Then to get a complete set, only to lose it? I cried. I seem to have gotten over the fact that on the first day of kindergarten that same year, I threw up all over poor Mrs. Malone's blue dress but I still can't reconcile the loss of that complete set of hockey cards.

So you get the point. If one is a product of his environment, Mike never had a chance.

He was just thirty-two days old when we made our first father-son hockey road trip—to the 1986 Ontario Hockey League midget priority selections, better known as the OHL draft, at North York Centennial Arena. Little did I know at that time that sixteen years later Mike would actually be chosen in the OHL draft and, as fate would have it, some of the truly lousy things that happened to Mike as a hockey player occurred in that very same arena.

Suffice to say that when your father is the Editor-in-Chief of *The Hockey News*, as I was at the time, you are going to be surrounded by hockey in one form or another as you grow up. And so it was for Mike, which apparently was fine by him, right from an early age.

Mike was crazy for all things hockey. As soon as he could walk, he had a mini-stick in his hand, batting around a ball and chasing after it. From the time he could talk, so much of his conversation revolved around hockey. Cindy has what I would call only a minimal or passing interest in professional hockey, but she knew that if she wanted to get toddler Mike to brush his teeth at night, she would say, "Mario Lemieux brushes his teeth every night..." So Mike would brush his teeth every night, as he would say, "like Mario Le-Moo."

When he got to the age where he liked to draw pictures, they were invariably pictures of hockey players. Mostly goalies. He loved to draw goalies. And NHL team logos. He would sit at the kitchen table for hours at a time, drawing hockey picture after hockey picture. We still have a huge Tupperware bin full of his drawings from those early years. I'm not sure how many kids, at the age of five, drew a crayon picture of Detroit defenseman Yves Racine, but Mike did. He had a particular fascination with Stephane Richer and Patrick Roy and spent hours with his Panini sticker book, looking to get a complete set. Sound familiar?

If I said a city name in the NHL, he would say the team name. If I pointed at an NHL logo, he would name the city and the team. He would get them all, too, although for some reason the Hartford Whalers were always the "Hartford Blakers." He would ask question after question and they were always about hockey. I loved that he loved hockey, but this kid would wear even me down.

His favorite song was "Big League" by Tom Cochrane. Hockey, hockey and more hockey. Mike was hockey mad, just as I figured he would be. Hockey-mad Mike; Hockey-mad Dad.

Lucky Cindy.

BREAKING THE ICE
It's Never Too Early

ONE OF THE MOST FREQUENTLY ASKED questions by neophyte Hockey Dads is at what age should Junior hit the ice for the first time—when is a good time to learn to skate?

As a proud Canadian, and an incurable wise guy, I like to say, "Well, the child should first be able to walk, but that's not necessarily a hard-and-fast rule."

Remember, we're not talking here about actually playing hockey in an organized form or even playing hockey at all. We're talking about what used to be one of the rites of winter passage for Canadian kids, especially in the good old days when it was no big deal to find an outdoor skating rink or pond close to home.

To the best of my recollection, I was probably four years old when my dad first took me to the local outdoor rink—no boards, just a rink—at Bendale Public School to see if I would be able to stand up. And really, that's all it needs to be. The first skate isn't about taking skating lessons or playing a game of hockey. It's not about structure; it should be, if at all possible, a social event for the whole family that underscores what it is to be a Canadian—ignoring how cold, windy and snowy it is and thumbing your nose at Old Man Winter. Go out as a family, note the momentous occasion of Junior's first attempt to skate, laugh uproariously at his or her first pratfalls, pick 'em up and go have hot chocolate, or maybe something a touch stronger.

For the record, Mike was two years, nine months and twenty days old when he first put on skates, but hey, who's counting? Some might think that's too young, but like I said, he could walk, why not try skating? Seriously, what's the point of waiting? If he didn't like it, he would tell me.

It was Saturday, February 18, 1989, when Cindy, who was four months pregnant with Shawn at the time, Mike and I took a drive down to the frozen marshlands near the mouth of Duffin's Creek, just a stone's throw north of Lake Ontario in Ajax. It was cold—blistering cold, with a wicked wind, the kind that feels like it could cut you in two, howling in off the lake.

We know this was the exact date of Mike's first time on skates—double-runner bob skates, mind you—because we have the video evidence to prove it. Actually, the video date and time code show us skating on the morning of Sunday February 19, 1989, and while it's marked on the video cassette as Mike's first day on skates, I know better. The truth is it was only after we were coming back from Mike's actual first skate on Saturday afternoon that I stupidly realized we should have captured this grand occasion on the family camcorder. When we went out the next day to skate again, we took the camera, filmed it for posterity's sake and wrote on the tape "Mike's first time on skates." Not quite, but close enough.

Mike loved it and I must admit I loved that he loved it. The video shows him all bundled up in a green and red snowsuit, wearing a toque under my old Cooper SK10 red helmet that I got for Christmas as a peewee—that, by the way, was a classic bucket...think Steve Shutt, Dave Gardner and Billy Harris in their Toronto Marlie days—with his snowsuit hood pulled up over the helmet and a scarf wrapped around his face.

I put on his skates—they just strapped onto his little winter boots—and gave him the left-handed hockey stick I had cut down for him. Wait a minute, you're saying, didn't I just say those first steps don't need to be about hockey?

True enough, but the boy said he wanted to play hockey. Who am I to spoil his fun?

I immediately asked Mike if he was cold. He said yes. I asked him if he wanted to go home. He said no. I was thrilled, not that we were going home if he said yes anyway. I may have been guilty of playing to the camera a little on that magnanimous but wholly insincere offer to go home. I put on my skates. Cindy manned the video camera and we were out there, considering the temperature and wind chill, for a good long time, the better part of an hour. He would whack a puck with his stick and chase it. He'd fall down occasionally. He'd get up and do it all over again.

I had kind of expected it might be a failed exercise; that perhaps it was too early to put him on skates, that he would cry when he fell or say he was too cold to skate. But he didn't cry when he went down and he didn't complain about the cold. Therein lies the answer of when you should put your child on skates for the first time—the sooner the better. If he or she doesn't like it, they will let you know. If it's the wrong time, you can try again, in a week or a month or a year. Whatever. But if they do like it, well, you're off to the races.

And we were.

3 FAMILY EXPANSION AND OUR LITTLE NERD

LEST YOU GET THE IDEA the McKenzies led a one-dimensional life that revolved solely around Mike's love of hockey, I must tell you there were other significant events in our lives at that time which are central to the telling of this story.

About five months after Mike's first time on skates, July 11, 1989, to be exact, Cindy, Mike and I welcomed Shawn Patrick McKenzie into the family. Another boy. I will spare you the "I told you so" on that one. Been there, done that. I was thrilled to add another player. You will get to know Shawn and his story intimately in due course.

Life started becoming a lot more chaotic in our household. I've always believed that when it comes to taking care of kids, one child equals one but two does not necessarily equal two. When you have more than one, it's like the little darlings work to a higher power. They wear you down exponentially. One is one, two might as well be four and, given how much time I spend on my job, Cindy and I never had any intentions of finding out what three equalled, but I'm guessing nine. Bless those who go for it, but one thing you can say about us—we knew our limitations.

Big changes were happening on the career front for me, too. In January of 1990, in addition to my fairly onerous responsibilities at *The Hockey News*, I started doing color commentary on TSN's weekly Canadian Hockey League (CHL) broadcast on Sunday nights, featuring a game a week from January right through to the Memorial Cup in May. I was already working a lot at *THN*—sixty-plus hours a week managing a staff and a couple of publications—and now I was taking on work that required many more hours of preparation to say nothing of the travel and time away from home.

If the CHL game of the week was in the West, and on average it was once every three weeks, I would work twelve-hour days Monday to Friday at *THN* and then fly out of Toronto around noon on Saturday to go to Medicine Hat or Lethbridge or Seattle or Portland or wherever. I would usually be able to catch a red-eye flight out of Vancouver or Edmonton or Calgary on Sunday night because I absolutely had to be back in my office at *THN* first thing Monday morning, which was the long, difficult (often eighteen-hour) day when *THN* was published.

It was a lot for me and no doubt even more for Cindy to handle, given she had a busy three-year-old, a demanding sixth-month-old, and her husband was off gallivanting across the continent.

All of this work I was doing at *THN* and TSN was putting a serious crimp in my efforts to be a Hockey Dad to Mike. Certainly on the Saturdays when I was at home in that first few months of 1990, Mike's hockey activities were limited primarily to playing ball hockey with me in the basement (which we did a lot) or me taking him public skating—he had graduated to real skates as opposed to the bobs—at the Pickering Recreation Complex.

He loved to go pleasure skating with me but would get bored pretty quickly—round and round we would go—and say he wanted to go home, but I would appeal to his competitive instincts and bet him he couldn't beat me around the rink. Off he would go, pumping away to beat Dad. I'd play that delay-and-distraction card as many times as I could before he finally rebelled and made it clear he was outta there. Fine by me, he was skating well, he enjoyed it. It was all good.

———— ● ————

Just before Mike was set to launch his so-called "organized" hockey career that fall of 1990, at the beginning of his junior kindergarten year, something happened that in a million years I never would have expected.

Mike got glasses.

No big deal, right? *Au contraire.*

Mike wasn't the least bit happy to get the news that he needed to wear glasses as part of everyday life—he was diag-nosed with astigmatism—and for me it was like being hit in the face with a bag of doorknobs. It never occurred to me a four-year-old might need glasses.

It's a funny thing about glasses, isn't it? I mean, on one hand, it's not really that big a deal. When you think of your kid being diagnosed with something, well, astigmatism and need-ing glasses is nothing. I know that. But it does change their appearance and, who's kidding who, not necessarily for the better. The perception, amongst kids and with a lot of adults, too, is that glasses equal nerdiness. Glasses on little kids are perceived as a sign of weakness.

On every level, it's an absurd and ridiculous notion and the ultimate in superficiality, but it was as plain as the glasses on Mike's face. Without them, he was a cute kid. With them, still sort of cute but, uh, what's the word I'm looking for? Poindexter? Yeah, that's it. If that view is held generally in society, and I would suggest it is, multiply it by ten in the athletic world. Like all good parents, we went to great lengths to convince Mike wearing glasses was no big deal. Cindy found a children's book that dealt with this very subject—*Tipou and His New Glasses*—and read it to Mike. Which is all well and good, but last time I checked, Tipou, a little French mouse, didn't have to play hockey or lacrosse wearing glasses.

I am no child psychologist but I would say now that Mike getting glasses had an impact on his self-image at that time. I am not sure I noticed it as much then, but looking back, I really think he was a little different after he started wearing the glasses, a little more self-conscious, a little more introverted with people outside of our family.

I only brought up Mike's glasses because it's funny how many times over the years in hockey they became part of the story or, for some time, even his identity. As a quick aside, I am firmly convinced that Mike's glasses were the catalyst that prompted him, the summer after he turned eighteen, to get a (hockey-oriented) tattoo on his left shoulder and bicep. I am not going to lie, Cindy had a tough time with that one. Me, I wasn't sure what to think, but I will tell you this: I'm blaming the damn glasses. A classic case of compensation if ever there were one. All those years of perhaps being perceived as a little nerdy, the first chance Mike had, he was going to show his bad-ass side. And now he has, as the kids like to say, "a sweet tatty" to prove it.

4 "I HATE LARRY MARSON" AND DISSING MR. HOCKEY

WHERE WE LIVED—IN PICKERING, Ont., the first community east of Metropolitan Toronto—was probably as good as, if not better than, any place for Mike to begin his minor hockey journey in the fall of 1990. While the Pickering Minor Hockey Association House League didn't start with actual game competition until a player was six years old—there was a Squirt Division, which combined six- and seven-year-olds—it had programs in place to accommodate kids as young as four and five.

They called it the PMHA hockey school. There was one session, an hour a week, for four-year-olds and another session for five-year-olds. They ran them back to back on Saturday afternoons at Don Beer Arena. It was obviously modeled on the Hockey Canada Initiation Program, which was introduced in 1986. The Initiation Program was in response to the criticisms that Canadian hockey was too structured too early and that kids who couldn't even skate were being dropped into game situations and never touching a puck, never developing their skills. The Initiation Program was a blueprint for a less structured, more sensible approach to introducing first-time players at young ages to the fundamentals of the game (skating, stick handling, etc.) in a fun, positive atmosphere devoid of pressure associated with winning or losing.

The PMHA had a couple of brothers, young guys in their twenties, who oversaw the hockey schools and they did an excellent job. These guys knew what they were doing. They asked up front for as many parent volunteers as wanted to be involved. This, of course, was right up my alley and I was out there with Mike each Saturday, at least the ones when I wasn't out of town working.

Mike loved it. So did I. Mike was fully decked out in his Montreal Canadiens gear—red Habs sweater, red, white and blue gloves, blue pants, Canadiens socks and a white CCM helmet, which is kind of funny for a Toronto-area kid. But since I had no real rooting interest for the Leafs or any team in the NHL, Mike just sort of formed his own likes and dislikes as far as teams. At that time, for whatever reason, Mike was absolutely loopy for Stephane Richer, who was reeling off fifty-goal seasons for the Canadiens, and netminder Patrick Roy.

As good as the PMHA hockey school was, and it was outstanding, I didn't think it was quite enough. One hour a week? Nope, not nearly enough. Now, as "crazy" as I might be about hockey, I am also one of those people who believes if you want to do well at anything—it's not enough to just do it; you should try to excel—you go the extra mile.

Welcome to the Larry Marson Power Skating School.

Like a lot of people, especially the really crazy Hockey Dads, I believed, and still do, that the foundation for everything in hockey is in the skating. So it only made perfect sense to me that while the hockey school was good, an extra hour a week of specialized instruction in just skating was exactly what Mike needed.

Larry Marson was a good college player who played at Ohio State. Larry is the younger brother of Mike Marson, who became the first black player to be taken in the first round of the NHL draft when he was chosen by the Washington Capitals in 1974. Larry was teaching skating to kids of all ages, although they didn't have to wear hockey equipment or use a stick. It was just helmet, gloves and skates. It was held Saturday at 8 a.m. This, I decided, was precisely the kind of basic training Mike needed. Awesome, I was pumped.

There was just one problem—Mike didn't seem to share my enthusiasm. In fact, he hated the entire concept, every minute of it. Once he realized he was going to a skating school where he didn't get to carry a hockey stick or wear hockey equipment, it was a little too much like work for him. Larry and his group of instructors were terrific. But Mike quickly decided it wasn't "fun."

We would get up early every Saturday morning and drive to the arena and most weeks Mike would start whimpering in the car on the way there. "I don't wanna go to Larry Marson," he would say. Occasionally, the odd tear would even roll down his cheek. I would try to pump him up, tell him, "It's fun, you will enjoy it once you get out there." He would do it, reluctantly, but on the way home in the car, he would pout, grimace and tell me, "I hate Larry Marson."

This scene would, more or less, play itself out week after week all winter long and you might be wondering what kind of monster makes his four-year-old go to power skating when the kid has made it clear he doesn't want to. That kind of monster would be me, and even now, upon sober second thought, I am not about to relent.

I am a big believer, for the most part, in once you start something, you finish it. As long as it doesn't apply to me, of course (I lasted six weeks at Wilfrid Laurier University in my first year of post-secondary education). So unless Mike absolutely refused to get into the car with me on those Saturday mornings, he was going to finish that first year of Larry Marson Power Skating. Mike was still loving to go to the PMHA hockey school on Saturday afternoons, so it's not like the power skating was so turning him off that he didn't want to play hockey. I was thinking he would eventually buy in.

Hey, it could have been worse. My parents put me in piano lessons...and we didn't even have a piano. So as far as Larry Marson was concerned, Mike was going to finish out the year. Tears on the way there? Not nearly good enough. Suck it up, sonny boy. Life is tough. Besides, it's not like he wasn't getting some perks along the way.

Even before that 1990–91 season, four-year-old Mike had already been to his first Stanley Cup final game. I had Cindy and Mike—Shawn stayed home with family because he was just ten months old—fly into Boston for Game 2 of the Bruins–Edmonton Oilers 1990 Cup final. Two funny things happened on that trip that I bring up when I want to embarrass Mike a little.

The first was that Mike, wearing his No. 4 Bruins sweater I had made up for him with MIKE on the back, found the crowd noise so loud at the old Boston Garden he told Cindy he wanted to leave the arena and go back to the hotel before the first period had ended. Mike just shakes his head at that now.

The second was Mike's first and very memorable meeting with Gordie Howe. I ran into Gordie in the Boston hotel lobby just as Mike and I were heading to the Garden for the game-day skates. Mike was eager to get to the rink because, a day earlier, Bruin defenseman Greg Hawgood had been nice enough to give Mike a stick at practice, and Mike was all revved up to go back to see his new hero, Greg Hawgood. But when I saw Gordie Howe, I stopped to chat. I introduced Gordie to Mike and Mike to Gordie. Gordie being Gordie, he was terrific with Mike, but Mike was starting to get impatient, tugging on my arm.

"C'mon, Dad, let's go," Mike said.

"In a minute, Mike," I responded.

"Dad," he pleaded. "I want to go to the rink; I want to see some hockey players."

Gordie's eyes were twinkling.

"You want to go see some hockey players, do you?" Gordie said to Mike.

"Yup," Mike said to Mr. Hockey.

"Well, it's too bad there's no hockey players around here, eh, Mike?" Gordie said as he winked at me. "You better get going."

Good job, Mike, way to diss Mr. Hockey.

It was in the middle of that season of Larry Marson that Mike also got to go to the 1991 World Junior Championships in Saskatoon. It would be the first of seven trips to the World Juniors over a ten-year period for Mike, so it's not like I felt the Larry Marson experience was going to scar him for life.

As it turned out, though, that was his first and last year of Larry Marson Power Skating.

The irony of all of this will become painfully apparent. Let's just say that if there is one part of Mike's game that was, and still is, found wanting, it would be his skating. I still like to give him the gears about it today:

"You should have stayed at Larry Marson."

5 BIG CHANGES AND THE GRAND DECEPTION

THE SUMMER OF 1991 brought big changes for the McKenzie family—we decided to move, I changed jobs, and Mike started playing "organized" sports.

Our house in Pickering was nice enough but we were thinking of getting an in-ground pool at some point and we had neither the space nor the privacy we really wanted to do it properly. So we sold the place in Pickering, moving in June of 1991 a little farther east to Whitby and buying a slightly bigger house with a slightly bigger backyard and a ravine lot. We knew the house well enough, too, because we bought it from a very good friend—NHL player agent Rick Curran, who was moving his business and his family to Philadelphia.

I first got to know Rick as an agent when I was starting out in the business because he represented Cindy's brother, John Goodwin, an outstanding OHL player who won rookie-of-the-year honors in his first junior season (1978–79) and then won the OHL scoring championship in his final year (1980–81).

Rick and I just seemed to hit it off in our dealings and to this day, we remain the best of friends. One of the reasons for that, I'm sure, is that Rick is also a Crazy Hockey Dad. Rick's son Michael is an '84, who played his minor hockey with the Philadelphia Junior Flyers. Michael Curran went on to have an outstanding college career, playing club team hockey and setting all sorts of records at the University of Rhode Island.

It's funny how one becomes a Crazy Hockey Dad. Michael was born late afternoon on December 31, 1984, and at that time, Rick was absolutely thrilled to get the child tax credit on the final day of the year. Penny wise, pound foolish, as it turned out. It wasn't too long after that Rick realized December 31 is just about the worst day for a hockey-playing youngster to be born because he's guaranteed to be the youngest player, almost by a year in some cases, on every team he plays on. We still laugh about it today, that if Rick knew then what he knows now, his lovely wife Lisa would have been in the hospital pushing Michael into the world and Rick would have been pushing right back, trying to delay Michael's arrival until the clock struck midnight to make him an '85 instead of an '84.

At roughly the same time we were moving from Pickering to Whitby, I was leaving *The Hockey News* after nine years as Editor-in-Chief to become hockey columnist for the Toronto *Star*. I was weary of being a manager at *THN*, responsible for myriad things that had a lot more to do with publishing and business than hockey and journalism. I also thought the job change would likely give me more flexibility and time to get more involved with the kids and their sports.

I was thinking that this move from Pickering to Whitby would be a positive for Mike's and Shawn's athletic endeavors, too, because I perceived Whitby to be a very good place for kids' sports. Even before the move became official, we had already registered Mike for house-league lacrosse in Whitby. Plus, I had always heard really good things about the minor hockey organization in Whitby. It was all systems go. I could see no downsides to it.

It was around April of 1991—the house deals weren't closing until late June of that year—that I discovered how wrong I was about no downsides to the move. Mike had just finished his first year in the PMHA hockey school and I was looking forward to getting him registered in the Brooklin-Whitby Minor Hockey Association (BWMHA). But when I called the BWMHA to get details on Mike's registration for the next season, I was stunned and horrified to discover they didn't take any players under the age of six. Unlike Pickering, Whitby had no provisions for four- or five-year-olds, no hockey school, nothing. Yikes, what had I done!

So I did what any self-respecting, manipulative, lying, cheatin' Hockey Dad would do—I took advantage of early registration in Pickering for the hockey school there as soon as it was humanly possible in the spring, using my Pickering address, which I knew I wasn't going to have after late June when we moved. I was both naïve and a little paranoid, telling Mike that if anyone asked him where he lived, not to answer. I can laugh now, but I do recall being unusually tense about our little deception.

Though we were busy with the preparations to move into the new house and the anguish that goes with making a decision on whether to take a new job, we still found time for Mike's first stab at organized sports. The house-league lacrosse season in Whitby runs for just two months (May and June), which parents love because it's all over by the time the kids get out of school and doesn't affect vacation plans. Mike was just five but was thrilled to try lacrosse, a game I played as a kid—not very well, mind you—in the Scarborough Lacrosse Association.

And he loved it. What was not to love? It was fun. It was great exercise. And it was competitive. There is no better summer sport, period, than lacrosse and if you're looking for a sport that so perfectly complements hockey, well, lacrosse is the game.

When the lacrosse season ended in June, and we were all moved into our new house and I was awaiting the new job at the *Star* to start in September, we did what most young families do in the summer—catch our breath, chase two-year-old Shawn and five-year-old Mike all over the new house and enjoy what was to be our last "sport-less" summer for quite some time.

"C'MON, DROP THE DAMN PUCK ALREADY"

FALL ARRIVED and even though we were living in Whitby, we were driving back to Pickering each Saturday for the five-year-old hockey school, our grand Whitby-Pickering residence deception apparently having gone undetected. I laugh about it now because over the years I saw married couples get legally separated or rent an apartment or even buy a house in another community to enrol their kid in a new school to satisfy a residency requirement they perceived as beneficial to their children's hockey-playing future. It was hilarious, actually, that I was fearful of Mike getting busted out of the five-year-old Pickering hockey school because we lived in Whitby.

After a summer of playing games in house-league lacrosse in Whitby, the PMHA hockey school seemed a lot less exciting than it had the year before. Mike had gotten a taste of playing games and competing and being on a team with other kids and he liked it, and so did I. Now he was headed back to just an hour a week of drills and you could plainly see he wanted more, though "more" did not include another session with Larry Marson, much to my chagrin. I knew, though, in the grand scheme of things, that another year in the hockey school really wasn't such a bad thing.

This whole issue of when Canadian kids should begin playing games as opposed to learning the skills and finer points was a raging debate at the time. The Canadian game was under fire for being too organized, too competitive at too early an age, and the Europeans were being lauded for a much more sensible approach in "developing" kids in sports clubs with little or no emphasis on competition or games where scores were kept. In many respects, the PMHA hockey school was in direct response to the debate of the day.

So while I could see Mike hungered to play games, I told him it was important for him to learn how to skate, stickhandle and shoot.

As it turned out, Mike's stint in the hockey school was short-lived that year anyway. The PMHA Squirt House League (six- and seven-year-olds) was short a handful of players, so a few weeks into the season they "promoted" the kids from the five-year-old hockey school who were best equipped to make the jump. Mike was one of those who was promoted.

Mike was happy to be joining a team and while I was mildly concerned about how he might fare playing against kids a year or two older, I was more excited he was one of those chosen to move up.

Mike joined a team sponsored by the Pickering Optimists. They had double blue as their colors—a foreshadowing of the colors Mike would wear much later in his favorite hockey seasons—and he wore No. 2 in a sweater that was miles too big, so long he would have tripped on it if Cindy hadn't hemmed it up.

Mike would have one practice and one game per week with his new team. Naturally, we videotaped his first "official" hockey game at Don Beer Arena but if you watch the video, you won't see much. Cindy made the mistake of putting me in charge of the camera. When Mike came onto the ice for his first shift, or any shift for that matter, I started with the camera on him. But as play started, I found myself letting the camera drift and actually watching the game with my eyes instead of through the camera viewfinder. The videotape shows herking and jerking all over the place with only the occasional glimpse of Mike. From that point forward, Cindy would be our designated camera person.

I'm not sure Mike even touched the puck in that first game. Actually, I am sure. He didn't. He got close to it a few times. Some would say that's a good reason to have kept him back in the hockey school, where in an hour of ice he would get all sorts of puck touches. But Mike skated hard all over the ice in his game, chasing the puck wherever it went. He didn't look out of place in relation to some of the older kids, but he didn't really do anything either.

Hockey, at that age, especially in house league, is so much about a few kids dominating. The best player on Mike's team was a little seven-year-old whirling dervish who could skate like the wind. His name was Darryl Lloyd and he would go on to have a very good OHL career with the Windsor Spitfires.

Mike loved playing the games, tried hard to keep up and whatever he gave up by not touching the puck much he may have made up in being pushed to skate harder to stay up with the play. Plus, he was still getting a full hour of practice time with his team in addition to that one game a week, so you could argue he was getting more ice time than he would have had he stayed in the hockey school.

Mike scored at least one goal that first season. While I don't remember exactly how the goal was scored—wait, ah, yes, it's coming back to me, a shot along the ice from the high slot that the goalie fanned on—and I can't honestly tell you whether he scored more than once that year, what I do clearly recall is Mike saying to us on the way home after his first goal: "I was smiling under my face mask for the whole game because I scored a goal."

I guess that is what they call the simple pleasures in life. For him, and for us.

All things considered, I was a reasonably well-behaved Hockey Dad that hockey season, at least outwardly. But I do recall getting agitated by a few things.

One, Mike developed in his squirt year this annoying habit of dragging his right skate blade behind him every few strides. He would get up a head of steam and then slow himself by dragging the toe of his right skate blade behind him. Take three strides and drag. Take three strides and drag. It drove me crazy. I would tell him on the way home not to do it, and next time out, he would be dragging it again. Where the hell is Larry Marson when you need him? (Note: somewhere along the line Mike just stopped doing it and there's probably a message there—kids sometimes figure it out on their own.)

The other thing that used to drive me crazy was refereeing. The refs were just kids themselves, thirteen or fourteen years old. House league, of course, is on the buzzer system. Three-minute shifts, running time. So if a player scored a goal—and trust me, little Darryl Lloyd was scoring more shifts than not—the referee would, way too slowly for my liking, go pick the puck out of the net, amble over to the timekeeper's bench to report who scored the goal and the assist and then make his way back to the center face-off dot to get the kids lined up. Then, finally, if the *^%$#*@ buzzer hadn't gone to change lines, he would drop the puck for whatever few seconds were left of the shift.

I was beside myself, especially if it was Mike's turn on the ice when a goal was scored. The teenage kids reffing had no sense of urgency at all, which is about what you would expect, not that I was prepared to accept that. I would mention this to Cindy—I had to tell someone how I felt and, crazy as I might be, I wasn't yelling out loud at some poor teenager wearing the stripes, although I might have once said loud enough for someone to hear, "C'mon, drop the damn puck"—and Cindy would look at me with strong disapproval, tell me to zip it up and relax.

Honestly, I would like to tell you now that I feel differently, that I was out of line back then, but I don't and I wasn't (except maybe the one time I used my outdoor voice when I should have been talking to myself). This is precisely what was wrong, and probably to some degree still is, with little kids' hockey in Canada. We are a little too organized sometimes. We do worry too much about protocol, about lining up correctly for face-offs. Ice time is precious. It's expensive, it's hard to come by and far too much time is spent coaxing kids to get on the right side of the circle for a face-off. I know there have been some changes since Mike was a squirt, but with a three-minute running time shift for six- and seven-year-olds in house league, why not simply give possession to the team that got scored on and let them skate it back up the ice? Or just toss it back down the length of the ice and let them all chase it?

I know some house leagues back then went to two-minute, stop-time shifts to combat this very problem of precious seconds ticking off the clock while the ref did his business at the timekeeper's bench. And while that would salvage the odd shift here or there for the kids who were on the ice, this face-off protocol, the reporting of who got the goals and the assists, still ultimately cut short the amount of actual playing time in a one-hour slot.

Of course, critics of the Canadian way and our fixation with structure would say we should go a step further—that with kids of that age it's ludicrous to be playing full-ice, ten-skaters-at-a-time games with double that number on the bench, that we would be far better off with three simultaneous cross-ice mini-games that involve twenty-five to thirty kids on the same sheet of ice at the same time. But we Canadians can still be a hard-headed bunch when it comes to change.

When it comes to hockey, I tend to be a little schizo-phrenic—some days I'm a dinosaur; some days I'm a visionary, or so I think—and I suppose the line between them is some-times a fine one. Let's just say there were days back then when I couldn't figure out whether I was part of the problem or part of the solution.

CROSSING THE LINE; GIVING MIKE THE "TAP"

IF MY EXPERIENCES IN THE SUMMER OF 1992 were any indication, I was more part of the problem than the solution.

There was never any doubt we were going to register Mike for another year of house-league lacrosse. He played Junior Paperweight the first year; this would be the summer of Senior Paperweight. And it wasn't long into his Senior Paperweight House League season that we discovered there was going to be a rep team chosen from the house league.

Rep? Did someone say rep? Rep is, of course, short for representative or all-star. Well, whatever you call it, I was certainly game to kick things up a notch and Mike was, too. He quite enjoyed lacrosse. It really is a wonderful game. The kids run hard, work up a sweat and for those of us who appreciate the physical and competitive elements of sport, it has those, too, even at the youngest ages.

In Paperweight lacrosse, the kids are taught to knock the ball out of another player's stick by using their stick. Aggression is by all means rewarded—and encouraged. And unlike hockey—where kids starting out have a tough time mastering skating, so puck control is but a pipe dream for most—kids playing lacrosse are stable on their feet and able to scoop up a ball and really run with it, maybe even throw it to a teammate, with all the other kids chasing after it, trying either to knock the ball out of the stick or knock down the ball carrier. Team play, the ability to complete passes and get some flow to the game, is so much greater in little kids' lacrosse than in little kids' hockey.

Mike could run fast, had a good stick, loved to get involved, was one of the better kids in the house league and, well, I needed details on this whole rep thing. I was given the name and number of the fellow who would be coaching the rep team. His name was Kevin O'Brien. I recognized his name only because his son, Kyle, a little red-haired kid, was known as one of the really big scorers in the Senior Paperweight league. I gave this Kevin O'Brien a call and told him I had a son who was interested in trying out for the rep team, did he have any information?

This guy was very noncommittal, very cool to my request, almost to the point of being aloof. He asked me what team Mike played on and what number he wore. Then he said he was coaching the yellow team, their next game was against Mike's white team: "I'll have a look at him and see how he does."

I hung up the phone and recall thinking, "Yeah, we'll see all right..."

Do you remember in the prologue, when I tried to make a case that I'm not really crazy? Well, this is the point where it gets hard to do that.

On the way to Mike's next game, which was against Kevin O'Brien's yellow team, I was giving Mike the pregame pep talk in the car. I told him about the rep team, explained the concept—trying out for a team of the best players in his league who would get to go in tournaments against all-star teams from other towns and cities—which he seemed to like a lot. I told him the coach of the yellow team was going to be the coach of the rep team and if Mike wanted to be on this rep team, this would be a good night to play a really good game to show the coach that he was a good player. Then I crossed the line, although that never really occurred to me at the time. I told Mike the best player on the other team was the coach's son, a red-haired kid with a big white Cooper helmet, and that he was maybe the best player in the league. I told Mike that every time this red-haired kid got the ball, Mike should do everything possible to prevent him from scoring a goal—check him, hit him, whack his stick, chase him down, run him over, whatever, but try to stop him from scoring a goal—and that every time Mike got the ball Mike should do everything possible to score a goal.

I didn't think of it as telling Mike to "goon" this other kid. But here I was, taking my bespectacled little six-year-old to his house-league lacrosse game, and I was pumping him up to go mano-a-mano against some other six-year-old, all in the name of making a good impression to make a rep team? It was ridiculous and shameful, although I obviously didn't think that at the time.

In any case, Mike proved to be a good listener. He played a very good game that night. Scored some goals. Worked extra hard to prevent the red-haired kid on the yellow team from scoring too many goals, although anyone who knows anything about lacrosse knows good players always get their goals, even in Paperweight house league, and little Kyle O'Brien did that night.

After the game, Kevin O'Brien told me he had taken a look at Mike and, yes, Mike would be invited to play for the rep team. Yeah, baby.

We, Kevin O'Brien and me, can laugh about it now because the kicker to this story is that the O'Briens—Kevin, his wife, Wendy, son Kyle and daughter Katie—are amongst our very best friends and you will get to know them all too well in the pages that follow. Mike and Kyle played their entire Whitby rep hockey and rep lacrosse careers together on the same team and became great friends and teammates. Within a couple of years of that day I told Mike to take it to Kyle O'Brien, we convinced the O'Briens to move from Oshawa to our street in Whitby. When Kevin coached the boys in lacrosse, I was his manager and/or assistant coach. When I, or anyone else for that matter, coached the boys in hockey, Kevin was always there as the team trainer. Together whatever the weather.

But still, the moral of the story is you don't tell your six-year-old to "target" another six-year-old in the hopes of making a rep team. You just don't.

———— 🏒 ————

Once we were fully settled into Whitby, we were looking forward to Mike playing hockey there for the first time.

Cindy's brother John, a '61 who had retired from pro hockey following a six-year career in the minors after being a star in the OHL, lived not too far from us in Whitby. He had two boys—Mathew and Thomas—the same ages as Mike and Shawn and would later add a daughter, Kathryn, who would go on to play girls' hockey. So we requested Mike and his cousin Mathew to be on the same team. John put on his registration form that he would help out with coaching. I helped out when I could, too.

Outside of the fact practices often took place as early as 6 a.m. on Saturday at the very chilly but character-laden Luther Vipond Arena in Brooklin, Ontario, it was an enjoyable and largely uneventful year.

You will be happy to know I behaved myself, for the most part. Some of those 6 a.m. practices were hell on wheels, though, especially when Cindy and I might have friends over on a Friday night and, well, there might have been a few times I had a few cocktails and didn't get to bed until 2 or 3 a.m. Mike wasn't difficult to get up at 5 a.m. if it was for hockey. Me? That depended on Friday night. When practice was over, like all good Canadians, my brother-in-law John and me and the boys would hit Tim Hortons on the way home. There's another one of the simple pleasures in life on a cold morning after practice—hot chocolate at Tim's with the kids. It just doesn't get much better than that.

Games, of course, were a much different story than practices, played on Sunday mornings (at respectable hours too). Just going to the arena as a family was a great feeling. There's still something really special about walking into a cold rink on the weekend, taking in all the sights and sounds of so many families there off the ice and the kids out there on the ice, the sounds of sticks and pucks echoing throughout the arena. It was wonderful, the highlight of my week. Mind you, I was still allowing myself at times to be highly agitated by teenage refs with no sense of urgency, but now that Mike was six, and playing against kids his own age, he was scoring a little more often. It's funny how less agitated I was about the shift being lost with the ref at the timekeeper's bench reporting a goal when it was my kid who scored the goal. But it was still one heck of a lot of wasted time.

I really only tried to impart one piece of wisdom to Mike that season—play hard every shift. And I imparted that message morning, noon and night. On the way there. On the way home. When I tucked him into bed at night. When I had breakfast with him in the morning. It's the mantra for the

McKenzies in all things we do, then and now. Don't let up. Don't worry about the score. Just play as hard as you can every time you hit the ice. Give it your all, all of the time. That's how my dad raised me in everything I did and that's how I was going to try to raise my boys, not just in sports either, but in life. No excuses. Work hard. Hard work. On the ice. At school. At work. One hundred percent effort one hundred percent of the time.

All of that can get a little old or clichéd sometimes but, hey, it's just how I'm wired. It's in the genes. No sense fighting it and of all the things I might consider apologizing for, going overboard on extolling the virtues of hard work isn't one of them.

THE STRAIGHT POOP ON PLAYING UP

IF YOU ARE FULLY COMMITTED to and entirely engaged in the minor hockey experience, there is nothing quite like the seven-year-old season. That's because it is, without question, the busiest hockey season a player or parent can have. It is all so new to you. In addition to playing house league, a player can play select level at the same time. For the uninitiated, select is when they take the best kids from house league and play them together on a select team that competes against other towns or organizations. The net effect is your kid is really playing on two teams at the same time. One practice and one game in house league; usually one practice and at least one game in select, sometimes more. The player is on the ice at least four times a week, often more than once a day on the weekends. It's awesome. It's also nuts, although nuts in a good, what-would-you-rather-be-doing kind of way.

For those parents whose kids play select and house league for their entire minor hockey careers, not just the seven-year-old season, I applaud you. You deserve a medal because it's even more demanding and time-consuming than the AAA, AA or A levels.

But for the truly ambitious hockey parent—and yes, that would be me—it was possible to bypass the seven-year-old house-league/select year and go directly to rep, which did not normally commence until the eight-year-old, or minor novice, season.

The Brooklin-Whitby Minor Hockey Association had a policy that allowed seven-year-olds to try out for the minor novice AA team, that is, "play up" a year, but not all the way up to the minor novice AAA team. The seven-year-olds had to be very good players, beat out some eight-year-olds to make the minor novice AA team on merit, and no more than three seven-year-olds could play on the AA team.

In Whitby, in Mike's age group of '86s, the first two spots were spoken for. The best player in Whitby at that age was Liam Reddox, and he was head and shoulders better than any other '86. Steven Seedhouse was clearly the next best.

That left just one potential opening and I was, to put it mildly, eager for Mike to get it. But there was competition from some other talented seven-year-olds, as well as the eight-year-olds, so it was far from a slam dunk. It all came down to the final tryout. It looked to me like the third seven-year-old spot was going to go to either Mike or a boy named Brandon Davis. I kind of thought Mike had the edge going into the final tryout, just as I'm sure Brandon's dad, Scott, figured his son would get it.

On the day of the final tryout, which was scheduled for 5 p.m. at Iroquois Park Arena, Mike came home from school at lunch and complained of a tummy ache. Before long, it was worse than that. Diarrhea. He had really bad stomach cramps.

Poop. Literally.

Mike said he didn't think he could go back to school because he was afraid he might get caught short, if you know what I mean. I didn't like where this was headed.

"But you'll be okay for hockey tryouts, won't you, Mike?" I said plaintively.

"No," he said. "I can't go. My tummy hurts. I might have to go to the bathroom."

Aw, crap.

"Oh, you'll be fine," I said, but he wasn't.

It was all over but the crying. And it was me who felt like crying.

So while Liam Reddox, Steven Seedhouse and Brandon Davis were the three '86s who played up on the minor novice AA team that season, Mike was left to play house league and select. Whatever my initial disappointment at Mike not being on the AA team, it passed quickly, because for all my faults, and I have many, I tend to believe everything happens for a reason. And besides, I do firmly believe that kids find their own level and, generally speaking, it's better to play and play well against kids your own age than to be less of a factor against older kids. Now, if the powers that be had come along and said Mike could play up on the AA team, we'd have been gone so fast it would make your head spin.

———— ● ————

This was the season when Mike actually started to wear glasses when he played hockey. Up until then, even though he had been wearing glasses for almost three years, he hadn't been wearing them for sports, but the truth is he couldn't see very well without them. I'm not sure why we allowed him to not wear glasses when he played hockey or lacrosse as a six-year-old, but it probably had a little to do with vanity—we, I mean I, didn't like how it would look under his face mask—and a lot to do with safety. We weren't keen on him wearing his conventional gold, wire-rimmed glasses with glass lenses—think Harry Potter—in a contact sport and we had not yet found sport glasses that would fit a boy that young.

I finally located a pair of sport glasses that looked as though they might do the trick. They were a little on the large side, rather heavy looking but with thick, clear plastic frames with large and fairly thick plastic lenses, the same sort of shape as aviator sunglasses. I think they were designed for racquetball or squash. I'm not sure words do this picture justice. Just think of a seven-year-old Kurt Rambis. Or maybe even a young Bubbles from *Trailer Park Boys*. (Sorry about that one, Mike.)

Hey, he could see. They were safe. They fit, barely, under his cage, it's not a frickin' beauty contest. He may have looked a little, or a lot, like a nerd that season but he didn't play like one.

With his uncle Johnny as the head coach and me helping out, Mike ripped it up in the seven-year-old house league. He would score more games than not and it wasn't unusual for him to get two, three, four, or sometimes even five or six goals a game. Regardless of how many he did or didn't score, I was preaching to him the value of consistency—play hard every shift, don't take shifts off, give it your all, all the time. Lest you get the wrong idea, I was also stressing to him the importance of passing the puck, helping his teammates score goals. And I was also telling him he should skate as hard on the backcheck as he did to score a goal.

Honestly, even now, I'm a little conflicted about how to handle a situation like this one. But only a little. I suppose a good sport, or a more easygoing guy than me, might instruct his son who is scoring a lot of goals to back it off at some point, but my attitude then, and I suppose not much has changed now, is how do you tell a seven-year-old kid not to try? I mean, in a forty-five-minute running-time house-league game, there were a total of fifteen three-minute shifts. So with three lines of skaters, that's no more than five shifts per game per player. Five shifts. Think about that.

And now you're telling a kid to back it off or take it easy on some of those five shifts? I don't think so.

I know there are many Hockey Dads who just take their kids to the game and tell them nothing more than to have fun. Nothing wrong with that. Heck, I told Mike that every game he played—I still do now—because if you're not having fun when you play, hockey is way too much like work. But I'm not going to apologize for the way I am either. My dad, who had an absolutely voracious work ethic, preached to me every chance he got the value of hard work. I've tried to do the same with my kids, even when they were seven years old.

I know there were some parents who weren't too thrilled to have a player score as often as Mike did that season. But most took it for what it was, the same as I took it when little Darryl Lloyd was making a shambles of the squirt house league in Pickering. But one mother was so incensed that she phoned and complained to the league about Mike. There was some talk she was going to start a petition to get Mike kicked out of the house league, although I'm not sure where exactly he was supposed to go.

All I knew is that if it was the minor novice AA team with Liam Reddox, Steven Seedhouse and Brandon Davis, I'd have been the first one to sign that petition.

Diarrhea, pfffft.

IT'S FAIR TO SAY WE'RE NOT MORNING PEOPLE

FOR A HOCKEY-CRAZED FATHER AND SON, Mike and I were livin' the dream that seven-year-old house-league/select season.

Mike was the captain of the select team (we didn't know then he wouldn't wear the "C" again for another twelve years). The schedule was hectic, nuts at times, and that was fine by us. There were the obligatory house-league practices on Saturday mornings and games on Sundays. There was at least one select practice and one select game each week. We were pretty much guaranteed four times on the ice each week.

The Whitby Select 7s were coached by John Velacich, who was Mike's coach for the next two seasons after select. John, whose son Jason played on the team, liked to win (that, by the way, is not a criticism), but he treated the kids well. They were having fun.

The select team played in what was known as the North York League, which basically meant all the games were played in arenas in the expansive suburb/city that runs both east and west of Yonge Street just north and south of Highway 401 across the top of Metro Toronto. But here's the kicker. In the North York League, which wasn't so much a real league as it was a clearinghouse for select-level exhibition games, you never knew when you were playing until the night before you played. Seriously.

So we'd be sitting around at home on a weekday night and the phone would ring about 9 p.m.—Mike and Shawn were long gone to bed—to find out that Mike had a game at 5 p.m. or 6 p.m. the next day somewhere in North York. It was like a fire alarm going off, suddenly rushing to make arrangements to get to the game the next afternoon. All that was missing was the sliding down the pole, the siren and the flashing red lights, and we could have used the flashing lights and siren. There's no easy way to get to any arena in North York for 5 p.m. on a weekday. Toronto rush-hour traffic was horrendous.

It wasn't all smooth sailing for the McKenzies in that select season.

There was quite an ice-time crunch happening in Whitby at the time and there were weeks when the Select 7s' assigned practice time was from 7 to 8 a.m. on a weekday at Iroquois Park. That's not ideal on a school day, but hockey parents tend to resign themselves to their fate.

Besides, children who swim, for example, have long used early-morning workouts before school as the standard training times, so one weekday morning hockey practice now and again wasn't such a hardship, was it?

Uh, yeah, it was for us.

Cindy was never fully on board with the concept from the beginning—she feared Mike would be too tired at school to do well—and I didn't necessarily disagree with her, but what choice did we have? Mike was the captain of the team; he needed to be there. So he was.

He attended the first practice and we rushed him straight from the rink to school. That wasn't so bad, was it?

Uh, yeah, it was for us.

Mike came home from school for lunch and he was a mess. Tired and cranky, he was done like dinner. He was barely functioning. He was so out of sorts he fussed big time about going back to school and once we finally got him back, which required no small effort, Cindy said we couldn't go through this routine every time there was a morning practice. We decided right then that was that, no more weekday morning practices for Mike.

Still, I felt sheepish. I explained the circumstances to John Velacich. He wasn't too thrilled, not that I expected him to be. When these weekday morning practices were scheduled, they were the only practice for the select team that week. So if Mike, the captain, refused to attend, it wouldn't be long before other players on the team might follow suit and what's the point of having a practice if only half the team is there?

John's concern was understandable. I knew we had put him in a tough spot, but this one was for us non-negotiable. Things were a little—or maybe even a lot—tense for a week or two. I do recall this being the dominant issue in our lives for a few days, but fortunately the weekday morning practices were not an every-week occurrence and the whole issue eventually blew over. If you have never been through the minor hockey experience, this may seem like no big deal but it's one of those issues that can snowball and cause major headaches on a team and lots of hard feelings. Somehow, we avoided it ballooning into a major problem, but that was Mike's first and last before-school practice that season.

Still, it would have been difficult for anyone to question our commitment. I'll never forget the one weekend that season when Mike was on the ice six times, including five games, on Saturday and Sunday alone. There was a house-league practice early Saturday morning and the house-league team was entered into a tournament in Bowmanville. There were two house-league tournament games on Saturday. There was the regularly scheduled house-league game in Brooklin on Sunday morning, followed by the tournament final in Bowmanville and then a select game all the way in Toronto at North York Centennial Arena.

There was a little breathing space between the Sunday morning game in Brooklin and the midday tournament game in Bowmanville. But there was, when you take into account travel time, virtually no time between the Bowmanville game and the select game in North York. I remember taking Mike off the ice as soon as the game in Bowmanville was over, literally tossing him over my shoulder in full equipment, including skates and helmet, and putting him in the front seat of the car that way for the fifty-mile drive to North York. When we arrived there I just picked him up out of the car with his skates on, threw him over my shoulder and dropped him on the ice just in time for the select game.

When it was all over, we were driving home and Mike was completely exhausted, hair matted down with sweat, cheeks bright red but he was still smiling after being on the ice six times, including five games, over two days and he said to me: "That was a really fun weekend. I love to play hockey."

It's funny, but for all the things that happen over the years, those are the moments you recall most fondly so many years after the fact.

On the ice, Mike was doing well, scoring lots of goals in house league and getting his fair share in select too, but there were some caution flags being waved at us.

The more success Mike had, the more he expected it to happen. On those occasions when maybe it didn't go as well as Mike would have liked—sometimes it was just a shift, sometimes it was a full game—he started to let his feelings be known, and in a not-so-nice way. It might come in the form of banging his stick if he missed a shot. And if he had a bad game, failing to score or whatever, he could be a little brooding afterwards. I am not sure if I was alarmed or encouraged by these emerging emotions. It's a sign of competitiveness and what Hockey Dad doesn't want his kid to be competitive? Besides, what had I been preaching to him about going as hard as he could every shift? Still, there's no excuse for acting like a spoiled brat when things don't go your way. So I would try to explain to Mike that there's no place in the game for banging his stick or getting mad or angry after a game is over. But those things are sometimes easier said by Dad than done by Mike.

———— ● ————

The one game that epitomized this developing issue was one I didn't even attend. It was a Sunday and I was in Sault Ste. Marie to broadcast a Greyhound game on TSN that night. That afternoon, Mike was playing in a very important select game at North York Centennial Arena, which is now known as Herb Carnegie Centennial Arena. If Mike's team won, it would qualify to play in the Timmy Tyke tournament semi-finals at Maple Leaf Gardens the next weekend. This was a big deal. In fact, it doesn't get any bigger for Select 7s.

I remember phoning Cindy from Sault Memorial Gardens just before we were getting ready to go on the air and I asked her how Mike's game went that afternoon. Not very well, she said. Whitby lost 4–3. I asked her where Mike was and she said he was in his bed. Crying.

"Crying," I said. "Why is he crying?"

"Because he's upset they lost," she replied.

"The game was two hours ago," I said.

"I know," Cindy replied, "he's been up there since we got home."

I got Mike onto the phone and asked him why he was so upset. He said because they lost and they wouldn't get to play at Maple Leaf Gardens. I told him that's the way it goes, someone has to win, someone has to lose, not to be upset and I asked him if he did his best. He said yes, that he scored three goals but some really big, good kid on the other team—and Mike just butchered the kid's name trying to pronounce it—scored four goals to win the game. He also told me he was upset because some of his teammates were "laughing" after the game and he didn't understand how they could laugh after losing such an important game.

I consoled him a bit, told him to stop crying, gave him the "be a big boy" speech and hung up. If I recall correctly, I kind of liked the fact he was upset his team lost and he took it more to heart than his teammates, but I didn't have any clue then that harnessing emotions in hockey would be a long and winding road for my son, a road that he's still traveling.

Oh, by the way, that kid whose name Mike butchered on the phone that day?

Wojtek Wolski of the Colorado Avalanche.

10 BREAKING THE GOLDEN RULE
"Grab Your Sticks"

AS WONDERFUL AS the house-league/select scene was, the first season of AAA—the highest level of play in minor hockey—was even better.

Whitby was, at that time, one of the smallest, if not the smallest, AAA centers in Ontario. But with Liam Reddox, Steven Seedhouse and Brandon Davis returning to their own age group after a year of minor novice AA, plus Mike and others moving up from the Select 7s, Coach Velacich's team was competitive with most of the teams they faced. A big part of the reason was Liam Reddox, who if he wasn't the most dominant eight-year-old in southern Ontario was awfully close to it.

Everything Liam did was at a higher level than everyone else. He was a very strong skater, extremely athletic, and his puck-handling skills, his shot and his competitive instincts were off the charts. It was difficult to imagine Liam not growing up to be a professional hockey player and that is, in fact, what he is. A fourth-round pick of the Edmonton Oilers in 2004, Liam scored his first NHL goal for the Oilers on

November 15, 2008. Unlike some of the stories you hear about kids who dominate when they're very young and are never heard of by the time they get to peewee, well, that's not Liam.

There were many games back in minor novice AAA when Liam was a veritable one-man band. He was that good.

John Velacich decided a position change was in store for Mike, moving him from center to left wing. Were we thrilled about that? At the time, no. We had just sort of presumed center was the position Mike would always play. But the coach wanted him to try left wing on a line with Liam. So that was that. Mike, by the way, didn't have any problem with it.

As an aside, more minor hockey blood, figuratively speaking (for the most part) has been spilled over position changes than any other issue. I've seen players drop down a level, change teams, move out of town or quit hockey altogether, all in the name of combating a position shift. In rep hockey, especially AAA, every coach reserves the right to determine which position a player will play. While center to wing isn't a seismic shift, watch the fireworks when a coach takes a forward and makes him a defenseman or vice versa. It can get ugly and, in fairness, some kids simply don't enjoy playing a different position. But it's also amazing how many kids will give anything a try even though their parents fight it every step of the way.

So Mike became a left winger and John Velacich must have been on to something—Mike never played anything but left wing after that.

As for playing on Liam's wing, it had its obvious benefits but there was one significant drawback. Liam was such a good player, he would often just take off. Because he could skate right through the other team, he would do exactly that. Mike and the other Whitby Wildcats on the ice might as well have stood and watched Liam. And some games, they did.

In one particular game, Liam scored a bucketful of goals and the Wildcats won big. I couldn't have been angrier. The way I saw it, Mike might as well have sat in the stands and watched the game with me because that's all he was doing while Liam went end to end.

I was steamed. It was then I committed my second big minor sports parenting faux pas—you will recall the first one was revving up Mike to rough up Kyle O'Brien to make the rep lacrosse team—and this was probably worse than the first.

I went into the dressing room after the game to untie Mike's skates and he was sitting right beside Liam. Liam's dad, John, a ginger-haired Glaswegian who is an ardent member of the Glasgow Rangers Supporters Club, was untying Liam's skates beside me. I was seething and not saying anything when Mike asked me a question: "How did I play, Dad?"

"Great, Mike, you played great. It's not your fault if no one will pass you the puck."

Unlike the targeting incident in lacrosse, where it took me years to realize what an ass I was, I knew I had made a big mistake the second the words came out of my mouth. Mike just looked at me. Liam looked at me. John Reddox, a good guy but every bit as much a Crazy Hockey Dad as me, just looked at me. No one said a word, which was good because it died right then and there. Under different circumstances, it could have evolved into quite a scene.

I was immediately embarrassed. These were eight-year-old kids, after all. Completely innocent. Liam was just playing on instinct, doing what he could do because he could do it, exactly the same as Mike did in the house league the season before.

And John Reddox had nothing to do with it either. He was up there in the stands with the rest of us parents.

A valuable lesson or two was learned that day as I waited for the embarrassment to drain out of my face in that dressing room.

One, no matter how upset you are, regardless of how justified you think you are, hold your tongue. There needs to be an emergency brake between the brain and the mouth. The dressing room right after the game is no place for an airing of grievances, not in front of kids and parents.

Two, and this I found out from personal experience of being on the other side of it, the parent of a player should not necessarily be held accountable for what his kid does or doesn't do on the ice.

But the bottom line is when you're bent out of shape about something in kids' hockey, just shut the hell up and get home without making a fool of yourself.

———— ● ————

One of the great aspects of the first AAA year is the newness or novelty of virtually everything. The caliber of play is terrific and while Mike's team was competitive most of the time, it was far from the elite squads from the Greater Toronto Hockey League (GTHL) or the Detroit area.

Cindy, however, was not quite as impressed with every part of the minor hockey culture. Don't get the wrong idea. She was an extremely supportive mom who was there for her kids and recognized there is much wonderful family time to be spent as part of the minor hockey experience. But she didn't blindly accept every part of it without question. One of Cindy's favorite lines over the years was "Minor hockey would be a lot better if it were run by the Moms instead of the Dads."

She never understood or embraced the concept of kids having to miss a day of school (Friday) to play in a minor hockey tournament because all tournaments are three-day affairs that start early Friday morning. (Neither did my TSN colleague Gord Miller, who was astonished that it happened with great frequency.) Oh, Cindy understood the ice-time issue, but the basic premise that kids have to take off a day of school to play hockey? And the fact most teams start with two tournaments in the first three weeks of the new school year? She was not impressed.

Me and Mike? We loved it. There's nothing quite as fine as playing a little hooky, from school or work, to drive to, say, Kitchener, on a crisp autumn morning and have the first game over before noon. Then grab lunch as a team, check into the hotel, let the kids run wild for a bit while the dads hash out the morning game over a couple of adult beverages before gearing up for the second game of the day.

As much fun as out-of-town tournaments were, that isn't to say there weren't dangerous pitfalls to be wary of. Like the postgame hospitality suite, especially on the Friday or Saturday night, when all the parents and sometimes the coach would be together in a social setting in the hotel.

Alcohol, minor hockey parents and the coach in the same room after a couple of tournament games and with another one the next morning is not always the wisest of recipes. It can be nitro. The hospitality suite can turn into the hostility suite in no time.

Smart coaches avoid them or are wise enough to get out while the going is good, before the alcohol-inspired courage/stupidity has bubbled to the surface. In Mike's minor novice year in Kitchener, one of the moms on the team was overly refreshed late in the evening and launched into a very public tirade outlining specific shortcomings of this player and that player. Suffice to say, that didn't go over too well with the other well-oiled parents in the room. The tension meter was on high; the fun meter on low. Had the words been delivered by a dad instead of a mom, I don't doubt for a moment there would have been fisticuffs. As it was, it was still ugly and raw and nasty. Some tears were shed, angry words were exchanged and there was residual bitterness that never fully went away.

The other thing about minor hockey Cindy could never understand was why they had young kids play games on Halloween night. Outside of Christmas, there is no day of the year that means more to kids of virtually all ages. When Mike and Shawn were young and of the trick-or-treating age, they would invariably have games scheduled on Halloween. This always caused major problems. It was the one night of the year when the kids, every one of them, would choose *not* to play hockey if they could. The funny thing was that when the kids were older and not trick-or-treating, there were no games scheduled. A mom, Cindy always maintained, would take care of this.

Alas, common sense is nice in theory but often difficult to achieve in the real minor hockey world.

Example.

Once Mike started to play rep hockey, the golden rule was that if he didn't go to school that day, he would not be permitted to play hockey that night. It's a sensible approach. Lots of families do it. We did, although what is it they say—rules are made to be broken?

There was a day in Mike's minor novice season when he had to miss school because of a nasty ear infection, although he had already started on antibiotics. Cindy was out with Shawn for a few hours, so it was just me and Mike at home.

Mike's team was playing at Northcrest Arena in Peter-borough at 6 p.m. It was around 4 p.m., Mike was in his pajamas, lying on the couch, looking a little worse for wear.

"How you feeling, buddy?" I asked him.

"Okay, I guess," he replied.

"Hey, I've got a great idea," I said to him. "Why don't you get dressed and we'll take a drive and go watch your team play."

"Can we?" Mike asked. "I didn't go to school today."

"Sure," I said, "but we're just going to watch. A little fresh air will do you good."

Mike got dressed and we were about to leave. "Hey, Mike, why don't you grab your sticks and your hockey bag?"

"Why?" Mike said. "I can't play, I'm sick, I didn't go to school today."

"Well, you never know, maybe you'll feel well enough to sit on the bench, maybe you can serve a bench penalty or something."

So we took the one-hour drive from Whitby along the 401 and up Highway 115 into the Borough, as we like to call it, and pulled into the parking lot of Northcrest.

"How you feeling, buddy?" I asked Mike.

"I think I feel a little better," he said.

"Great," I said, "grab your bag."

Well, I don't have to tell you what happened after that. Mike played. That was the good part. Then reality set in. Once the game was over, I had two major concerns. One, I was now afraid Mike might get even sicker because he played when he really shouldn't have. (Thankfully, he didn't.) Two, how was I going to explain this to Cindy? (Sheepishly, if you must know.)

So much for the golden rule.

11 SO, THAT'S HOW YOU WANT TO PLAY THE GAME, IS IT?

I AM NOT GOING TO LIE, writing this book isn't easy at times. I don't mind highlighting my shortcomings to get a laugh or make a point, but I also don't want you to think I was some kind of loon bar 24/7, because I wasn't. I look back at Chapter Eight, where I told you about Mike's scoring exploits in house league, and I worry you might think I'm one of those self-centered Hockey Dads who are so full of themselves and run around bragging about their kids. I would be devastated if that were the case. That's not me at all.

But the real conflict in writing parts of this book isn't as much about how I characterize myself—because I am ultimately driving the bus on that—as it is my family and whether, in the telling of this very personal story, I am doing Cindy, Mike and Shawn justice in terms of how they are portrayed. I mean, it's possible some of these snapshots I'm providing could create the wrong impression, or least an imbalanced one.

So as I prepare to tell you about some of the things that happened in Mike's major novice AAA year, and throughout his hockey-playing days, maybe some things that are not so flattering to Mike, I feel the strong need to tell you this up front about him.

Mike was, as a boy, and is now, as a young man, a great son, a terrific person.

As a kid he was fairly quiet and could, when in the company of people outside of our family, be quite shy. He was extraordinarily respectful of all authority, conscientious at school, a very good student who worked hard at all times. He cooperated and played well with others, including his little brother, Shawn, and really was never any problem to his parents or teachers or anyone else.

But when it came to anything where competition was involved, winning or losing, well, this quiet, well-mannered, well-behaved, bespectacled little kid could go from Jekyll to Hyde in a heartbeat. Probably the first time Cindy and I saw this manifest itself was with video games when he was four or five. He would be playing Super Mario on the old Nintendo system. If the game was beating him, look out, because that video game controller used to go flying all over the place. I lost count of how many times we had to ban video games for a week or a month.

The same was true when he played sports.

Mike was over-the-top passionate about playing hockey and lacrosse. He just loved his sports. He couldn't wait to get to the rink. He would always be one of the first kids dressed. While other kids would horse around in the dressing room, thinking and talking about anything but hockey, Mike would go out and watch the game being played before his.

My friend Kevin O'Brien, who coached Mike in lacrosse and was the trainer for hockey, said in all his years of being around kids playing sports, no player ever prepared himself for games the way Mike did.

As calm and quiet as Mike was at home (except when he was playing video games), the intensity came off him in waves in the sporting arena. He was driven on the ice, gave his all every shift and badly wanted to be successful as an individual—scoring or setting up goals—and ultimately wanted team success in the form of a win. I would like to tell you he was this way because I was drilling it into his head that a good player works hard every shift and never lets up, but who's kidding who? It was just his nature and my words only reinforced what came naturally to him.

There was one time I was driving Mike home from a minor novice AAA game. He told me that in the middle of his game he had to go to the bathroom but that he didn't want to leave the bench and miss a shift by going to the dressing room.

"So what did you do?" I asked him.

"I just went on the bench," he said.

The good news was it was No. 1, not No. 2. And between his long johns, jock, pants, socks and shin pads, any of the evidence would have been soaked up so it was just our little secret, until now, but it gives you an idea of how intent Mike was to not miss a single shift. (Cindy gave Mike's equipment a good cleaning that night.)

Kids on other teams would call Mike "Four Eyes"—at the younger ages they hadn't yet twigged to the fact his dad was on TV; all that nonsense would come later—and that only added fuel to Mike's fire.

In his second year of rep, major novice AAA, the Wildcats were playing in a December tournament in Lindsay, hosted by the Central Ontario Wolves organization. The team and Mike were on top of their game. The Wildcats went 6–0–0 to win the tournament and Mike, who had eight goals and eleven points in the six games (we know the precise stats because the newspaper story is in an old scrapbook), was named tournament MVP.

Cindy and I should have been thrilled, but we weren't. In fact, we were really quite upset. Throughout the weekend's play, Mike's intensity level was too high. We talked to him about it a couple of times after the tournament games on Friday and Saturday, warned him that if he was going to continue to play like that, we weren't going to put up with it. But right into the championship game, he was getting worse instead of better. As well as he played, and he was on fire, he was banging his stick when things didn't go his way, waving his arms or getting flustered and agitated, at times almost to the point of tears.

We had seen enough. Before Mike had even emerged from the dressing room with his trophy and the MVP award, Cindy and I had decided to "suspend" Mike for one game. The next league game the Wildcats played was against their arch rivals from Oshawa, so we determined that would be the game he would have to miss. He needed to understand he couldn't keep playing like that, even if he was playing well and being successful.

We told Mike on the way home from Lindsay and he begged us to relent, promised us he would behave himself from now on, but we had heard that story on previous car rides and it hadn't happened, so we were sticking to our guns.

We told John Velacich about our plan at practice that week and, not surprisingly, he tried to talk us out of it. As a coach, he didn't want to be without Mike for the game against Oshawa. But Cindy and I felt strongly about it and wouldn't relent.

I would like to tell you that Mike sitting out that game against Oshawa did the trick, but there was a game later that season when Oshawa was really putting the boots to the Wildcats. In that game, a ticked-off, frustrated and angry Mike turned a noncontact major novice AAA game into full contact and had the six—six, count 'em, six—minor penalties for body checking to prove it. Remember when I told you before that parents shouldn't necessarily be held accountable for what their kids do or don't do on the ice? Well, I was speaking from experience.

And let's just say this whole discipline thing with Mike has remained a work in progress.

———— ● ————

The Wildcats were having a good major novice AAA year. When the playoffs arrived, we were all hoping the team would be good enough to get to the Ontario Minor Hockey Association championships. That's the Holy Grail for every OMHA team. The league we played in was called the Eastern Triple A (ETA); there were eight to eleven centers depending upon the age group (Barrie, Richmond Hill, Markham, Ajax-Pickering, Whitby, Oshawa, Peterborough, Central Ontario, York-Simcoe, North Central and Quinte) and they competed for the right to get to what we simply called the OMHAs. Two teams from our ETA league would advance, two teams would advance from the South-Central Triple A (SCTA) league (Brampton, Oakville, Halton, Hamilton, Burlington, St. Catharines, Welland,

Niagara Falls and Guelph) and there would be one host team, from either the ETA or SCTA, depending upon who had won the OMHA title in that age group the year before.

Oakville had won the OMHAs in minor novice so the SCTA would get three teams in the major novice AAA OMHA championships. Only two would go from the ETA, so the Wildcats were going to have to win two playoff rounds to get a berth in the OMHAs.

Our first-round playoff series was against Barrie and it was a barn burner. The Wildcats were leading the best-of-five series 2–1 and Game 4 was being played at Iroquois Park Arena. But Barrie rallied for the win and tied the series. Late in the third period of that game, Coach Velacich got tossed from the game for arguing a call with the referee. Minor hockey rules being what they are, if a player or coach gets a game misconduct in the last ten minutes of the third period, he or she must sit out another game in addition to the one they were ejected from.

So we weren't going to have our head coach for Game 5 back in Barrie. But the kids overcame that. The boys played well in Game 5 in a really tense nail-biter and it was Steven Seedhouse who scored the game-winning goal for Whitby with only a minute left to play. We were on to the next round, against our neighbors from Ajax-Pickering, one playoff series victory from getting to the OMHAs.

We showed up for our next practice and were told there was going to be a parent meeting. We then found out the OMHA had reversed the outcome of Game 5, which Whitby won on the ice 2–1, after Barrie filed an official protest. Barrie protested the fact that our suspended head coach was seen coming out of our dressing room before the game. John Velacich had apparently gone in to tie his son Jason's skates before the game and wish the boys good luck, but according to OMHA rules, a suspended coach is not permitted to even be around the dressing room before the game. So the OMHA ruled in favor of Barrie's protest, and reversed the outcome of that game and the series. Barrie, not Whitby, would be playing Ajax-Pickering the next night, and the Wildcats were destined to play in what's called the ETA playoffs, or ringette/consolation round, as it's disdainfully known.

Poor John Velacich felt terrible. It was such an innocent thing. No one was trying to pull a fast one. I really felt bad for the poor guy. Mike's team was done as far as the OMHA playoffs were concerned and it was because of some technicality which, on one level, made sense (you don't want suspended coaches permitted to "coach"), but the punishment (reversing the outcome of a game and a playoff series) was ridiculously heavy-handed, penalizing a bunch of innocent kids.

Games are won and lost on the ice, especially with nine-year-olds, and there was no advantage, real or imagined, to the coach innocently being in the room before the game to tie his son's skates.

I was outraged. All of the parents were. And the kids? They were all crying; it was quite a scene.

You hear about really ridiculous things happening in the name of minor hockey and this was one of them. What was the OMHA thinking? What was the Barrie team who lodged the protest thinking? Was that how Barrie wanted to advance in the playoffs, winning a series in the boardroom, not on the ice? We couldn't imagine a more unfair scenario. I've been known to spin a good yarn in front of a keyboard so I wrote a scathing letter, epic length too, to both the OMHA and the Barrie Minor Hockey Association. It was just blistering. But it obviously fell on deaf ears because no one ever responded. We were done.

But I learned an important lesson that day about how minor hockey operates. I didn't forget it.

And, as they like to say, payback's a bitch.

12 "I DIDN'T REALIZE YOU HAD ONLY ONE SON"

HOUSTON, WE HAVE A PROBLEM.

We are eleven chapters into this epic and Shawn Patrick McKenzie has just now offered up this wry, albeit accurate, observation.

"I didn't realize you had only one son," Shawn said with, if I didn't know him better, a tinge of sarcasm.

True enough, the story thus far has been a little Mike-centric, but there are reasons for only now getting to No. 2 son in any great depth. Good reasons, too. Or at least that is our story and we're sticking to it.

First, you show me a family with more than one kid and I'll show you a family who in a variety of different ways doesn't lavish quite the same amount of undivided attention on the second as the first received. For the first three years of Mike's life, with Shawn not being born until July of 1989, Mike had a captive audience.

The reality is that when Mike was three years old, my focus was solely on getting him to skate. When Shawn was three years old, my hockey-related efforts were split between Mike's first year in the six-year-old house league and getting Shawn on the ice for the first time. So if my recollection of specifics about Shawn's early hockey days isn't quite as sharp as it was for his brother, I suppose I stand guilty as charged.

There's another factor, too, though. While Mike was absolutely maniacal about all things hockey—playing it, watching it, drawing it, talking it, singing it—Shawn was, shall we say, somewhat less enthusiastic. Oh, he liked it well enough. Like his older brother, he would as a toddler pick up a mini-stick and bat a ball around the house. And if little Mikey and I were in the basement "taking shots" on each other, Shawn would join in. Mike, especially if I wasn't around, would get Shawn all suited in the goalie pads and gloves and drill shots at him. Shawn would stand in there, get unmercifully pelted with a tennis ball and take whatever Mike was dishing out without so much as a whimper.

But Shawn didn't sit for hours at a time and draw hockey pictures. He had no interest whatsoever in learning which logos belonged to which teams and couldn't have cared less about how Mike's friend Mario Le-Moo brushed his teeth.

Shawn's attention span was fleeting. He would go from one thing to the next in rapid succession. His hockey stick wasn't going to get any more attention from him than his toy truck or toy car or toy gun or Super Soaker or toy sword or his action figures. He was much more likely to plant himself in front of the TV to watch cartoons than a hockey game, which is to say he was a pretty normal little kid.

That said, Shawn was still going to be given every opportunity Mike had when it came to hockey.

The first time I recall having Shawn on skates was just after Christmas of 1992, when he was about three and a half years old. That's when the Griswolds—I mean the McKenzies—decided to do the Christmas Vacation thing in Gavle, Sweden, site of the 1993 World Junior Championship. I obviously had to work the tournament for TSN and since the first game started on Christmas Day, Cindy and I agreed it would be nice for the whole family to be together for a family Christmas in Sweden.

So we sort of celebrated Christmas in Canada with our families four or five days before the actual day. Then the four of us—Cindy, six-year-old Mike and three-year-old Shawn and I—jetted off to Sweden. If that sounds exotic and glamorous, great, but anyone who has traveled with kids that age, they know only too well what it's really like.

There was, with a seven-hour time difference, the seven-hour overnight flight from Toronto to Frankfurt and a six-hour layover in Frankfurt before the two-hour flight to Stockholm, followed by the two-hour drive north to Gavle. I recall getting into the nice Volvo station wagon rental we got at Stockholm's Arlanda airport and everyone (except me, of course) immediately, for the first time on the trip, falling asleep in the car.

As we drove north from Stockholm to Gavle on that snowy afternoon and the family slept, I did what I could to stay awake, but it was difficult, compounded by the fact I was starting to feel extremely warm, so much so that I thought I might be getting sick with a fever. I started sweating. My shirt and jeans became drenched. The hotter I got, the more tired I got. Every so often I would have to put down the window to get a blast of cold, fresh air to keep me awake. I was never so happy on the early evening of Christmas Eve to finally arrive at our hotel in Gavle, wake up the family, unpack the car and check in.

It was only as I exited the car and happened to put my hand on the driver's seat that I made an amazing discovery—this car had heated seats, which was a totally new and foreign concept for me. Let's just say that drive might have been a lot more enjoyable if I'd realized the heated seat was on high and frying my backside for the entire time.

I mention the Gavle trip because, to the best of my recollection, that was where Shawn first skated. I had gone out in advance of the trip to buy Shawn his own skates. We took the same bob skates Mike had learned on but I figured Shawn was a little older than when Mike first tried skating, so he needed to have single-blade skates.

There was a great outdoor rink close to the hotel in Gavle where kids and adults played shinny all day long. That is where we spent a considerable amount of our free time. Mike loved it because there were little pickup games going on all over the ice and it took him no time at all to mix in.

It was also a time when the McKenzie family got to hang out with Darryl Sittler and his family. Darryl's son Ryan was playing for Team USA. Darryl and his lovely wife, Wendy, who passed away in October of 2001 after a battle with colon cancer, and their daughters Ashley and Meaghan, were staying at our hotel. The Sittler girls were older than our boys by quite a few years but they got a great kick out of Mike and Shawn, especially three-and-a-half-year-old Shawn, whose energy usually made him the center of attention.

Shawn and Mike couldn't have been more different as kids. Mike was a little quiet and shy. He was always as neat as a pin, polite and well spoken. Shawn was not quiet and not shy. He would talk to anybody anywhere. No matter how hard Cindy tried to dress up Shawn, he always looked like an unmade bed. His shirt was always untucked, his hair was all over the place. As much as he talked, he wasn't what you would call a great talker. He couldn't say his name very well because he couldn't pronounce his Ss or Fs. So if you asked him his name, he would say "Gawn." When he was four, if you asked him how old he was, he would say "Gore."

It turned out he didn't have a speech impediment as much as he was either just too lazy to say his Ss and Fs or simply liked the reaction he got from saying things incorrectly because he went to precisely one and a half speech classes before saying his Ss and Fs the right way. Our theory was once he realized he would have to commit time and effort to speech lessons, he just decided to say words correctly and be done with it. But that was Shawn. Tell him to walk, he would run. So it was obvious to me, as a Hockey Dad, that I was dealing with someone completely different than Mike.

Mind you, it wasn't as if Shawn didn't like hockey. When he first hit the ice in Sweden he had a great time. But I probably spent as much time carrying the lazy little monkey in my arms and whooshing him around the rink as he did actually skating. But he was having fun out there, so were all the McKenzies and the Sittlers, too.

The Sittlers didn't bring their skates to Sweden, but I would take off mine and let Darryl go out for a twirl with Mike and Shawn. We have video of that, which is kind of neat. Darryl would skate for a bit and then his daughter Meaghan, who went on a few years later to be a star hockey player at Colby College in Maine, would use my skates, too. It was a wonderful time. The Sittlers were great fun. Darryl is about as nice a guy as you could imagine and Wendy was wonderful, too. She took a real shine to Shawn, as did the Sittler girls. For as much video as we have of the kids skating in Sweden, we've got the Sittler girls putting a Harley-Davidson handkerchief on

Shawn's head like a biker bandanna—Shawn was on some sort of crazy Harley-Davidson kick at the time.

As an aside, years later, Cindy and I were having a garage sale. Those old Bauers of mine, all beat up and with no laces in them, were on a table in our driveway with a price tag of $2. A guy picked them up and looked at them, and was contemplating whether to buy them.

"Those were once worn by Darryl Sittler," I told the guy. The guy looked at me like I was crazy. He put them back down and walked away.

———— ● ————

Okay, so here's the bottom line. At this age, Shawn liked hockey but didn't love it; he liked the Power Rangers more than the New York Rangers and I, thankfully, was not dumb enough to fall into the trap of believing Shawn should be exactly like Mike. It was probably easier for me to accept that about Shawn because I was so busy with Mike's hockey, to say nothing of work. For instance, when Shawn was four, I was up to my eyeballs in the craziness of Mike's Select 7 season. But however immersed I was in Mike's hockey, I still wanted to make sure Shawn was given every opportunity Mike had because it wasn't like Shawn hated hockey, he just wasn't as over the top about it.

So for the 1994–95 season, when Mike was playing his first year of AAA, I was adamant Shawn should start playing because he was five, a full year older than when I started Mike in the Pickering hockey school as a four-year-old. But now that we were living in Whitby, not Pickering, there was no five-year-old hockey school for Shawn. It turned out there was a program within the Oshawa CYO (Catholic Youth Organization), which had a house-league system based on the various parishes in

Oshawa and Whitby. The Oshawa CYO hockey school, though, was almost identical to the PMHA hockey school in that it was mostly instructional. Like I was with Mike, I was able to help out on the ice with Shawn.

Shawn liked it well enough—at least he never complained about going—but when it was over, it was over and he moved on to other stuff. The big excitement that season, probably more for me than Shawn, was when he got "called up" from the hockey school to play one game in the league. Our parish, Holy Family in Whitby, was going to be short some players for a game in the Squirt house league and Shawn got the call to fill in. Not unlike Mike, Shawn never touched the puck in that first game he ever played, not even close actually, but it sure seemed like the big time to me. The stars of the CYO back then were the Neals, a Whitby family with four hockey-playing boys. The player who dominated the CYO back then was James Neal, an '87 who has gone on to star for the Dallas Stars.

Like his older brother, Shawn had already developed a skating habit that was driving me nuts. Mike used to drag his one skate to slow himself down if he felt like he was going too fast. Shawn decided, for a period of time, that he would only push off with one skate, the same skate, over and over again. If you know anything about skating mechanics, you can envision what that's like. I used to tell him he had to push with both skates, one and then the other, but sure enough, he'd go back and push with just one. Like Mike, he eventually figured it out.

If I didn't know better, I would have thought Shawn was just trying to torment me.

13 WAS IT COMMITMENT OR SHOULD I HAVE BEEN COMMITTED?

IN SPITE OF MIKE AND SHAWN being different in their approach to hockey, no one can ever suggest I didn't show the same commitment to Shawn as to Mike. You could argue I should have been committed, but there was never any doubt about commitment. Registering Shawn for the six-year-old house league in Whitby was a case in point.

Whitby was one of Ontario's fastest-growing communities at the time and the by-product was a severe ice-time crunch. Even in the few years since Mike's six-year-old season in Whitby, ice time had become a major problem. Whitby had just three pads—two at the Iroquois Park Arena complex just south of the 401 and one at Luther Vipond Memorial Arena in Brooklin—for its rapidly expanding population. Between the WMHA (they dropped Brooklin from the name), ringette, figuring skating, etc., there just wasn't enough ice to go around.

It got so bad the WMHA had to scale back its operation. One of those affected was the six-year-old house league. When

Mike played, there were six teams with seventeen players apiece, so approximately one hundred six-year-olds were accommodated. But for the 1995–96 season, there were only thirty-four slots for six-year-olds and thirty-four slots for seven-year-olds; they would play together in a four-team league of six- and seven-year-olds.

Everyone knew it was going to be difficult to get one of those thirty-four spots so the expectation was there were going to be long lineups and hard feelings.

House-league registration was set for a Tuesday in mid-August in the lobby of Iroquois Park. On the prior weekend, we were away at Mike's provincial lacrosse championship in Hamilton. The lacrosse provincials were always a hoot. Lots of games, not much sleep, lots of partying with other parents and by the time we got home Sunday night, we were exhausted, physically and emotionally drained.

I just wanted to go to bed, but I mentioned to Cindy that I better take a run by Iroquois Park just to make sure no lunatics had started lining up for the registration that would commence at 5 p.m. on Tuesday. You can imagine my surprise when I walked into the lobby and saw 6 people sitting in lawn chairs and chaise lounges with sleeping bags and coolers. Of the 6 people lining up, three of them were guys I knew who were registering '89s, the same birth year as Shawn. Thirty-four slots had just become thirty-one.

I did two things. One, I phoned Cindy and told her to drive down a lawn chair and cooler to me at the arena. Two, just barely under my breath, I conjured up about every English curse word known to man because I knew that the spot right in front of the Coke machine by the entrance to Pad One was going to be my home for the next forty-six hours.

Some people might say I'm crazy. Fine. It was a no-brainer for me. I figured Shawn had to play hockey. I wanted him playing hockey in the town where we lived. If this was how it had to be done, so be it. I was resigned to my fate.

The Town of Whitby dimmed the lights for us in the lobby overnight so we could sleep but the Coke machine illumination wasn't helping my cause. Slowly but surely that night, more and more people started to show up and camp out. I went from feeling bitter to fortunate that I was in a spot where I knew, if I simply invested the forty-six hours, Shawn would get one of the thirty-four spots.

On Monday morning, Cindy came down and relieved me for a few hours so I could go home and have a shower. Did I mention there was quite a heat wave going on at the time? It was hot and very humid. After getting cleaned up, I returned to my post and she went home. The line really started to grow on Monday once word spread around town. It went right out the front door of the arena and ran alongside the parking lot. The Town of Whitby was a little concerned with that many people being outside for that long, so they directed the line into a side door of Pad One. The lineup then started snaking through the dressing room corridor of the arena on Pad One and right out on the floor of Pad One.

Monday night was more like a party than Sunday night, which is to say there was a lot more drinking. It was the minor hockey equivalent of Woodstock. There were hundreds of people lined up inside the lobby, outside the building and then back inside through the side door of the complex. It was quite a night, especially when a mouse ran through the hallway near the dressing room corridor, sending many into the parking lot screaming.

The air-conditioned comfort of the main lobby, even with the Coke machine glow, was never as welcome as it was then. The registration wasn't supposed to start until 5 p.m. on Tuesday but the WMHA personnel started it earlier in the afternoon. Those of us who toughed it out for forty-plus hours in that lobby will always wear it like a badge of honor even though others might think us crazy. All I know is Shawn had one of the thirty-four spots; he better appreciate it.

As a side note, there were never again lineups for that length of time. The WMHA, in future years, went to a wrist-band system or a lottery. Iroquois Park Arena eventually went from two pads to a glorious six-pad facility, the envy of every community in Canada, and another new facility, McKinney Arena, was built with two hockey pads and a full-time designated figure-skating surface.

I always like to tell people I "lived" at Iroquois Park Arena when the kids were young. For two days, I actually did.

———— ● ————

As house-league hockey players go, Shawn did fine. He wasn't the best kid on his team; he wasn't the worst. He enjoyed going to his games and practices but when they were over, that was fine, too. He was a happy-go-lucky kid who had a smile on his face whatever he was doing and took none of it too seriously.

On the bright side, he was now pushing off with both feet so I wasn't being traumatized on that front. But he had developed another annoying habit that was threatening to put me in a rubber room. On several occasions in games during his first house-league season, Shawn would skate onto the ice for his shift and line up facing the wrong way. He was usually playing on the wing and there he'd be, facing his own goalie

for a face-off, with some confused kid on the other team wondering why Shawn was standing where he was supposed to be.
I don't know how many times I explained to Shawn how to
line up. I gave him all manner of explanations.

"Shawn, make sure your back is to your goalie."

"Shawn, make sure you can see the other team's goalie."

"Shawn, just wait until everyone else on the ice has lined
up and go to the player on the other team who doesn't have
anyone standing beside him."

I don't know how else I could have explained it; I don't
know how many times I told him, but I do know how many
times he ignored me.

This, I figured, was my payback for being stupid enough to
line up for forty-plus hours. God was clearly telling me I was
an idiot, but I wasn't listening to Him any more than Shawn
was listening to me.

As time wore on in Shawn's first house-league season, he
did manage to figure out the face-off configuration more often
than not. But even the next season, when he went into the
seven-year-old house league and played on the Whitby Select
7s, he occasionally lapsed and lined up on the wrong side.

There was one game in particular when Shawn lined up
incorrectly. We were driving home—me and Cindy in the front
seat, Shawn in the back—and I made my most impassioned
plea ever to the little guy.

"Shawner," I said to him as we started the drive home,
"buddy, you know I don't ask you for much. I don't expect
you to take your hockey as seriously as Mike takes his hockey
because you're different than Mike, and I'm fine with that. You
don't prepare for games like Mike, and that's fine. You don't
try as hard as Mike in your games and that's fine, too, because

you're having fun and I like to see you have fun. But Shawner, you have to do me one favor, just one thing, please, for Dad. I lined up forty-eight hours to get you into hockey, I would do anything for you so I'm just asking you this one thing—can you please, please just promise me that you're going to line up on the right side of the face-off circle from now on?"

I looked into the rear-view mirror and saw he was looking at me. I was waiting for him to say something and I said, "So what do you have to say about that, buddy?"

"I'm hungry," he said. "What's for dinner?"

14 TALKING THE TALK, WALKING THE WALK
A Coach Is Born

IT WAS ONLY A MATTER OF TIME.

Most every Hockey Dad feels as though he's got what it takes to be a better coach than the guy who's doing the job. Scotty Bowman could be coaching a kids' team and the dads would all stand around at practice or a game and say they could do better.

The line combinations are never quite right; the practice drills could be better; the shifts are too long or too short; this player plays too much; that player plays too little; or maybe the wrong goalie is started. It's always something. Trust me, it's always something.

All that separates the Hockey Dads who endlessly critique their kids' coaches is that some of the very brave—or is it the very foolish?—decide to walk the walk and not just talk the talk.

So it was only a matter of time before I took the plunge to become a coach, or at least an assistant coach to start.

John Velacich's two-year stint as a rep coach with that group of kids was up and there were a couple of groups interested in applying to succeed him. I was part of one of them. So were my good pals Stu Seedhouse and Kevin O'Brien, both of whom already had a foot in the door, having jumped on board in the major novice year to help out John Velacich. Stu was an assistant coach under John; Kevin was the trainer.

To be honest, I think it's easier to become Pope than a minor hockey coach. By the time you fill out all the forms, get the obligatory police check, go through the interview process with the association, to say nothing of the coaching and training certifications (there's a weekend of your life you're not getting back), and let us not forget the anti-abuse seminar/clinic, well, let's just say a *lot* of time and effort, and some money, is required in order to become drunk with power and finally get to put together the line combinations you've been thinking of for two years.

Honestly, though, the best part about coaching kids' hockey is spending time with your buddies, the camaraderie that goes with time spent together before and after practices and games and "coaches' meetings" over adult beverages. As gratifying or as frustrating as coaching kids can be, and it can be both to extremes, it is best when done with good friends. And Stu Seedhouse, Kevin O'Brien and I were like the Three Amigos, spending our winters together in the hockey rinks and our summers together in the lacrosse arenas. Our boys—Stu's son Steven, Kevin's son Kyle and my son Mike—played eight consecutive years of AAA hockey together and even longer than that in competitive lacrosse.

Coaching with Stu, who was named head coach of the minor atom AAA Wildcats, was terrific because it always seemed like we were on the same frequency on just about everything. Stu is a really bright guy, an engineer who is really high up the food chain for Ontario Power Generation (formerly Ontario Hydro) but a lot of fun to be around. Once he gets laughing he has a tough time stopping. Kevin has always been involved in industrial security/fire prevention and safety and as serious as he is about his profession, he's equally off the wall in everything else he does. He tells more jokes than a stand-up comedian, tosses out more puns than Ron MacLean and can generate as many groans as laughs, a real practical joker. If you were there that summer night at the Holiday Inn in Burlington, Ont., when, in front of about one hundred lacrosse parents, he stretched a condom over his head and, using only the air coming out of his nostrils, blew it up three feet tall on top of his head...now that's talent.

But for all the laughs we had, Stu and Kevin were great with the kids, too. Stu is a level-headed guy who rarely, if ever, loses his cool or raises his voice and really knows the game of hockey inside and out. From a health and safety perspective, the kids and parents couldn't have had a better trainer than Kevin, who is safety certified on so many levels that he actually teaches classes on how to be certified to administer CPR. Kevin's sporting expertise is more lacrosse than hockey but that allowed us, and the kids, to make fun of his skates (ancient) and how he skated (badly).

I should take a brief moment to tackle two subjects— parents coaching their kids and minor hockey coaches being paid to coach kids.

I understand the former can be a problem at times because there are occasions when a parent-coach will favor his child and that causes hard feelings, but there are likely more occasions when a parent-coach is a little harder on his child to ensure there isn't that accusation of bias. I know that is how Stu, Kevin and I always operated. In any case, the minor hockey system would cease to exist without parents who coach and my experience has been, more often than not, especially at the younger ages, it's a positive to have parents involved.

As for the recent trend and now somewhat common practice of paying minor hockey coaches a salary, which was unheard of when I first started coaching, I think it's mostly ridiculous. The argument in favor of it is that by paying people you end up with more qualified coaches and they do a better job, but I don't necessarily see evidence to support that. Actually, I see the opportunity to make a buck as drawing more undesirables than qualified people, guys who are in it for all the wrong reasons. Minor hockey is an expensive enough proposition for parents without paying coaches anywhere from $20,000 a year to two and three times that.

I fully understand the need to sometimes offer financial remuneration to one individual who oversees an entire minor hockey organization or someone who acts as an organizational mentor for a bank of volunteer coaches. That makes sense, because you're hiring just one super-qualified individual whose references and background check out and he is able to coordinate a large group that makes everyone better. But to give individual minor hockey coaches five-figure salaries to coach kids' hockey teams? There has to be a better way than that.

It is not, after all, professional hockey.

———— ● ————

I don't know where exactly the following was taken from, so I apologize if it appears here without the proper credit.

I only know I got it as an e-mail from a friend many years ago and truer words were never spoken when it comes to the relationship between minor hockey coaches and parents. Here you go:

A store that sells quality hockey coaches has just opened. The store has six floors and the quality of coaches available increases as the shopper goes up each floor. There is, however, a catch. As you open the door to any floor, you may choose your quality hockey coach from that floor but once you go up a floor you cannot go back down unless you directly exit the building.

So the father of a ten-year-old up-and-coming NHL superstar goes shopping to find a quality hockey coach for his son. On the first floor, the sign on the door reads: **Floor one—these quality hockey coaches enjoy coaching kids (not afraid to use discipline when necessary).** The parent reads the sign and says, "Well, that's better than my child's last coach, but I wonder what's on the next floor?" So up the stairs he goes.

The second-floor sign reads: **Floor two—These quality hockey coaches enjoy coaching kids (not afraid to use discipline when necessary) and have a detailed game plan for the season.** The father says, "That's great, but I wonder what's on the next floor?" And up he goes again.

The next sign reads: **Floor three—these quality hockey coaches enjoy coaching kids (not afraid to use discipline when necessary), have a detailed game plan for the season and possess a tremendous amount of hockey knowledge and experience.** "Hmm," the father says, "that's great but what could I get if I go higher?"

On the fourth floor, the sign says: **Floor four—these quality hockey coaches enjoy coaching kids (not afraid to use discipline when necessary), have a detailed game plan for the season, possess a tremendous amount of hockey knowledge and experience**

and run a great practice. "Wow, that's very tempting," the father says, "but I have to know what's on the next floor up."

Up one more he goes. **Floor five—these quality hockey coaches enjoy coaching kids (not afraid to use discipline when necessary), have a detailed game plan for the season, possess a tremendous amount of hockey knowledge and experience, run a great practice and believe strongly in fair play and making sure each player gets equal ice time.** "This is incredible," the father says, "but I just have to see what's on the next floor." So he ascends the final flight of stairs and comes upon the final door with the final sign:

Floor six—congratulations, you are visitor No. 3,458,987 to this floor. There are no quality hockey coaches available here. This floor exists solely as proof that hockey parents are impossible to please. Thank you for shopping Quality Hockey Coaches Mart, and have a nice day!

15 FALLING INTO THE TRAP, IN MORE WAYS THAN ONE

AS A COACHING STAFF, we were probably a little, or a lot, naïve, idealistic and intent on trying to do things the right way, but what we knew for sure before we started is that we would be doing it that season without the best player in Whitby.

Liam Reddox had decided to leave Whitby to play in the Metropolitan Toronto Hockey League (MTHL, now known as the Greater Toronto Hockey League or GTHL). He wasn't actually moving—he and his family were still residing in Whitby—but at the time it was possible to transfer out of the OMHA to the MTHL (it has become much more difficult to do that now; not impossible, but difficult). The OMHA is a residence-based league for the most part. You are supposed to play where you live and towns compete against other towns. The GTHL consists of as many as a dozen AAA organizations (Toronto Young Nationals, Toronto Marlies, Toronto Red Wings, among others). Any player in the GTHL is free to play on any team that wants him, regardless of where in the Greater Toronto Area he lives.

My personal preference has always been for my boys to play where they live, alongside many of the kids they go to school with or play summer sports with. But I also understand if a player or parent has an issue with the coach, or does not want the extra travel of going to OMHA centers east and north of Toronto; the OMHA system doesn't offer a lot of flexibility. Each to their own, I say.

In Liam's case, I fully understood why he was leaving. Liam was such an elite player, so much better than any of the Whitby kids; he clearly longed to play with the best players in the province on one of the very best teams. He wasn't going to be able to do that in Whitby. He could, though, achieve that by going into the city because the GTHL is well known for having two or three stacked teams. I understood the motivation.

Generally speaking, though, I'm not a fan of the GTHL model. Recruiting players is big business in the GTHL and before one season is even over, many of the players have already committed to playing on a different team for the next season. The old joke is that when the two best teams in the GTHL meet in the championship at the end of the year, half the players on one team are already committed to playing on the other team, and vice versa, and everyone knows it. It's like prepubescent unrestricted free agency gone wild. That said, the best players and best teams in the '86 age group were definitely in the MTHL.

Meanwhile, the minor atom AAA Wildcats were a reasonably competitive, middle-of-the-pack team in the OMHA's ETA (Eastern Triple A) league. We would usually get the same twenty-five or thirty kids trying out most years. There was no recruiting or anything like that. You'd get three or four tryouts to pick the team and that was that.

Whitby was still one of the smallest AAA centers in the province at the time and we had to play a new minor atom entry, the York-Simcoe Express, which drew on a very large region that includes Aurora, Newmarket and north all the way to Lake Simcoe. That's a big area, with a large population base, and the Express were a very good team in their first year in the league. They beat us badly in our first meeting so, as a coaching staff, we were brainstorming how we might make it closer for the coming rematch.

York Simcoe seemed so much faster than our kids. We were working hard at making our kids better skaters and puck handlers but the truth of the matter was that York Simcoe's athleticism was simply superior.

So I made a suggestion: How about we throw a little different look at them?

I'll get in big trouble with this story—from Wayne Gretzky to Bobby Orr—because what I did is considered one of the cardinal sins of coaching kids in minor hockey. So be it. I'm a big boy, I can take it.

We taught the kids to play a "system" for the next game against York Simcoe. There, I said it. Others would call it "neutralizing skill" and say it's a symbol of everything that is wrong with minor hockey.

Fair enough. All I knew is that our kids didn't have any fun getting beat by double digits the first time they played York Simcoe, I knew we were doing everything humanly possible in practice to make them better skaters and puck handlers, but I still didn't like our chances of doing it fast enough to not get blown out in the next meeting. Winning and losing is not the end all, be all—I understand that—but ask a bunch of ten-year-olds how much they enjoy getting blitzed 10–1.

We called it "The Trap," but it wasn't really the trap system employed by NHL teams that clog up the neutral zone.
Our trap was a little more aggressive and worked as follows:
The two forechecking wingers would go in hard and "lock off"
the other team's wingers, who were waiting on the boards for
the breakout pass. Our center would go in a little bit passively
to forecheck the other team's defenseman with the puck and
try to steer or angle him towards the boards, preferably on his
backhand, as he came out from behind his own net with the
puck. One of our defensemen would step up aggressively and
lock off the other team's center, who was usually curling in the
middle of the ice awaiting a breakout pass. Our other defenseman would stay back and assume a defensive posture at the
offensive blue line. Keep in mind, this was back in the bad
old days before zero tolerance on restraining fouls. If executed
properly, the other team's puck carrier had no passing options
at all. If he was angled towards the boards, he had nowhere
to go.

The kids on our team maybe weren't quite as athletic as the
York Simcoe players, but they were smart, coachable, eager and
they followed instructions well.

Whitby 8, York Simcoe 3.

The poor kids and the coach on the other team didn't
know what hit them. York Simcoe kept turning the puck over.
We kept scoring. It wasn't even close.

Now, I'm not saying there wasn't a temptation to use "The
Trap" over and over again, because it initially confused the hell
out of opposing players and coaches at the minor atom level.
But Stu and I both favored aggressive, two-man forechecking.
Besides, it wouldn't take long for opposing coaches to figure
out the easy way to beat our trap. That is, don't set up behind

the net, just wheel that puck as soon as you get it and skate by the first forechecker.

But we did trot it out from time to time when we thought we were really overmatched in the talent department. We were playing Detroit Compuware, one of North America's best teams, in the Kitchener-Waterloo tournament in November. There was no comparison between our team and theirs. They were the crème de la crème of minor hockey. It was a double-digit disaster just waiting to happen.

So we employed our version of the trap and kept it close. Compuware won 4–1. I think they outshot us 55–5, but we confused and confounded them long enough to keep it closer than it should have been. When it was over, Stu and I looked at each other on the bench. We were just drained. I shook Stu's hand and said: "Never have so many worked so hard for so long for so little." Our kids felt like they won the game, they were that happy not to have been blown out.

When the game was over one of the Compuware coaches started to give me the business about our "system" and lecturing me on how wrong it is to teach that to ten-year-olds. I let him have it right back; I didn't need a lesson in minor hockey values from this guy.

"I'll tell you what's wrong," I said to him. "Recruiting ten-year-olds from all over the state of Michigan and beyond, giving them skates and sticks and free equipment and putting together a team of little superstars that wins most of their games by twelve goals, with a bunch of obnoxious A-hole parents in the stands cheering every goal like it's the first, that's what's wrong."

I would like to tell you we were perfect coaches in our first year, but when things aren't going well, it's easy to get going down the wrong road.

Late in the regular season, the Wildcats went on quite a losing streak, up around eight or nine games. With each passing game of that streak, we became more and more desperate. In minor hockey, desperation usually means shortening the bench, playing your best players more and your weaker players less. It's an insidious thing, really. We never planned on doing it—equal ice time was going to be our foundation—but the losses piled up and suddenly the good players were getting all the power play time and some of the weaker players weren't seeing ice in the final few minutes.

I've told you enough embarrassing and stupid things about myself that I won't be accused of trying to make myself look too good here, but I do recall phoning Stu one night and telling him we needed a coaching meeting. So we got everyone together and I basically said we were losing sight of what's important, that equitable ice time was the platform on which we ran as coaches and we were getting away from that. It wasn't right. I said I would rather lose all our remaining games than coach a team where we regularly shortened the bench. Not surprisingly, everyone agreed. We would go back to doing it the right way, regardless of the results.

Which was not to say we would sit idly by and lose every game without pushing some buttons. Being a rookie coach, a rookie assistant coach at that, I felt I needed input from a veteran, so I called Roger Neilson, who was coaching the St. Louis Blues at the time. Roger, by the way, was one of the greatest people ever involved in the game of hockey and he's sorely missed after passing away in 2003 after a valiant battle

Right: Mike's first Christmas and we try to get him to sit up to show off his hockey pajamas as we take photos to get one for our family Christmas card.

Below: Shawn, as he is wont to do, hams it up on the kitchen floor as he gets ready to go to the Oshawa CYO five-year-old hockey school.

Bottom-right: Our little angels (in this portrait shot anyway), five-year-old Mike and two-year-old Shawn, thankfully, behave for the photographer.

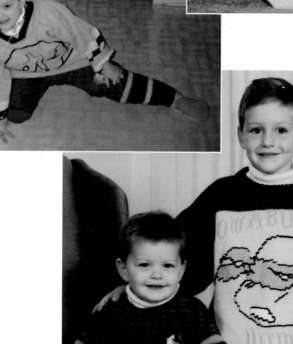

Portrait of the artist as a young boy: Mike was eight when he drew Toronto's Doug Gilmour and five when he drew Montreal's Patrick Roy.

Mike is all business as he sorts through his Panini hockey sticker collector book. A serious young man doing a serious job, and why wouldn't he be? It runs in the family.

Shawn takes a break from Mike's Tyke A provincial lacrosse championship weekend to get his picture taken alongside his obsession at the time – a Harley Davidson motorcycle. Mike looks on.

Mike (got something in your eye, kid?), Cindy and Shawn pose for a Christmas day photo with Nana and Pops, my Mom and Dad. Note my Dad's ever-present tie and my wheelchair-bound Mom's festive green paper crown.

Shawn, and his Teddy, and Mike take a little break from their hockey-card collecting in Mom and Dad's bed. Mike is wearing the classic Sudbury Wolves' blue sweater.

Above: Captain Mike's individual photo from his Whitby Select 7 season, the year Wojtek Wolski made him cry.

Left: Mike and his glasses – not the ones he wore under his cage – as a member of the AAA novice rep team.

Above: Mike (middle row, second from right) and me (top row, far right) at the Pickering Hockey Association five-year-old hockey school.

Left: Mike is resplendent in his Montreal uniform, his homage to Patrick Roy and Stephane Richer.

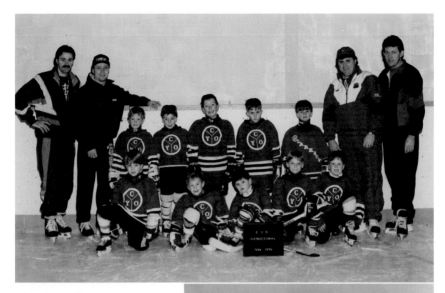

Above: Shawn (front and centre) and me (red track suit and hat), at the Oshawa CYO five-year-old hockey school.

Right: Shawn in his first year of six-year-old house league, which required me camping out for two nights to get him registered.

Work buddies Steve Dryden (right) and Bob Amesse (left) play some basement ball hockey with Mike and me.

Shawn, with his painted face, Mike and I celebrate a provincial lacrosse championship. Lacrosse is a great game.

with cancer. Typical of Roger, he was absolutely thrilled that I thought to call him and immediately began peppering me with questions about how we were losing games.

Roger, of course, was a great tactician and after pondering the data I gave him, he came up with a prescription for what he thought ailed the Wildcats—better puck support, especially on the breakout.

It was really just a little tweak to the standard controlled breakout, having the center come over to support the winger on the boards with the puck and keeping the weak side winger from flying the zone until he saw the other winger or center was safely on the way out of the zone before leaving himself.

We taught it to the kids and called it the "St. Louis Blue breakout." They thought it was cool to have a breakout named for an NHL team. We rediscovered our winning ways, to a point, and though we didn't make it to the OMHAs, it was, all in all, a successful year. The kids had fun; so did we.

16 VENGEANCE IS A DISH BEST SERVED CURVED

IT WASN'T REALLY CHILD ABUSE. Not really, although I suppose I could see how some might see it that way.

I have already told you Mike was a good kid, a good player but, at times, a little on the volatile side. Gee, I wonder where he got that?

It was Mike's major atom AAA (eleven-year-old) season and we were in Kitchener for a tournament. We were down to our last round-robin game on a Saturday afternoon and were playing the Detroit Little Caesars, who were being coached by Viktor Fedorov, father of then-Red Wing Sergei Fedorov. All the Wildcats needed was a tie to advance, but midway through the game we were down 2–0 and our prospects looked a little bleak.

Stu Seedhouse was, of course, still the head coach, but I was responsible for changing the forward lines. Mike had just completed a shift where things hadn't gone particularly well for his line. He came off the ice in what I would call a "mild to moderate" state of agitation.

"Relax, Mike," I said to him cheerily, sensing he needed to be calmed down. "You're not playing bad, the team isn't playing bad, there's lots of time left, just relax and we'll be fine."

It was not only textbook coaching, it was textbook parenting. Potentially volatile situation; take the emotion out of it; everybody take a deep breath and relax. I was kind of proud of myself because I'm not usually that calm, cool and collected.

But Mike didn't feel like relaxing, apparently. He turned and looked at me through those big glasses of his and more or less snarled a few words, waved his arms in my direction and suggested he didn't need to relax and I didn't need to remind him to relax. He started getting bent out of shape.

It was on. What follows, it goes without saying, was not textbook coaching or parenting.

Mike had his back to me, I put my hand on his shoulder and, much more forcefully and emphatically, told him to not talk back, keep his mouth shut and don't get excited. Well, Mike didn't like that too much. He twisted his shoulder to get my hand off him, started talking a lot of emotional nonsense and kicking one of his skates against the boards. He was having quite a little tantrum, he was on the way to out of control and my fuse was lit, too.

I hopped off the bench and stood just behind it. I reached around to the front of Mike, grabbed two fistfuls of his hockey sweater right in the middle of his chest and picked him up off the ground, feet up and over the bench, and deposited him in front of me as I pivoted to put my back to the game.

Mike continued to squirm and fuss a bit as he stood there so I tightened my grip on his sweater with both hands and pulled him in really close so my face was right up against his cage. I was trying to use eye contact to snap him out of wherever he was and I really blasted him, telling him only one thing—"Settle down!"

As quickly as it got heated, it suddenly cooled. Just like that, the two of us were there, face to face and not saying a word to each other. I realized that whatever had possessed him to lose his cool, and mine as well, had passed. Recognizing we needed a quick reconciliation—there was still lots of hockey to be played—I very calmly explained to Mike I wasn't mad at him, that he had been playing fine and I only wanted him to focus on playing the game, that we were down two goals and we needed him to be at his best if we were going to get a tie and move on.

All of this transpired in less than one minute—it started and ended in a flash—while the game was still going on. I patted him on the back, he took his place on the bench and was ready to go again. It was almost as if it had never happened. As I jumped back up on the bench, though, I started to worry who in the stands might have seen me pick up Mike by his sweater and get into his face.

I sidled up to Stu on the bench, folded my arms across my chest to look really casual and relaxed, I tilted my head in Stu's direction while I watched the game and said, "Stu, uh, could you do me a, uh, little favor? Just have a look up in the stands and tell me if Cindy is staring at me right now?"

"Nope," Stu said. "She's watching the game."

Whew. Close call. Cindy hadn't seen what happened with me and Mike and that was just as well.

No coach should ever, and I mean ever, lay hands on one of his players. It's just not acceptable. But in that instance, for that moment, I wasn't Mike's coach as much as I was his father. Some will say it shouldn't matter; it was unacceptable in any case, or that's a good reason for parents not ever coaching their kids.

Fair enough, but I did what I felt needed to be done at the time and the moment passed and we all lived happily ever after. After that, though, Stu and I agreed in the future he would handle all "situations" with Mike and I would do the same with his son Steven because there was no question the father-son dynamic complicated things that day.

Now, here's the kicker to the story.

After he got refocused, Mike assisted on one goal and scored the tying goal himself. The game finished 2–2; we advanced, knocking out the Little Caesars.

Perhaps there was something in the air in that Kitchener arena that day because in the lobby right after that game, a couple of parents from the Little Caesars' team tried to physically accost their coach, Viktor Fedorov. It was quite a nasty scene.

"Wow," I said to one of the other Detroit parents in the lobby after the melee, "that's crazy. Why did they go after the coach, their kids not get enough ice time?"

"No," the Detroit parent responded, "those were the parents of the good players who thought he [Fedorov] didn't shorten the bench enough to win the game. They were mad because he played everyone, we tied and we're not moving on."

Go figure. Another day in the paradise we call minor hockey.

The final word on this episode, though, goes to Mike himself, who even today still likes to needle me: "Hey, Dad, remember that time you physically abused me in major atom?"

To which I say, "Yes, Mike, I do remember."

And, without fail, with a big grin, he replies: "Thanks, Dad, I needed that."

———— ● ————

Again, I find myself having to make sure you don't think one snapshot of a Mike–Bob "snap show" was in any way indicative of the whole major atom AAA season, because it wasn't. It was a great year. The kids, the coaching staff and the parents had a great time. The team was reasonably competitive most nights and, from a personal perspective, Mike was scoring a lot of goals, racking up points and playing quite well. As coaches, we put a lot into it and I believe the kids got a lot out of it, too. The funny or memorable moments are too numerous to recount but there are two stories that have to be told.

Whitby was playing Quinte at Iroquois Park. It was a great game, really intense. We scored the go-ahead goal with less than a minute left, but a talented and somewhat theatrical Quinte defenseman answered back with the tying goal just seconds later. He celebrated it by skating to the center ice dot, turning towards our parents in the stands and bowing to them. Well, that got everyone all worked up, on and off the ice.

With four seconds left we had a face-off in the Quinte end and Stu called time out, pulled the goalie for an extra attacker and drew up a play for the kids to try to get the winner. But when he finished explaining the play to the kids—and this is just one reason why Stu is a very good coach—he told the players in no uncertain terms that he did not want any shenanigans, whether we scored or not. He instructed every player on the bench to stay there when the game ended. Anyway, long story short, we scored a miraculous buzzer-beater goal right off the face-off, just as time was expiring, to win the game. While the kids on the ice were celebrating like crazy, Stu and I were making sure to hold our bench.

The next thing you know—and this image is indelibly burned into all of our minds—we see our trainer Kevin O'Brien, in his blue and gold Whitby track suit, running full speed off the bench and onto the ice towards the on-ice celebration. He dropped down onto both knees as he passed the Quinte bench—sliding, hootin' and hollerin'—all the while waving his white trainer's towel over his head in a circular motion.

Stu and I looked at each other and completely cracked up. The kids on the bench were laughing so hard at "Mr. O'Brien" that they were almost crying, especially since he had lectured the kids before the game on "good sportsmanship."

I guess there was one "big kid" Stu forgot to talk to about staying on the bench.

The other story that has to be told from the same season is the one that inspired this book and the whole notion of Crazy Hockey Dad.

We had been knocked out of the OMHA playoffs and had dropped down to the ETA (Eastern Triple A) playoffs, or "ringette round," as we called it. It was the final game of a series with Barrie in venerable Dunlop Arena and we were losing 5–2 with about five minutes to go.

"Hey, Stu," I suggested, "why don't you let me call a stick measurement to see if we can't score a power play goal to try to light a little fire here?"

Stu thought about it and although the look on his face was one of reluctance, he said, "Go for it."

In one of the previous games against Barrie, I had been looking at their kids' sticks in the rack between the benches and noticed about half of their team was using wildly illegal curves.

I had one of our players, an alternate captain, Kenny Henry, ask the referee for a stick measurement on a Barrie player. The referee looked at poor Kenny like he was nuts and then shot me a dirty look on the bench. You could tell he was really ticked a coach was calling a stick measurement in major atom. He asked Kenny, "What kind of measurement do you want?" This ref was playing it by the book, because when you request a stick measurement, apparently you have to specify if it's for the curve or the length or whatever. Kenny guessed "curve" and the ref was obliged to do the measurement.

The ref confiscated the Barrie player's stick for the measurement and the whole arena erupted. Their bench and their parents went a little nuts. The ref had to go to the referees' room to get a stick-measuring gauge. It was quite a scene.

Sure enough, the stick was illegal, the Barrie player went to the box and with only seconds left in his penalty, we scored a power play goal to narrow Barrie's lead to two goals with just over three minutes left in the game. The goal lit a fire under our guys. We started to play a lot better. With less than two minutes remaining, there was a stoppage and I went back at Stu.

"Let me call another stick measurement," I said. "Their kids are still using the illegal sticks."

Stu started laughing. "Go ahead," he said.

If everyone in the rink went a little nuts on the first stick call, you should have witnessed the scene when we called the second. Their bench was in bedlam. Kids were throwing sticks up to their parents in the crowd, presumably to get the illegal sticks off their bench. Some of their parents were screaming at me and our bench. The referee was looking at me like he wanted me dead.

Less than twenty seconds into the power play, we scored to make it 5–4. There was lots of time, more than a minute, left. The worm had definitely turned. You could see the Barrie bench was in a state of disarray. Our kids were all fired up.

There was a stoppage with about one minute left. I noticed one Barrie player on the ice still using a stick with a banana curve.

"Stu, let me call another one," I pleaded.

Stu laughed, thought about it briefly: "No, we're good now. We're going to be fine."

Stu pulled the goalie in the final minute and one of our defensemen, Bobby Scott, who hadn't scored a goal all season, tried to one-time a shot. He chunked or sliced the puck and it went straight up in the air and came down, bouncing wildly, in the slot. One bounce, two bounces and right over the goalie's glove and into the net. With nine seconds left, the game was tied 5–5. It was pandemonium.

Time expired, we were going to overtime and our message to the kids was very basic. Go for it. Hold nothing back. We had all the momentum. You could tell by looking at their bench they were crushed.

Sure enough, Matt Snowden scored the game-winning goal about twenty seconds in on the first shift of overtime.

Our kids and parents were celebrating. I seem to recall some of the Barrie parents yelling at me, although it looked like a few of them were yelling at their own coach, too. The referee was looking at me and shaking his head. If looks could kill.

Once our kids and coaching staff had gone to the dressing room to celebrate the win, I told Stu I had better go over to the Barrie side of the lobby, where their parents were waiting outside their dressing room, and take any medicine that was coming my way.

I went over and, sure enough, as soon as I got there, one of their parents let me have it.

"What a cheap way to win a hockey game," he said. "You should be ashamed of yourself, and to think you go on TV and talk about hockey. You're an embarrassment."

I asked this guy how long his son had played on the team and he responded it was his first year with the club. I then told this dad to ask one of the other parents on the team whose kid had played there for two years to explain to him why I might be calling stick measurements in a major atom game.

If you haven't already figured it out, the coach of this Barrie major atom team was the same guy who had coached the Barrie major novice AAA team two years ago, the same team that protested and overturned a playoff game that they lost to Whitby because our suspended coach was seen coming out of the dressing room.

Those two stick measurements—and I still wish Stu had let me call the third one, just for the hell of it—were my first, second and last calls of that kind. Ever. I never, in a million years, would have even considered calling a stick measurement if not for the history with that coach and what the Barrie organization had done in Mike's major novice AAA year.

But, like I said at the end of Chapter Eleven, payback's a bitch.

And if you talk to any of the '86s who played AAA hockey in Whitby for a good long time and ask them for one of their most memorable moments, chances are good they'll mention the "Barrie stick measurement game." It will still bring a smile to their face.

Mine, too.

17 THE BEST REWARD, BAR NONE, AND HOCKEY PARENTS FROM HELL

WHEN LAST WE LEFT YOU with regard to Shawn, he was wrapping up his Select 7 experience and looking as though he might be on his way to figuring out on which side of the face-off circle he belonged. It was now time for Shawn to enter the rep phase of his minor hockey career and it was fairly obvious to all of us, including Shawn, that he wasn't exactly AAA material.

That never bothered me in the least and it most certainly didn't bother Shawn. He had no desire to even try out for AAA and was content to try to make his mark with the minor novice AA team.

Mike and Shawn could not have been more different in their on-ice temperament. Mike was competitive and driven, sometimes too much so. Shawn was far more relaxed and happy-go-lucky. Which is not to suggest Shawn wasn't a good AA player in his own right. He was just motivated by different things than Mike.

There was a game early in his minor novice year that illustrated this perfectly. Shawn found himself in the penalty box. The timekeeper was the son of Shawn's head coach, Norm Orviss. Shawn was chitchatting away with Norm's son in the penalty box when The Proposition was made. "If you come right out of the penalty box and score a goal," the timekeeper said to Shawn, "I'll buy you a chocolate bar when the game is over." This kid was talking Shawn's language.

As fate would have it, Shawn stepped out of the box at precisely the same moment the puck was cleared up the ice. He found himself on a clear-cut breakaway. He went in and buried it. It was the winning goal in a 2–1 game, the team's first win of the regular season. In the days that followed a community newspaper ran a little write-up with a photo of Shawn that was taken immediately after the game. The black and white photo is a little too grainy to see it clearly, but if you look very closely at Shawn's hands, he's holding onto something. It's a Twix chocolate bar, which the timekeeper had given Shawn at the end of the game.

By the time I got into the dressing room to take off his skates, Shawn had already started munching on the bar and happily told me the story of how he got it. He was on Cloud Nine, as much or more for the bar as the goal. All these years later, it's as funny and cute and brings a smile to my face now as it did then.

———— ● ————

I would be lying if I told you I was as heavily involved with Shawn's hockey, from his Select 7 season through the next three years of his rep hockey, because those were the four years I was coaching Mike. Cindy picked up the slack for driving

Shawn and being there when I was absent because of conflicts with Mike's games or practices or my work schedule, but any chance I got to be at Shawn's hockey, I was most definitely there. Even if it meant I had to do a little Crazy Hockey Dad crazy driving.

Mike was fortunate throughout his minor hockey career to have some nice continuity in coaching. He had John Velacich for three years. Then it was Stu Seedhouse, who was an assistant under John, for the next two years. Then it was me, who was an assistant under Stu, for two years, followed by Bucky Crouch, who worked on my staff as the goalie coach, for two more years. Mike played eight years of AAA hockey and had only four head coaches. His new head coach was always someone who had been an assistant the year before.

Shawn, on the other hand, had three different head coaches in his first four years of competitive hockey and never had the same coach in two consecutive years until I coached him in major atom and minor peewee. Jeff Sisson, a good guy who lived in our neighborhood and whose son, Kyle, went to school with Shawn, was the Select 7 coach. Norm Orviss was Shawn's minor novice AA coach. Jeff Sisson came back to coach the major novice AA team for a year and then Don Houghton took over in the minor atom AA season. I suppose there's nothing intrinsically wrong with having a new coach each year, but there is a lot to be said for continuity, for the coach getting to know the boys really well and vice versa. Every new coach comes in with big ideas on how he wants to do things. If that philosophy or approach changes year after year, it's a lot harder for kids to adapt.

Shawn's first year of rep hockey, though, did feature our first experience with The Hockey Parents From Hell (THPFH).

It's funny, really, that for all the minor hockey and lacrosse teams Mike and Shawn played on, I could count the real problem people on one hand and have a finger or two left. Sure, over the course of time, there might have been isolated incidents involving a parent on a particular issue, but there was, from our personal experience, just one extreme case of THPFH.

THPFH generally fall into two categories. The first is THPFH lifers, who in spite of being a cancerous blight on the minor hockey landscape, manage to go the distance and be a royal pain in everyone's ass for an eight-to-ten-year period. For reasons no one can explain, they bounce from team to team wreaking havoc but have inexplicable staying power. The second is THPFH flaming burnouts, who roar onto the scene with reckless abandon, lighting fires, abusing coaches, insulting kids and parents and generally proving to be antisocial deviants who were born without a clue. The former is bad; the latter is worse. The lifers have some—not much, mind you, but some—sense of boundaries, knowing that if they push too far they'll ultimately be expelled from minor hockey culture. The flaming burnouts, though, know no bounds. They come, they go, they scorch the earth and then pull their kid out of hockey because of the "politics." It's always the politics, never the fact that they are usually rude, ignorant, selfish, malicious and truly crazy.

THPFH on Shawn's team were flaming burnouts, there for just one season. It was obvious at the first tournament of the year when the patriarch of THPFH showed up to the game with a stopwatch and a pen and notepad to keep track of Junior's ice time. He had actually enlisted another parent on the team to help him out because, well, as anybody in the game knows, keeping track of nine forwards' ice time on the fly is no mean feat. And, of course, misery loves company. The other dad should have known better but then that's the real danger of THPFH.

What is it they say about the universal truth of coaching in minor hockey? Five parents love you, five hate you and five are neutral. The challenge is keeping the five who are neutral away from the five who hate you. I love that. It's so true. Even in the NHL, coaches will tell you it's the same, not with parents of course, but players.

Shawn's coach that year, Norm Orviss, had come out of minor hockey retirement, along with three of his best buddies who had once coached their own kids. They were a little older version of Stu, Kevin and me, just looking to relive some of the glory days. And they got THPFH as their reward.

In the wake of the tournament where everyone saw THPFH and his accomplice feverishly recording ice times, Norm called a parent meeting in a dressing room at Iroquois Park, where he tried to put out the fire. He explained as best he could their philosophy and while it all made perfect sense, the patriarch and matriarch of THPFH weren't satisfied. They began peppering the staff with questions and accusations. It was very uncomfortable with most of the parents just looking at the floor and hoping it would end soon.

I'd finally had enough of this inquisition—being a coach for Mike's team at the time, I had great sympathy for Norm—and in the middle of it all, I just said: "Well, I think we can all agree that the coaches are doing a good job. I would say this meeting is over."

All the parents made for the door except of course THPFH, who continued to grind Norm. It was just them and me and Norm. I was seriously concerned this verbal confrontation might escalate to physical, so I put my arm around Norm and said, "Excuse me, but I need to talk to you about something outside."

And that was that. We just left them in there. Long story short, THPFH were never heard of again after that season. I used to occasionally see them around the rink the next season—it wasn't long before they disappeared entirely—and isn't that the most unfortunate aspect of all?

Their boy seemed like an okay kid and was a decent little player, too. I always felt sorry for kids like that. They never stood a chance. Kids like that don't get cut from hockey teams; their parents do, not that THPFH would ever figure that out.

THE FOUR-POINT PLAN
Not as Stupid as I Look

THE PREMISE OF THIS BOOK is I am not the least bit shy about holding myself up to ridicule and revealing to one and all that I can be a horse's ass at times. I'm okay with that. But if you're going to read the stories that make me look like an idiot, you're also going to have to put up with the occasional parts where I tell you how smart I am. If that doesn't appeal to you, skip this chapter entirely and forge ahead because there are many examples of stupidity to come.

But right here, right now, it's time to tell you I'm not as stupid as I look. I do actually get it; I fully understand what minor hockey is about, at least what it should be about. This, of course, is the preface to me becoming the head coach of the Whitby minor peewee AAA team.

Coaching as an assistant with Stu Seedhouse in atom, I knew I wanted to be the head coach in minor peewee, but my fear was I wouldn't be able to because of work commitments. Exacerbating the situation was that Stu was not going to be involved this year as he was going to coach his daughter Ellie's team in girls' hockey. Kevin O'Brien was back as trainer and I shanghaied another parent, Ron Balcom, whose son Aaron was on the team, to be the manager/treasurer.

The challenge, though, was finding minor hockey coaching expertise—one or preferably two experienced assistants—for the times when I wouldn't be able to be at a practice and/or a game. In my business, that could be anytime, anywhere.

I was at the Nagano Olympics in 1998 and my biggest concern was not whether Wayne Gretzky should have shot in the shootout against Dominik Hasek, but whether I could, long distance, convince a friend, Mark Rowland from Oshawa, to help out as an associate coach. Mark had coached his own son back in the day, had been "retired" and wasn't sure he wanted to do it again. But I was persuasive on the phone from Japan and managed to convince him to give it a shot, for one year anyway. That was great; it was even better that Mark had a friend, Steve Hedington, who had played in the Ontario Hockey League (Niagara Falls and Sudbury) and wanted to help out, too. That took care of that. I was going to be a head coach for the first time. I am often asked how, with such a busy work schedule, I ever find the time to coach. The answer is simple really. If you want to get to your kids' practices and games, it's actually easier if you coach. Who decides when practices and games are scheduled? The coach, of course. It's all about control. For the most part, I had control of when the team would practice or play and I set it up in such a way to minimize conflicts with work. When I went to the OMHA scheduling meetings I was like General Norman Schwarzkopf on Operation Desert Storm. But there are always going to be conflicts and that's why you need a large and able support staff who you trust implicitly and I most certainly had that. Coaching is a weighty responsibilty.

Ultimately, the head coach of a minor hockey team is charged with safeguarding seventeen kids, whose parents may or may not be present, for many hours each week from late August to early March, in places that could be many miles away from home. Outside of a kid's parents, a minor hockey coach can have as much, if not more, input and influence as that kid's teacher at school.

I have very strong opinions on what minor hockey should be. So now you're going to get the same four-point philosophy I outlined for the parents and players at the start of that season:

1. Have Fun. If it isn't fun, what's the point? That doesn't mean it can't be challenging or there won't be bumps in the road, but if the players and parents aren't having fun, why do it? It costs too much money and takes up too many days and nights for it not to be fun.

   I firmly believe that once a month or so, outside of practices or games, the team needs to have fun as a group away from the arena. It could be an excursion to the Hockey Hall of Fame; a pregame meal at Pizza Hut or Don Cherry's Restaurant; the ever-popular trip to Laser Quest in Oshawa; a game of touch football or ball hockey; or perhaps a bus trip to a road game to make the kids feel like they're (minor?) pros.

   On the ice, I started every practice with five-minute mini-games at each end of the ice, four-on-four at one end and four-on-three at the other with a goalie in each net. The attacking team had to score a goal and then go on defense or the defending team had to get the puck back out over the blue line in order to switch to offense, just like a half-court game of one-on-one basketball. The only rule was the kids had to go hard, keep their feet moving, and that was rarely a problem. Of all the things I ever did as a coach, nothing got a more favorable reaction from the kids than a mini-game to start every practice. It's the best warm-up for practice because they not only worked up a good sweat, they got excited about practicing. The kids worked harder, competed harder, got more creative and had more fun playing that mini-game than any drill. They were eager and pumped up to do whatever hard work we threw at them in practice after that.

The fun, I always believed, should extend to the parents, too. We had many good parent parties. It didn't hurt that the group of parents on Mike's team were a terrific, level-headed bunch who were always up for a good time.

At the end of it all, as much as what takes place on the ice is of value, it's the other stuff the kids really remember, like the time Nick Cotter zipped himself inside his hockey bag or when Kyle O'Brien got Walter Gretzky to autograph his jock. It's about the relationships, friendships and many memories. If you make it just about the hockey, you have made a critical mistake.

2. Instill the Right Values. Teamwork. Sportsmanship. Discipline. Work ethic. Commitment. Dedication. Sacrifice. Cooperation. Respect. All that good stuff.

If, at the end of the season, the players, and the coaches and parents for that matter, have learned more about those qualities than they have about how to take a slap shot or break the puck out of their own end, I would consider it a successful season. If you're going to invest that much time, effort and money, there has to be a bigger payoff than what happens on the ice.

3. Improve Individual Skating and Skills Development. This one is pretty obvious. As a coach, you are responsible for making sure the kids are better skaters, puck handlers and shooters at the end of the season than at the beginning. While skill development happened every time we took to the ice for practice, we tried to designate at least one practice a week to just skills. We often brought in outside help who specialized in power skating or puck handling or off-ice conditioning. I had a high-performance trainer, Dennis Lindsay, to introduce the kids to rudimentary plyometrics and core work. I had Jari Byrski—my wonderful Ukrainian friend and a true character who has worked with countless Toronto-area kids over the years, including so many that have made it in the NHL (Jason Spezza, Brent Burns, Wojtek Wolski, among others)—to work on skating and puck handling in his fun-infused fashion.

4. Teaching Team Concepts, Strategies and Systems. Yes, there's that dirty word again—systems. There are those who will tell you it is evil incarnate in minor hockey. If that's all you're doing for instruction, shame on you. But if you are ensuring the kids are having fun on and off the ice, extolling the proper life values, giving them well-designed personal improvement programs for skills etc., there is nothing wrong with teaching them how to break out of their zone, forecheck, regroup, work a power play, set up a penalty kill, block shots and take away passing or shooting lanes. In other words, teaching them how to play like a team.

Like anything in life, it's all about balance and finding the right emphasis at the right time.

In many ways, hockey is a complex game. In so many others, though, it really couldn't be simpler. It doesn't matter if it's the NHL or minor peewee AAA, it's basically the same game. I am not so naïve to believe coaching a minor peewee AAA team is the same as coaching in the NHL. Being around the NHL every day, I know that as well as anyone.

But the same basic principles of the game still apply.

We gave each kid a different slogan to memorize that related to a specific aspect of the game and how we thought it should be played. If an NHL team were to successfully execute the majority of these slogans on any given night, that team would win a lot more than it loses:

Keep your feet moving.

Shoot the puck.

Pucks and bodies to the net.

Support the puck all over the ice, no fair fights (in other words, always try to outnumber the other team in battles for loose pucks).

Short, hard shifts.

Don't be afraid to make a mistake.

Fight from and/or get on the right side of the puck (back-check like your hair is on fire).

The puck moves faster than anyone can skate, head-man the puck.

No turnovers at either blue line.

Discipline, discipline, discipline; initiate, don't retaliate.

Play the game, not the scoreboard (that is, don't get discouraged if you're down three and don't get complacent if you're up three, just play the same way every shift).

Always make yourself a threat to score a goal.

Say nothing when you lose; say less when you win.

It's all about *respect*. For your teammates, your coaches, your parents, your opponents, yourself and the officials.

———— 🏒 ————

There is an old saying in hockey that goes something like this: "What goes on in the dressing room stays in the dressing room."

If you are going to coach kids' hockey, DO NOT embrace that slogan. If you do, you are asking for trouble. The dressing room is not Las Vegas and these players are not adults.

As difficult as some parents can be by being overly involved and interfering when you are coaching, the parents ultimately have the right to know what goes on behind closed doors with their kids. There must be a high level of transparency. And that is for your own protection as much as anything.

As a coach, you must be aware of what is going on at all times in your dressing room. It's important for kids to develop some independence and not feel like there is someone watching over their every move—the dressing room needs to feel like it is "their" place—but a common mistake many minor hockey coaches make is to leave their players unsupervised in the dressing room for too long. You need to know if your kids are locker-boxing (pounding each other in their helmeted heads with their gloves on) or if kids are being picked on or harassed. Or whatever. I don't have to tell anyone reading this book how cruel kids can be and how the mob mentality can take over if you permit it. All of that is the head coach's responsibility as much as teaching them how to play the game.

As for the playing hockey part of coaching, I've always believed you don't ask players of any age or caliber to win. You don't ask them to score goals or prevent them. It's the old journey versus destination thing; the focus should be on the process as opposed to the result. Scoring goals and getting wins are the end result. You have to teach them all the little things—the journey, if you will—which are required to score or prevent goals. I never asked or expected the kids to win. I asked them to work hard and embrace the values, skills and concepts they were taught.

On the nights they did that, it was the most gratifying experience one could imagine. Other nights, well, maybe not so much gratifying as it was intensely challenging. That, however, is the magnet pull of coaching. If it was easy, they would call it being in the media.

Now, getting players to execute all of that with any degree of consistency? Well, that's something else entirely and, boy, did I find that out the hard way in my first year as a head coach.

19 TOUGH LOVE AND LEARNING OUR LESSONS THE HARD WAY

I SHOULD HAVE KNOWN my first year as head coach was going to be a challenge when I ran afoul of the Whitby Minor Hockey Association before the team had even been picked. Tryouts were in April. The WMHA rule was a coach couldn't release any players until after the second tryout.

My problem was that the second tryout ended exactly thirty minutes before I was scheduled to be on the air at TSN. Not *at* TSN, *on the air* at TSN. It was going to be a play at the plate just to finish the tryout, never mind release players after it, and get to work on time.

Now, I am nothing if not a practical man. I had to find a way to cut ten or twelve kids instantaneously after that second tryout. But the association also had fairly firm guidelines on how releasing players could be done—one-on-one meetings; letters; or posting helmet numbers (never names) assigned during tryout registration. I didn't have time for any of that. So I came up with my own idea, which, quite frankly, I thought was ingenious.

With about twenty minutes left in the ninety-minute try-out, I divided the kids on the ice into two groups. One was larger than the other. I took the smaller group at one end; the other coaches took the larger group at the other end. I ran a few drills and then gathered the kids at my end, explained my time constraints and how this may be unconventional, but they were being released. They went to the dressing rooms, where they got changed while the remaining kids finished the try-out. As the kids who were cut left the dressing room, I had Ron Balcom, the team manager, give them a letter saying I would be happy to meet one-on-one with any parent or player at any time to explain my decision, but not now, not at this moment.

Personally, I thought it was just about the best way to cut kids. None of the boys seemed to have any problem with it (kids rarely do, but more on that later). They were able to get changed and leave the rink without having to deal with those kids who didn't get cut. And I got to work on time. Barely.

But someone didn't like it. I caught hell from the association and was told in no uncertain terms not to do it again. All right, fine, although it only underlined what I have often subscribed to in life—it's easier to get forgiveness than permission.

———— ● ————

Nothing came easy in that minor peewee (twelve-year-old) year, for me or the kids.

It was the year body contact was introduced for these players. While there is always great debate on when is the best time to introduce contact in minor hockey, I can only say from personal experience that it's definitely not when the kids are twelve. Yet that is the standard in minor hockey in Canada.

It's been my experience that at the age of twelve, the size difference, in both height and weight, between the biggest players and smallest players is greater than at any other age. So I would say the potential for injury is far greater at twelve. It's also the age when many of the kids are going through puberty and their hormones are absolutely raging out of control. I personally prefer bringing in contact at age ten, the way it was done with Shawn's age group in a pilot program. But that's just me.

Bill Carroll, the former NHLer who won four Stanley Cups with the New York Islanders and Edmonton Oilers, would agree. Bill is a good friend. His son Matthew (who plays for the Toronto Rock in the National Lacrosse League) is the same age as Mike, and Bill's youngest son, Marcus (who plays for Owen Sound of the Ontario Hockey League), is the same age as Shawn. Our boys played lacrosse together and hockey against each other. I coached against Bill in minor peewee as he was behind the bench of the Ajax-Pickering Raiders and former NHLer Bobby Lalonde was one of his assistants.

Bill and I used to joke that in minor peewee they should change the name of the game from "hockey" to "hit" because that's all the kids focused on. Some games you could have played without a puck and the kids wouldn't have noticed.

Well, that wasn't quite true of my Wildcats. Remember that part about puberty? The kids on my team, for the most part, were very late to that party. This group of '86s had always been fairly competitive within their age group. But it became apparent early in the minor peewee season that wasn't going to be the case. Our kids—including Mike (maybe especially Mike)—appeared to be physically overmatched in just about every regard.

Bill Carroll's Ajax-Pickering team steamrolled us early that season. They were so much faster and physically stronger. They ran us out of the rink on repeated occasions. As an NHLer, Bill was the quintessential defensive specialist but he coached the kids exactly opposite to the way he played. His team played run and gun and, boy, did they run and gun us. We even lost the Rum Cup that year. That was just a little inside joke between Bobby Lalonde and me. Both of us like a sip of the demon rum now and again, so we talked about putting a bottle on the line for each game. Hence, our games against each other became known as the Rum Cup.

Puberty apparently wasn't an issue in Peterborough. The Borough Boys, who used to be the league doormat but were now a dominant team, had all grown up. They were huge. And mean. They looked and played like a men's team and, believe me, it was like men against boys in our games with them.

I never saw any of this coming, neither did the kids. Their reaction, as twelve-year-olds, was understandable but not what I would necessarily deem acceptable. They basically shut down—mentally, emotionally and then physically. Once they realized they were, for the most part, physically overmatched, the attributes they did possess (puck skills, hockey sense, team play and a decent scoring touch) went right out the window. They quickly lost their confidence. Once a kid's confidence goes, it is a long, slippery slope. They became rather timid and skittish, if not downright scared at times, and that, folks, is no way to go through minor peewee AAA and the first year of body contact.

Were we having fun yet? The losses were piling up. The margins of defeat were not pretty.

As the head coach, I had two choices. I could accept what was happening, try to keep the kids' spirits up as best I could and we could all take our lumps. You know, relax, it's just a game. Or I could try to come up with a plan, painful as that might be, to fight through the adversity and offer some pushback. The choice was obvious for me—I love a challenge—but in order to do that I was going to have to push the envelope a little. Or maybe a lot.

Competing is a skill, the same as skating or puck handling, but it's a lot harder to teach because to do it, you have to be a hard son of a gun. You have to get in people's faces, you have to push them and grind and take them out of their comfort zone over and over again so that they eventually become conditioned and confident enough to push back and push back hard. No one likes to go through that learning experience. It isn't fun. So I knew what had to be done, but I also knew it wasn't going to be pretty. Remember, these were twelve-year-old kids, not professionals.

But you know what? I really thought these kids were worth it. I liked them. They were a good bunch of boys from good families and they liked each other and playing hockey together.

I don't want to create the sense the kids had no fun. We still had social outings for them. They still had their mini-games at the beginning of each practice. They still had lots of horseplay at the rink. As hard as we pushed them, the kids knew we liked and respected them. The fact I knew so many of them and their families so well, from our years of minor hockey and lacrosse together, helped immeasurably. This was one case where being a parent-coach and having familiarity and relationships outside of the rink with a lot of the families was a real benefit. In fact, I couldn't have done it if there weren't already a high level of trust between me and many of the parents.

Man, did those kids get pushed in practice. Hard. There was lots of skating and even more battling. The three-on-three battle drills down low became unbelievably intense and a regular staple. There was lots of yelling and screaming, most of it from me. Our practices became harder than the games, and that was the idea. These kids simply needed to get much tougher—mentally, emotionally and physically. I don't think anything I ever did was out of pure anger or frustration as much as it was calculated, but that doesn't mean there weren't some times when people thought I was a little, or maybe a lot, nuts.

In a tournament in Kitchener, we fell behind 6–0 in the first period against a very good Team Illinois squad. They scored a couple of soft goals early and our guys just folded. The ice resurfacing was to be done at the end of the first period, but I didn't allow the kids to leave the bench to go to the dressing room for the intermission. I made them all stay seated there, watching the Zamboni go around and around. I literally walked up and down the bench while I figuratively went up and down each player with some really pointed criticism. All of this unfolded in front of the spectators, and their parents, in the stands. I don't doubt some of them thought I had gone too far.

Immediately after that game, though, I went even farther. I took the rare step of meeting with a couple of parents and reading them the riot act. It was my infamous goalie rant. Our goalies, like the rest of the team, had been performing poorly but in this game, they were particularly bad. As anyone in hockey knows, if you don't get a save now and again, it doesn't matter what else you do, you're toast.

One of the goalies was Kyle Clancy, whose parents, Sue and Dan, were friends of ours. Kyle was part of a group of five or six kids who played AAA hockey together in the winter and rep lacrosse in the summer all the way up. Kyle was a very good lacrosse goalie and a good hockey goalie, too, but like all the kids, his confidence was shot at this point.

I remember telling his mom, Sue, and the other goalie's parents, as well as the goalies themselves, that what I was about to say wasn't fair, I understand that, but that life wasn't fair. I told them that if life were fair, a goalie's equipment wouldn't cost more than every other player's. I told them goalies get too much credit when a team wins and goalies get too much blame when a team loses. I then told them their kids weren't mentally prepared to play the games, they weren't working hard enough to get better and that if the team had any chance of competing, we needed better goaltending. I told them if their kids didn't prepare better and work harder, I would have to find new goalies in mid-season.

The part about finding new goalies was a total bluff. I am one hundred percent philosophically opposed to any minor hockey team making a personnel change in mid-season just to get better. That's just not right.

But for my purposes I had to get our goalies out of their comfort zone and I didn't mind telling a white lie to do it. And I also told the goalies and their parents that night that we would get them some specialized instruction to help them out. Right after that tournament, we got ourselves a very good goalie coach, Bucky Crouch. It's all well and good to rant and rave at kids and parents that they need to be better, but the onus is ultimately on the coaching staff to provide them the tools to do it.

Then there was a game in Peterborough, where we were trying our best to get out of the Evinrude Centre in one piece against the OMHA minor peewee equivalent of the Broad Street Bullies. The Petes were a nasty bit of business back then with their size and aggression. In this game, some of our kids were competing surprisingly well, but there were still too many passengers. Going into the third period, I did something I had never done before. I sat down five kids and didn't play them a shift for the whole third period.

Included in the five were some key players who had been with the AAA team since minor novice. My attitude was that taking away only fifteen minutes (or the equivalent of about five shifts) of hockey from a kid is a small price to pay if that kid gets the message to compete harder. The kids didn't like it; their parents didn't either, nor would you expect them to. But there was one parent who lost it. During the middle of that third period, he started yelling loudly and repeatedly at me from the stands: "Put [his kid's name here] on. Put [name of player] on."

I couldn't believe it. No one could. It was so loud and clear. It was embarrassing for me but more for that father and his son, who was among the five stapled to the bench. That specific issue got sorted out with that father after the fact, but it reinforced how this whole notion of pushing the kids hard only works if the parents buy in, too. I had a parent meeting to explain exactly that; that if the parents were always going to give their kids a soft landing at home any time I put the kids' feet to the fire at the rink, I would be sunk as a coach and we would be sunk as a team. For the most part, the parents were great. They understood I wasn't being mean to their kids; I was only trying to teach them to compete.

Mind you, a coach has to be careful not to cross the line. That point was driven home to me at practice one day. Our best defenseman was Femi Amurwaiye. Femi was a smiley, outgoing kid with a lot of personality and I really liked him, but he had a little Eddie Haskell in him. "Hello, Mr. McKenzie, how are you today?" he would often say. Femi, who went on to play prep-school hockey at Holderness in New Hampshire and then NCAA Division Three at Amherst College in Massachusetts, could be a real character and wouldn't mind testing you a bit either. He would eat Skittles between periods. He wasn't above cutting a corner or two in practice drills.

We were doing a hard, full-ice, zigzag skating drill that included sprints and then quick-step lateral crossovers. From my end of the ice, I saw Femi fall down on the crossovers. He got up slowly and basically stopped doing the drill. I was yelling at him from the far end of the ice to keep going. He was shrugging his shoulders and not doing the drill, just sort of shuffling along. I kept yelling at him to get going but he wasn't moving. I just assumed he was pulling a fast one to avoid doing the rest of this drill. I wasn't amused. Kyle O'Brien then skated from that end of the ice to me and said: "Mr. McKenzie, I think Femi is hurt pretty badly."

My heart went into my mouth. I raced down to see what the problem was and Femi showed me his leg, the inside of his thigh. It was quite a nasty laceration. Femi had a habit of not pulling up his socks all the way in practice and when he fell, he somehow shredded his leg and was bleeding pretty good. I was devastated. Actually, mortified. Here I was, yelling at the poor kid to skate and the blood was running down his leg. If I needed a harsh reminder that, even in this atmosphere of pushing the kids to be better, common sense must still always prevail, I certainly got it that day.

Somehow, through all of the losing and my pushing and prodding of the kids, we all managed to maintain our sense of humor, perspective and sanity. Of the almost forty regular-season league games we played that year, we won a grand total of five.

The best players on our team in any given game that year were call-ups from the major atom AAA Wildcats. James Neal, who had a terrific rookie season (2008-09) in the NHL with Dallas, and David McIntyre, who was drafted by Dallas but subsequently had his NHL rights traded to Anaheim and New Jersey while starring for Colgate University, were both '87s but more talented than any of our '86s.

Because we finished in last place in our division, we didn't qualify for the OMHA playoffs but were automatically entered into the ETA (Eastern Triple A) playoffs or consolation round with the other non-playoff teams and the losers from the first round of the OMHA playoffs. Maybe it was because we had more incentive than other teams, but the kids came together really well in the ETA playoffs. They competed hard. The differences in physical play and speed that were so glaring early in the season were not nearly as great at the end and—surprise, surprise—we actually won the ETA championship.

It really was quite an accomplishment for those kids. I was unbelievably proud of how far they came that season. They deserved all the credit in the world and so did their parents, because while the kids invested the blood, sweat and tears—and believe me, there were all three of them—it was the parents who fostered and permitted an environment that allowed their kids to be pushed as hard as they were by their Crazy Head Coach.

I really like to think the kids learned a large life lesson that season, but even if they didn't, I know I most certainly did.

20 OF GUN-SHY DOGS AND A CRISIS OF CONFIDENCE

WHO STOLE MY TWELVE-YEAR-OLD SON MIKE and what the hell did they do with him?

That pretty much summed up my reaction to the beginning of the minor peewee AAA season, my first as a head coach. It was one thing for the whole team to have taken a surprising and precipitous fall from where they were in previous years; it was quite another for it to happen as strikingly as it did to my son in the 1998–99 season.

During his first four years of rep hockey, Mike was an above-average AAA player, not elite by any means, but above average. In his major atom year, for example, he led our team in scoring, averaging close to a goal and almost two points per game. He skated quite well, demonstrated good athleticism, showed tremendous self-confidence, competed hard (sometimes too hard), had great passion for the game (sometimes too passionate), exhibited great hockey sense and vision, made terrific plays and had nice soft hands for finishing.

But it wasn't very far into the minor peewee season when I could scarcely believe my eyes.

He no longer skated well; in fact, he looked slow and awkward. He was no longer aggressive; in fact, he appeared tentative and timid. His athleticism and confidence had seemingly disappeared. He didn't compete nearly as hard and while he still loved to go to the rink for practices and games, his offensive instincts and skills, which were so readily apparent in the past, weren't as much a factor now that he had become slower. What had happened to Mike in the space of mere months was symptomatic of our entire team, but I don't believe anyone's game had gone as far south as quickly or noticeably as Mike's.

I was crushed. I'm not going to lie. It was just so unexpected and presented some real challenges in my first year as a head coach.

Here I was, responsible for the performance of seventeen largely underachieving kids that season, and the one thing that I never used to have to worry about—Mike—was suddenly my most heartfelt and deeply personal concern.

There will be those who suggest the explanation was readily apparent and cite this being the first year of body contact as the reason Mike became a shell of his former self. Lots of kids notice a big difference when hitting is introduced. This is often the age when they separate the twelve-year-old men from the twelve-year-old boys, so to speak. And I might have considered buying that line of thinking if there hadn't been such overwhelming evidence to the contrary in Mike's previous years in sports.

While Mike had never played contact hockey until that season, he knew what it was like to be hit and hit hard. Having played rep lacrosse since he was six years old, Mike was well acquainted with body contact. He didn't take backward steps or show any hesitation to scoop up loose balls in traffic or go to the danger areas in front of the net in lacrosse. He'd been cross-checked hard off his feet too many times to count and it never had any impact on him. I always believed he would go through the gates of hell if he thought he could score a goal there.

Years later, I wondered if the fact Mike broke his arm playing Peewee A lacrosse in the summer of 1998 might have been a contributing factor. It happened in the annual Peterborough Early Bird tournament in May. It was just a freak accident. He tripped over his buddy Kyle O'Brien in front of their own net and fell. He used his hands to break his fall and broke his arm in the process.

Since we're on this subject, I might as well go the distance and expose myself as Crazy Lacrosse Dad/Coach, too. I was an assistant coach on the bench, running the front door where players go out onto the floor. Mike came in the back door holding his arm and our very capable trainer Mike Doherty was looking after him.

I could hear Mike crying and I looked down the bench.

"You okay, Mike?" I yelled.

"No," Mike said to me.

"I don't think it's good," Mike Doherty yelled down to me. Mike was still crying.

"Oh, he'll be fine," I yelled down dismissively. "Mike, come on down here. Your line is going on soon. C'mon, let's go..."

"I can't," Mike shrieked, "my arm is too sore."

More like too broken, it turned out. Cindy came and got him off the bench and took him to the hospital. I stayed to finish coaching the game. When it was over, I hooked up with Cindy and Mike at the hospital emergency room, where he was getting the fracture set and put in a cast.

I don't honestly believe the broken arm was the reason Mike regressed in the minor peewee hockey season, but I have always tried to make some sense of that year.

Or maybe it was his glasses? He had stopped wearing them under his helmet and cage. Samson's hair? Mike's glasses? Hmmm...

The more plausible explanation was simply that Mike, like a lot of the kids on our team, hadn't gone through puberty yet and found himself at a big physical disadvantage. I think once Mike lost his wheels and became a below-average skater, his moves and skills, which came so naturally before, became difficult, if not impossible, to execute. I think once he realized he had lost that magic, he spiraled into a real crisis of confidence that manifested itself with a wholesale mental and emotional shutdown. At least that's my theory.

There probably isn't any fate worse in minor hockey than being a kid who is deemed to be shy about contact and competing. Hockey is such a hard, physical game that when someone isn't prepared to play it that way, he sticks out like a sore thumb. Opposing players and teammates aren't shy about pointing it out and neither are parents.

There is also a theory embraced by many in the hockey establishment: "A gun-shy dog will never hunt." The implication is that if a kid ever demonstrates any timidity or fear, he'll never get over that; it's just part of his makeup; a flaw, a fatal flaw. You're either tough or you're not.

I don't necessarily buy that. I believe there can be a million factors contributing to a kid lacking confidence or not feeling comfortable with some aspects of the game. And I had some of my own experiences to draw on.

Later in the book, I will talk a little about my nondescript minor hockey career, but since it applies here, I went through a somewhat similar experience as Mike at around the same age. I was never even half the player Mike was or is. I had played a couple of years in the Scarborough Hockey Association, a caliber of play that was a couple of notches down from the highest level in the MTHL. But in peewee, I went up a level to the MTHL's Scarborough Lions—Brad Park's father Bob was my coach—and I can recall very clearly that season getting berated by my mom and dad on the drive home for sometimes being hesitant to get physically involved.

I am not sure then what prompted me to attempt to move up to the highest level of the MTHL the next season, trying out for and making the Agincourt Canadians minor bantam rep team. But I was even more out of my element there and my shortcomings were even more obvious, so much so that I was cut from the team a month or two into the season and replaced by a better, presumably tougher, player.

Naturally, I was devastated, but I just opted to go back and play house league for a couple of seasons, where I was one of the better players. I regained my confidence, scored a ton and just enjoyed playing the game. But in my minor midget year, when I was fifteen, some of my good buddies were playing for a new lower-level MTHL team and I decided to join them. I thought I was long past any fears, but fairly early in that season, I accidentally clipped an opposing player in the helmet with my stick. It happened to be the biggest, meanest, toughest guy on the other team and he indicated to me he was going to kill me. I was sitting on the bench awaiting my next shift, not to mention the end of my life, and some of those old feelings of insecurity, and, yeah, maybe even fear, started to well up inside me. I didn't like how I felt. Honestly, I was ashamed. I suddenly experienced another, far stronger emotion: anger and disgust with myself.

It was, in a way, a defining moment. I told myself in no uncertain terms this was no way to go through life; that I either needed to grow a set and be a man or just quit hockey and accept my shortcomings. So I worked myself up into a bit of a state, hit the ice and went looking to confront my demons. I went right after the big, tough kid who was going to kill me. I ran at him hard, we battled and I thought we were going to drop the gloves to fight. I was ready to do that, but a funny thing happened. I could see and sense some uncertainty—maybe even a little fear—in his face as he decided to pull back.

Not to be overly dramatic about it, but I can honestly say I never took another backward step in a hockey game for the rest of my life, and I got punched out more times than I care to remember because of it.

So I like to think I had a little insight into where Mike's mind may have been. I had been a gun-shy dog but I learned to hunt. I was convinced Mike would do the same if only we could find what buttons to push to get him to where he used to be.

I couldn't help but think it all came back to confidence. I wasn't entirely clear on why he seemed to lose his to the degree he did, but I was intent on finding ways to restore it. Keeping in mind Mike was still very eager and game to try anything that would make him better, we went on a quest of sorts.

Recognizing he first had to improve his skating, I took Mike to Jari Byrski's skating and skills sessions in Toronto at least once a week if it fit our schedule. I mentioned Jari earlier and he's one of my favorites of the people I've met in the long and winding road of minor hockey. He's an off-the-wall character—think of a Ukrainian version of Kramer from *Seinfeld*—but a brilliant teacher of skating and skills. Most important, though, he knows kids and how to reach them on so many levels. Everything he does is designed to instil confidence. I can still hear him saying it so loudly on the ice with his Ukrainian accent—"Con-*fee*-dence!"

I also took Mike to off-ice workout sessions with Mike Marson, the former NHLer who is now a Toronto Transit Commission employee and the older brother of "I hate Larry Marson" fame from Chapter Four. Mike Marson is one of the most fascinating people I've ever met, a martial arts expert with more black belts than Don Cherry has ties. His story—being the first black first-round pick in the NHL—is obviously remarkable but, for me, it pales in comparison to the story of his life after hockey and where he felt he was headed before making some significant changes for the better in his life.

Mike Marson worked with a variety of clients of all ages and stripes who wanted to improve their physical fitness or strengthen their mind or learn self-defense or other manly physical pursuits. I've seen Mike Marson hypnotize people and do some incredible things to demonstrate his mental prowess and mastery over pain. He was just what the doctor ordered for a kid like Mike, who needed a little help to rediscover his true self.

Now, it should be pointed out that not all that was being done that season was positive, educational and confidence-instilling. Truthfully, I didn't always do a very good job of navigating through those turbulent times for Mike and me. As I was trying to teach the whole team how to deal with adversity, which was an uphill struggle, I was absolutely embracing the concept of tough love. The kids on the team knew I liked them so when I got in their face, they were fairly accepting of it, although there were some occasions where maybe it wasn't so pleasant. But as I told you earlier, I did it because I knew those kids were better than they were showing. Mike knew I loved him dearly and that I only wanted what was best for him. I knew that hockey meant so much to Mike and he badly needed to get over this crisis of confidence, not just for hockey reasons but as a life lesson as well. So I went at him hard, just as my dad went at me hard.

As his coach, for example, I told Mike that, as a winger, if he couldn't get the puck out of our own end from the hash marks to the blue line on the breakout, I couldn't put him on the ice; that if a winger in hockey could have only one skill it would be to get the puck out on the boards because otherwise that winger is absolutely useless to his team.

As a dad, there were definitely some emotional and uncomfortable drives home that season, but there was the one horrible and truly regrettable night when it went way too far.

We were coming back from a game or a practice—I don't recall which one—and I was really laying into Mike about how poorly and softly he'd been playing. I decided to up the ante in terms of pushing a button to find the old Mike. As we were getting close to home, I told him that if he was going to play like a chicken or a coward, I was going to cut him from the team next season and I would stay on as the AAA coach without him. I told him he could go play AA or wherever.

I didn't really mean it. I thought I could shock him into rediscovering the way he had always played the game, but I had gone too far. Way too far.

Just as we pulled into our driveway, Mike lost it. He snapped. He burst into tears and ran into the house crying. Cindy came to see what all the commotion was about and through his tears as he ran upstairs to his room, Mike told Cindy that I called him a chicken and a coward and I was going to cut him from the team.

Cindy was not impressed. Not one of my finest moments; not a scene I enjoy recounting now. I will spare any further details and just say there was, in the wake of that night, a great deal of discussion, reflection and soul-searching on what's important in life. Fortunately for me, the father-son bond between Mike and me was so strong that it was able to withstand that episode. Mike quickly appeared to forgive, if not forget.

The good news, not to spoil the story by jumping way ahead, is he eventually got back to that good place. Not overnight, mind you. It was a process, somewhat gradual in nature, almost painfully so at times, but one in which Mike ultimately triumphed and triumphed large.

He did it and he should be proud.

Me? Maybe not so much.

21 NO NEED FOR A COIN TOSS
'Twas the Best Year Ever

THINK BIG. Why settle for good when you can be great?

Without getting too deep or philosophical, I really do believe in those attitudes. I've always told Mike and Shawn, "Don't ever be afraid to be excellent."

So while practicality and common sense might dictate that a coach who won only five regular-season games the year before establish a modest goal of, say, just making the playoffs, I was totally convinced we had to set our sights much higher than that.

And we did.

I knew it was going to be my last year coaching Mike's team so I was consumed by the feeling that it couldn't just be a good year; it had to be a great year. And for me, great would be defined by setting and achieving two lofty goals. One, get the major peewee AAA Wildcats into the prestigious Quebec International Peewee Tournament. Two, get the team into the OMHA championships, which would require not only making the playoffs but winning two best-of-five playoff series.

On the coaching front, my friend Mark Rowland had decided to go back into retirement. Stu Seedhouse returned as an assistant, so the Three Amigos—Kevin, Stu and I—were back together once again. Steve Hedington stayed on to help us. We added Bob Anderson, whose son Matt was our captain, as another assistant coach. (Bob, by the way, is the brother of Atlanta Thrashers' head coach John Anderson.) Our goalie coach, Bucky Crouch, was on board from the get-go. Ron Balcom was back as the manager. We had a bigger staff than the University of Michigan football team.

We had some key additions on the ice, too. I neglected to mention another factor in our struggles in minor peewee: one of the best offensive players in Whitby, Zack Greer, had decided to take a break to play AA for a year. Zack's first love was lacrosse and why not? He and Peterborough's Shawn Evans were the two best lacrosse players for their age in Canada. Zack went on to get a scholarship to play field lacrosse at Duke University— yes, *that* Duke University lacrosse team (but don't even get me started on how unfairly those poor kids were treated)—and all Zack did in his four years there was to establish myriad NCAA scoring records. A superb athlete, Zack was a bit of a heavy-footed skater but had a heavier shot and could really put the puck in the net. It was huge to get him back on the team.

We also had a new goalie, Blake Cross, who jumped up from the Whitby A level. He stepped in and immediately provided some top-notch netminding and Kyle Clancy returned to be on top of his game, too.

Mike was also slowly but surely making his way back. For all that he went through in minor peewee, Mike was still one of our top scorers that year. His skating still required major work, but he was at least showing signs of being on the right track. So was the whole team.

Getting into the Quebec tourney isn't easy. It's the crème de la crème of minor hockey events, the trip of a lifetime for any kid who plays the game.

I played in the 1969 Quebec Peewee tournament when I played for Bob Park's Scarborough Lions. Our team normally wouldn't have been considered good enough to go, but Bob Park coached the team that won the very first Quebec Peewee tourney in 1959, with his future Hall of Fame son Brad and Syl Apps, Jr. on the roster. He had an open invitation to go back and he took our team.

The Peewee tournament isn't just a hockey event for the kids. It's a life experience. It's as much about the team train ride there, being billeted with French-Canadian families, trying to make time with teenage girls from Quebec and playing in front of 14,000 fans at Le Colisée, the building that Jean Beliveau made famous in his days with the Quebec Aces, as it is playing hockey.

I knew I could use my connections in the hockey world to open some doors to get us *considered* for Quebec, but I also knew they weren't about to accept a crap team because it was coached by the Hockey Insider. And if only one team from our OMHA ETA league was going to go to Quebec, it was going to be the defending champions from Richmond Hill, who were head and shoulders better than everyone.

I talked to Patrick Dom, who runs the Quebec Peewee tourney, explained the situation (bad team last year) and the lofty goal (get invited to Quebec this year). He had me fill out an application, made no promises and suggested the team better start winning some hockey games for us to have any chance.

We did exactly that. In our first tournament of the year, we went to the finals and lost a close game to a very good

Brantford team from another league. Brantford which was an automatic to go to Quebec. That sent a strong early message—we could play with the high-end teams.

What a difference a year made. The kids were really dedicated to an off-ice program of plyometrics. We got extra ice time to continue working on their skating. They still weren't what you would call a high-speed or high-skill team, but they were smart, coachable and becoming a hard team to play against.

When we played Bill Carroll's high flyers from Ajax-Pickering, we would make like Ken Hitchcock's Dallas Stars, take away the middle of the ice and put the game on the boards, where we made teams fight for every inch of ice. Our kids backchecked ferociously; they were always trying to get themselves on the right side of the puck when we didn't have it. It was beautiful in its own ugly way. Most highly skilled teams simply didn't have the appetite to play that type of hard game, not for three periods. I think I even won the Rum Cup with Bobby Lalonde that season.

We got off to quite a good start in league play. Our record was comparable to the other ETA teams—besides Richmond Hill—that also had aspirations to go to Quebec.

In early November, I got a call from Patrick Dom telling me there was a spot for Whitby in the Quebec tourney. I was shocked. I asked him which other team from our league was going and he told me there wasn't any other team. To this day, I think he was just testing me, but for Richmond Hill to not be the one team going from the ETA was a travesty and I told him so.

"Bob," he said to me, "you realize you are turning down an invitation to the Quebec Peewee tourney? You realize no one does that?"

Tempting as it may have been, it was an easy call. Richmond Hill was head and shoulders better than any other team in our league. I wanted to go to Quebec but not that badly.

Not long after that, Patrick Dom called me back and told me Richmond Hill had been accepted into the tournament and that if we still wanted to go, they would take a second team from the ETA. Before accepting that, though, I asked him if I said no, what team would go in our place? St. Catharines (SCTA), he said.

As fate would have it, we were playing St. Catharines that weekend in a tourney in Peterborough, so I told Patrick: "Tell you what, if St. Catharines beats us on the weekend, give them the spot; if we beat them, we're coming."

I thought that was fair. If the Wildcats went to Quebec, there had to be some legitimacy. That said, our kids went into that St. Catharines game knowing a trip to Quebec was on the line; the St. Catharines' players had no clue. We hammered them, beat them by five or six, and they started gooning it up, so I didn't feel the least bit bad about taking that spot in Quebec.

Getting the team ready to go to Quebec, on and off the ice, became a full-time job for me. Crazy Hockey Coach was spending hours—seriously, hours—every day on preparations—sorting out the train travel, van transportation once we got there, hotels, billet lists, getting third jerseys made up, commemorative patches, right down to what kind of hats the kids would be wearing there, to say nothing of setting up practice and exhibition games once we got there. This will come as a surprise to those who know me (not!), but I can be a bit of a control freak at times.

But that was only because I wanted to make sure it was done properly. Too many teams go to the Quebec tournament and make it just about the hockey. They don't take a train or they don't billet their kids with families or they pack up and leave as soon as they're eliminated. I desperately wanted this to be a total life experience for our kids and their families, not just another hockey tournament.

And it was. The train ride there was the party of all parties as we had our own railway car. The kids were having fun but maybe not as much fun as the parents.

As for the hockey itself, our first game at Le Colisée is one the kids and parents will remember forever. There were at least 12,000 in the stands. We were playing a team from Fredericton, N.B. I had told our two goalies they would split the game down the middle. That's not the norm, but if we lost this game, it would be our only game in Le Colisée and I thought both kids deserved a chance to play in the big building in front of the big crowd.

Our kids were unbelievably nervous and I dare say the coaches were a little uptight, too. The kids were getting dressed and it was a far quieter dressing room than ever before. I noticed one of the players, Stephen Foston, was sniffing and rubbing his eyes as he got dressed. If I didn't know better, I would have thought he was crying. And he was.

"Stephen, what's the matter," I said.

"Nothing," he sniffed.

"Well, something has to be wrong, you're crying," I said.

"I'm fine," he said, wiping away tears.

One of the other kids said to me: "He's upset because he lost his Quebec Peewee tournament ring."

Prior to the game, a lot of the kids had gone out and bought souvenirs and some of them splurged for pretty nice commemorative rings. Stephen had apparently lost his and now he was upset.

"Stephen," I said. "Stop crying right now. We will find your ring. If we don't find your ring, I promise you I will buy you another %$#&*!% ring as soon as this game is over. I will buy you five %$#&*!% rings. Stop %$#&*!% crying right now because we're all so %$#&*!% nervous right now that if you don't stop crying, we're all going to start crying."

That broke the ice. Repeatedly swearing in front of thirteen-year-olds isn't standard protocol but it can be an icebreaker. Steven cracked a smile, the other kids started laughing uproariously and we were a little more relaxed after that.

We won the game, which was great because it would guarantee at least one more game in Le Colisée, which was very cool for the kids. Our next game was against a hometown team from Quebec so the place would be packed and we would be decided underdogs, but the winner of that game was going to face a Russian team next.

We lost that game 4–1 to the Quebec team—which eliminated us from the tournament—but the notable story, for the purposes of this book, happened before the game. As I said, we had these really nice third sweaters made up just for Quebec, like the St. Louis Blues' dark blue sweater but with our Wildcat logo. We wore them in the first game; the kids loved them. Prior to our second game at Le Colisée, we had to determine who would wear what color sweater and the Quebec team also had third jerseys and theirs were black. One team would have to wear their regular white uniforms and neither wanted to do that. So the tourney organizers said there would be a coin flip to settle this highly contentious issue.

The tournament official tossed the coin. The other coaches, there were two of them, called it heads. Sure enough, it came up heads, but before the coin had landed on the ground, it hit the top of my shoe. The two Quebec coaches were high-fiving each other after winning the coin toss and I'm saying, "No %$#&*!% way, bad toss, interference, do it over again." The tourney official shook his head and I'm saying, "Screw that, we have to do it over." No chance. So while these two imbeciles from the Quebec team were celebrating a victory in the coin toss of all things, the other imbecile—that would be me—was storming out there with a torrent of "%$#&*!% bullshit toss, interference."

I don't imagine those two guys who coached that Quebec team get TSN in Quebec City, but if they do, I've often thought if they ever turned on the TV after the fact and saw me, they would say: *"Voilà le maudit fou qui nous a fait perdre le pile ou face."*

Rough translation: "There's that crazy bastard who called interference on the coin toss."

Yup, that would be me...but you have to admit, it was a B.S. toss.

———— ● ————

The Quebec Peewee experience was everything we thought it would be, and then some. The hockey was terrific, but as I fully expected, it was just one aspect of it. If you ask any of the kids or parents now, they're likely to tell you the most memorable and enjoyable day was spent at the giant Snow Parc just outside Quebec City, which is like a full-fledged ski resort but with rubber tubes. It was an all-day venture and if any team goes to the Peewee tournament and doesn't get to the Snow Parc, well, shame on them. Between that excursion and just walking around the walled old town in Quebec City at night is something none of us will ever forget.

But Phase Two of our Dream Season still awaited us. We had accomplished our goal of getting to Quebec but now the focus was on making it to the OMHA tournament. And it was going to be a quick turnaround.

Our train from Quebec pulled into Oshawa on a Friday night at midnight. We were physically and emotionally drained, but our first game of the playoffs, against the first-place Quinte Red Devils, was the next day at twelve noon in Belleville's Yardman Arena, home of the OHL's Belleville Bulls. It was ridiculous scheduling and we weren't happy about it, but it was the price to be paid for Quebec. *C'est la vie.*

Somehow, we won that first game in overtime. It was a terrific back-and-forth series that ended up going to a fifth-and-deciding game in Quinte's barn. The game went into overtime and Zack Greer buried the game winner to send us on to the next round.

Next up was the York-Simcoe Express. It was an intense series that, at times, looked like it might get out of hand.

We had played, and won, in Aurora and after the game was over, one of their parents, incensed about something that happened during the game, tried to get into our dressing room. Bob Anderson, who is as thick and as strong as they come, intercepted this idiot. This guy foolishly decided he was going to mix it up with Bob. Not a smart thing to do. A bunch of us got in to break it up before any real damage was done.

When I got home that night, I called the Whitby AAA convener, Larry Dancey, and told him of the trouble in Aurora that day and how he might want to arrange for a little extra security for the next game at Iroquois Park. Sure enough, Larry attended the next game to keep a lid on things. We lost that game. It was an emotional finish. I was standing outside our dressing room unwinding and as the spectators were leaving the stands on the other side of the rink, one of their fans started heckling me. The guy was really giving it to me; stuff about the team, about losing, about me being on TSN, stuff about my kid. Not nice stuff, although it wasn't anything I hadn't heard before on countless occasions. I ignored it for awhile but he was relentless. Finally, I'd had enough and I yelled across to him, "If you want to talk to me so bad, come on over here."

He yelled back: "Why don't you come over here?"

I was off like a shot. Just as I got around to the other side, in the stands, with me going towards this loudmouth and him coming towards me, I was intercepted by none other than Larry Dancey.

"Geez, Bob," the AAA convener said to me as he put his hands on my shoulders, "I knew you thought we needed extra security for the game; I didn't think it was for you."

Larry's stab at humor made me laugh a little and I saw the foolishness of it all. I just turned around and walked back to the dressing room.

Like the Quinte series before it, this one with York-Simcoe was going the distance, to a fifth and deciding game, but because of the way points were awarded, York-Simcoe could win the series with an overtime tie and we had to win the game outright to get it to a sixth game. We were on home ice and, sure enough, the game went into overtime. With a minute left, Zack Greer had a wonderful chance to end it, but he was foiled by their goalie. Time expired. The game and the series were over, and our dream of getting to the OMHA tournament was dead, too.

We had come so close, but when one took into account where this group started at the beginning of the minor peewee season and where they were at when the major peewee season ended, it was an incredibly gratifying experience.

It was the best year of my life in minor hockey.

22 REJECTED: The Parents Always Take It Harder Than the Kid

THE TIMING WAS NOTHING if not impeccable.

No sooner was I done as Mike's coach than my services were desperately required elsewhere—with Shawn.

That was always the plan anyway. I knew once I finished coaching Mike I would turn my attention fully to Shawn for as many years as I could. And let's just say the light was never greener.

It seems young Shawn was a man without a team.

Shawn experienced what a lot of kids go through in minor hockey—he got cut. There was not going to be a spot for him on the major atom AA Wildcats for the 2000–01 season.

This was a whole new experience for the McKenzie family. In all the time Mike played hockey—right into junior and college—he was never once cut from a team, unless you count his diarrhea-induced, underage minor novice AA try-out absence when he was seven years old, or not making the Ontario Under-17 team (which was never a realistic possibility to begin with).

And because Shawn had chosen not to even try out for the AAA team in novice or minor atom, this was his first time experiencing legitimate rejection.

If Shawn was upset, he did a good job of hiding it. Don't get me wrong, he was a little disappointed. You could see and sense that on the way home in the car the night he was cut. No one likes to be told they're not good enough. No one likes to be told, "You're no longer on the team." And when your friends you've played with for a few years are still there, it can be a little tough.

But I was probably more upset and disappointed than he was.

Which, as a rule, is pretty much par for the course. Parents almost always take getting cut much harder than their kids.

I will grant you there are times when a kid is legitimately devastated. These extreme cases usually involve a player who has played on the same team for many, many years, forged incredibly tight friendships and then—usually in one of the older age groups, bantam or midget—gets the unkindest cut of all. That can certainly seem like the end of the world to a teenager because it's not just about hockey; it's about social standing and being part of a peer group.

But most kids, especially in the younger age groups, are incredibly resilient. They bounce back and bounce back quickly, a lot faster than Mommy and Daddy.

The truth was that as much as I may have been piqued the night Shawn was cut, I was hardly surprised. You could see it coming.

As I told you earlier, Shawn was a good little AA player from the time he started playing at that level in minor novice. But as he progressed into major novice and then minor atom, he certainly wasn't getting better. He started to go longer stretches without scoring goals or getting points and while he was never a liability and never looked out of place, he wasn't always accomplishing a whole lot either. If I were the coach of the team, I might have cut him, too, figuring it's sometimes better to take a chance on a lesser-known new player who might have a bigger upside than to take the middling same-old, same-old with a kid like Shawn.

Having been a coach myself, I knew that cutting kids is easily the worst part of the job. It's a gut-wrenching experience. There's no good way to do it. If you cut them en masse like I did with Mike's team, you're accused of not providing individual attention. If you meet one-on-one and tell the kid and his parents that, for example, the boy needs to work on his skating, they go out saying, "Who the hell does that guy think he is to say my kid can't skate?"

Cutting players is a dirty job, but one that has to be done. I've seen long friendships deteriorate or break up entirely because a coach cut a friend's kid. It can get very ugly and it's why some guys just aren't cut out, if you'll pardon the pun, to coach kids' sports.

After you coach awhile, you realize you can't win no matter what, so you try to do what you think is right for the team. If it costs you a friendship or two along the way, so be it. If that friendship couldn't withstand a rough patch from cutting a friend's kid, it probably wasn't a truly solid friendship to begin with. At least that is what you have to tell yourself. As for the parents whose kids get cut, I have this one simple piece of advice: Don't take it personally because it's usually not. Get over it. Your kid will and you will, too, if you allow yourself.

So, based on all of that, I actually felt a little empathy for Don Houghton, the coach of Shawn's team in minor atom and the guy who cut him. Don's son Bryant, or Buzz as he was called, and Shawn had played together on the same teams for the previous four years. Cindy and I were friends with Don and his wife, Paula, so it wasn't difficult for me to put myself in Don's shoes and realize this was no fun for him either. He was just doing what he thought was right for the team; you can't fault a coach for that.

Which is not to say I still wasn't a little ticked off, generally speaking, the night Shawn got cut. He's my kid, after all. It's only human nature to absorb or share some of that disappointment with your son. And to embrace a little bit of that "we'll show you" mentality. Shawn was, in my opinion, entirely capable of being a AA-level player; he just wasn't playing as well as he could on a consistent basis and was going to need some work.

I would hate to think the reason for Shawn's lack of progress as a player through novice and minor atom was tied to the fact I was a lot busier with Mike's hockey over those three years than I was with Shawn's, because I still did manage to make a lot of Shawn's games and practices. I was on him about work ethic and him getting more involved in his games; it's not like I neglected him or his hockey. He was just a pretty laid-back dude.

But all that was history; it was time to focus on the present. I told Shawn precisely that on the way home that night. I said I was going to put in to coach the major atom A team, that we were going to have a lot of fun together, that he was going to have a great season and if he played as well as he's capable of playing, I would put in to coach the AA team the next year and he would prove to everyone he was still a good player who deserved to play AA hockey. It was a good little pep talk—Shawn seemed to like it—and the best part about it was that I actually believed every bit of it.

Selfishly, I was also encouraged that the AA team had cut three more kids—a forward, Bryn McDonnell, and two defensemen, Breandon Barnett and Michael Ochman—who I thought were good AA-caliber players. For whatever reason, they had, like Shawn, underachieved that minor atom season and pretty much played their way off the team. Great, they would make a good nucleus for the A team.

Before I could commit to coaching the A team, though, I had to take care of logistics. There would be no Kevin or Stu or Ron Balcom to back me up, so I had to find a whole new staff. Steve Hedington, who had been such a big help the last two years with Mike's team, agreed to keep coaching with me. That was huge, because Heddy was an invaluable assistant coach— a level-headed, mature and responsible guy who had played hockey at a high level and an absolutely outstanding teacher who related extremely well with kids of all ages and calibers. Bryn McDonnell's dad, Paul, who I often watched AA games with, had indicated he would help out.

But the real problem was going to be finding a manager, because that is the most labor-intensive position. A head coach's life is nothing but misery without a good manager.

The A team the previous year had been coached by a guy named Mike Rostek, and his wife, Val, was the manager. Their son Matt played on the team. Mike Rostek's two years as coach with that group were up, so he was moving on to coach his other son, David, an '87. Shawn and Matt Rostek happened to be playing on the same house-league lacrosse team that spring and while I didn't know the Rosteks well at all, I was pumping them for information on the '89 A-level scene. Finally, I asked Val if I applied for the team and if her son Matt made the team—as a coach, you have to be careful you don't make promises you can't keep—would she be interested in managing? She thought about it and eventually said yes, so I was once again back in the coaching saddle.

I should point out the Rosteks, especially Mike, are completely and utterly crazy, far crazier than me. But that's crazy in an affectionate, good-friend kind of crazy. They're late for everything and the sight of Mike plowing that old, big blue Suburban over snow banks and going "cross-country" to get to games on time and roaring into arena parking lots all over the province will forever be burned into my mind. But the overriding quality of the Rosteks, above and beyond all the craziness, is they are inherently generous people who would do anything for their kids or anyone else's kids for that matter—anytime, anyplace, anything, you name it, no questions asked. In the world of minor hockey, there's no greater redeeming quality than that.

To be honest, I wasn't quite sure what to expect coaching at the A level after having been involved in only AAA hockey to that point. I was pleasantly surprised. The A kids obviously weren't as gifted as the AAA kids, but what I immediately realized was that, for the most part, the kids and their parents were no less committed to minor hockey than the AAA families. They were eager to learn, worked just as hard and while the execution wasn't there to the same degree, it was obvious to me that I wouldn't have to make many coaching adjustments, except maybe try to be a little more patient when teaching concepts or working on skills.

Speaking from my experiences in the Whitby minor system, there is no difference whatsoever in the time and effort commitment or passion levels between AAA and AA and single A. It's the same basic routine regardless of how many As you string together: two games and two practices, on average, a week and anywhere between four and seven tournaments depending upon what's available.

We had a competitive little team—not the best; not the worst—in an A loop that included Stouffville, Pickering, Ajax, Uxbridge, Clarington, Port Perry, Lindsay, Port Hope, Cobourg, Trenton, Belleville, Picton and Napanee. I like to think we followed my four-point plan (have fun; embrace and reinforce the proper values; improve skating and skills; and teach team strategies, tactics, systems and concepts) and the season was a success.

Best of all, putting on my parent hat, Shawn was excelling at this level. He was one of the better players on the team. He was scoring goals and points regularly, competing harder than he had been, playing more consistently and seemingly enjoying himself and having a great deal of fun with this group of kids.

As a parent, you can't ask for much more than that.

23 NEW-AND-IMPROVED SHAWN MAKES A U-TURN FOR THE BETTER

IT'S FUNNY HOW THE WORLD TURNS SOMETIMES. When Mike was a twelve-year-old, his game went totally into the tank, in large part, I believe, because he was a late arrival to the puberty party. Shawn, on the other hand, got to this occasion quite early. So while in the summer of 1998 I was asking what the aliens had done with twelve-year-old Mike, I was three years later wondering where did this new-and-improved version of twelve-year-old Shawn come from?

You could see the signs for Shawn in the major atom A season, the first year I coached him. Shawn was getting bigger and stronger than the other kids, but it really became most obvious in the summer of '01, although that didn't prevent Shawn from still experiencing the nastiest cut of all.

Shawn decided that summer to come out of "retirement" to play Peewee A rep lacrosse, which he had quit a few years earlier, so he could, as he put it, "just relax a little."

I'm not sure how many kids that age ever talk about the need to "relax a little," but that's our Shawnie. I wasn't happy about his decision to quit rep lacrosse when he made it, but what was I going to do? You can't force a kid to play something he doesn't want to play—as much, I admit, as I would have liked to—and Shawn had it in his mind he was going to have a "relaxing" July and August and play only house-league lacrosse.

This particular summer, though, he was feeling pretty good about himself, although he was probably motivated by something else as well—this Peewee A lacrosse team was scheduled to go on a much-heralded trip to British Columbia.

Being a Crazy Lacrosse Dad in the summer, I was thrilled Shawn wanted to get back to playing the game at its highest level. I was also thinking a Vancouver lacrosse trip might be nice, too. So off we went to tryouts.

To say Shawn was one of the better kids at the tryouts was, in my opinion, an understatement. He was, to my eyes, easily in the top five players on the floor, faster and physically stronger than most. He always had decent stick skills and a good feel for the game; at this point he had some physical prowess. I couldn't see any way he didn't make this team.

But he didn't. He got cut. I couldn't believe it. Neither could he. He was stunned. I was outraged, although I said absolutely nothing to anyone on my way out of Luther Vipond Memorial Arena in Brooklin that day. When I'm really seriously upset about something, I go out of my way to not give anyone the satisfaction to see me upset or bothered. So I plastered a phony smile on my face and headed home.

I told Shawn in the car I thought it was unfair; that I thought he was one of the best players on the floor. He was at a loss for words, which was rare with Shawn. There really wasn't anything else to say. He was clearly disappointed. I went home and thought about it for awhile and tried to come up with a logical explanation for what had just happened. And then it struck me: Maybe it was the Vancouver trip. It had to be. This trip was something the kids on that team had been shooting for, talking about doing for years and they were finally going to do it. This was a winning team with not a lot of turnover from year to year. It was a pretty tight group. As well as Shawn had played in tryouts, I could see how the coaches might still think of him as the laid-back kid who wanted to "relax" in the summer instead of play high-level rep lacrosse; or as the not-too-competitive kid who had played his way off the AA hockey team the year before. And I could also see how the coaches didn't want to cut a kid who had toiled hard for them the last few summers and deprive that kid of the much-anticipated trip of a lacrosse lifetime to B.C.

It all made sense and, to be honest, I didn't have a problem with it. The more I thought about it, the more sense it made to me. I know tryouts are supposed to be about picking the best kids, but sometimes other factors—loyalty and hard work and commitment and, yeah, sometimes friendship—come into it. And that can be fair, too, though it may not always seem like it at the time.

I sat Shawn down and explained all of this to him. I told him on one level it's not fair, reiterated that life isn't fair (I never get tired of telling my kids that), but asked him if it was fair for some kid, who ran his ass off in stifling hot arenas the last three summers, to miss out on a trip of a lifetime to Vancouver so some other kid who just wanted to "relax" the last few summers got to go?

The big question then was whether Shawn was going to play on the Peewee B team. At first, he wasn't sure. He was extremely disappointed at being cut. I asked him if he really wanted to play rep lacrosse or he just wanted a trip to British

Columbia. I told him if it was the latter, the Peewee A team was so right to cut him, but that if he really wanted to play rep lacrosse, then he would play on the B team and start proving to the A coaches and everyone else he was worthy to be on the top team.

He ultimately decided to play on the B team. Long story short, it was a great experience. He was, in my opinion, one of the best players on the team, if not the best; he was named the captain and became a go-to guy whose confidence soared. It was a good summer; a good lesson learned, I hoped.

There was no question in my mind that Shawn was, at the end of his first season of A-level hockey, good enough to go back and play at the AA level again. In fact, I thought he might actually have a chance to make the AAA team. But I also knew it wouldn't hurt him to spend another year in A and it would also allow me to continue as his coach, which I really wanted to do for at least another year. So I went ahead and committed to coaching the A team again for the 2001–02 season.

But Shawn did go out to the AAA spring tryouts, just for the experience of it. He fared quite well, especially considering the AAA team at Shawn's age was an OMHA championship caliber squad and one of the better teams in the province. John Annis, the head coach of the AAA team, told Shawn he was good enough to earn a spot but it wouldn't hurt to spend one more year in A with his dad. Shawn was fine with that, but quite proud for showing well at the AAA tryouts.

Later that season, John Annis and I worked out an arrangement where Shawn would be one of their affiliate players, or AP as they call it, which was unusual because normally only

AA players affiliate with AAA teams and A players affiliate with AA teams. But we got Don Houghton, who was still coaching the AA team, to sign off on it, so Shawn and I knew he would, at some point, get a chance to try AAA hockey for the first time. John Annis occasionally had Shawn come out and practice with the AAA kids to get a better feel for the level.

Shawn had a great season in single A. He was, more often than not, a physically dominant player. He played hard and wasn't afraid to punish people with hits and take the puck to the net to score or set up goals. He was aggressive and confident. On a couple of occasions he was called up to the AAA team by John Annis and he didn't look out of place at all. It was not a reach to think he'd play AAA hockey the next season.

Our A team was quite competitive that season, but the odds of us getting out of our league in postseason play weren't very good. Cobourg had a powerhouse team, one of the best in the province. Cobourg, a nice little town, is roughly halfway between Toronto and Belleville on the north shore of Lake Ontario. They usually had very strong A-level teams at all ages and were almost always supported strongly by the townspeople.

Part of the reason Cobourg was as strong as they were was because it was part of Quinte's AAA region, at the far west end of the area. A lot of talented Cobourg players, who were clearly good enough to play AAA for Quinte, didn't like the idea of driving all the way to Belleville or Madoc or wherever for AAA games and practices and instead decide to stay back and play the lower A level in Cobourg. So the Cougars usually had strong teams, whereas in Whitby, for example, the better players were generally playing at the highest level possible, either AAA or AA, not single A.

As I said, this Cobourg team won a lot and some teams when they win a lot, well, let's just say some parents develop a strong personality to go with a strong team. They would probably call themselves supportive and passionate; I kind of thought a few of them were a tad obnoxious. They used to really give it to me when I was behind the bench and, for the most part, I just ignored them. It wasn't anything I hadn't heard before.

Because Shawn was one of our most physical players—and he wasn't shy about getting involved that season—he attracted a lot of attention, on and off the ice. Over the years, Shawn didn't get verbally abused or centered out for being the son of the Hockey Insider nearly as much or as badly as Mike did. Because Shawn played at different levels against different kids from year to year and I had only just started coaching him, most people didn't even realize who Shawn was on the ice. Mike, though, took a pretty good beating almost from the get-go, because he played AAA every year against a lot of the same teams and kids. Everyone knew who the kid with the glasses was. But that didn't mean Shawn didn't get some abuse, too—and these Cobourg players and parents certainly knew who he was.

Our playoff series with Cobourg was getting pretty heated. Their fans were worked up and that got our fans going. It was actually great A hockey, fast and physical. Shawn had crushed a few guys in the series and they were starting to key on him and really give it back. In one of the games at Iroquois Park, he got absolutely flattened in open ice, right in front of where the Cobourg parents were sitting. When he went down, they all jumped up and began cheering and banging on the glass as he slowly got back to his feet. Some of them were yelling across the rink and asking me if I liked that. I was ticked; I am not going to lie. But I kept my game face on, never reacted in the least and just tried to ignore it, although I was seething inside.

We were giving a valiant effort in the series but Cobourg was too good. We weren't going to win this series. But that didn't mean I didn't get some personal satisfaction before it was over. The game was being played in Cobourg's wonderful old barn. The place was rocking pretty good. You just can't beat small-town hockey when the town gets behind one of its teams. A bunch of local teenage kids sat right behind our bench the whole game and banged on the glass and were really giving it to me and our kids. Keep in mind, this was minor pee-wee A hockey.

Shawn took a penalty in the game and was in the box. While he was in there, I noticed two dads from the Cobourg team behind the penalty box and saw that they were jawing at Shawn while he was in there. I also noticed that at some point Shawn said something to them. Suddenly, one of the dads raced down to right behind the penalty box and started banging on the glass, cursing and swearing at Shawn for some reason. At that moment, Shawn's penalty expired and he skated to our bench. Here's how our conversation went:

"What happened over there?"

"Those men were mouthing off at me."

"What did they say?"

"Oh, the normal stuff, stuff about you, TSN, me. They were swearing at me."

"What did you say?"

"Nothing, at first, but then I said something."

"Is that why the one dad went nuts?"

"Yup."

"What did you say to him to make him go crazy?"

"I told him to go f— himself."

Pause.

"Good boy."

And with that, Shawn and I bid adieu to A-level hockey.

24 TEACH YOUR CHILDREN WELL ON THE "BALANCE" BEAM

I MUST HAVE LOST MY MIND; there is no other explanation for this rare moment of clarity and common sense.

It was fairly early into Mike's minor bantam AAA season and I was watching him and the Wildcats get destroyed by their hated rivals from Oshawa. This game wasn't pretty. The final score was 10–2 or something along those lines. On this night, the Wildcats looked soft and slow—not unlike that dreadful minor peewee season—and the Oshawa '86s were, individually speaking, quite a handful.

As a side note, I was always amazed this group of Oshawa kids didn't accomplish more as a team—they were hard-pressed to win a few playoff series over eight years, never mind a championship—because they were loaded with individual talent. No fewer than five kids from that Oshawa team went on to be front-line players in the OHL—Adam Berti, who was a second-round pick of the Chicago Blackhawks, and Michael Haley (both of whom had played lacrosse with Mike from the time they were six), as well as Mike MacLean, Andrew Gibbons and Derrick Bagshaw. Three of them (Berti, Haley and MacLean) went on to play pro; Gibbons and Bagshaw went to Canadian university hockey after graduating from the OHL. When this group was "on," they could dominate and this was one of those nights.

Mike's game had, for the most part, improved markedly from that horrible minor peewee year, but there were still some nights when it was back to the bad old ways for him and his teammates. This was definitely one of them.

I don't want to say it was a revelation, but it did kind of hit me like a ton of bricks as I sat in that cold, damp, poorly lit North Oshawa Arena late on a weekday night—we were wasting our time here.

Come again?

You heard me.

I wouldn't go so far as to say it was like a brilliant stream of light coming into the building with a deep voice resonating from above, saying: "You're wasting your time here." But whatever it was, it had that kind of impact on me.

I started thinking about how much time, effort and money we had, as a family, committed to this minor hockey experience. Then I looked out onto the ice to see my kid and his team feebly trying to keep up. What was the point? Where was it leading? Was I nuts? I answered my own questions: There wasn't one; nowhere; yes, definitely.

Of course there were some outside forces at work here, too. Cindy, bless her rational heart, had always maintained we needed more balance in our lives. I'd ignored that message long enough, but there was some stuff happening on the school front for Mike that was quite disconcerting, even for myopic me.

Mike had always been a very good student. School was never an issue. His marks were excellent, his conduct exemplary. But now he was in his first year of high school at Father Leo J. Austin Catholic Secondary School and it wasn't going particularly well. This was a tough time for secondary school education in Ontario. Then-premier Mike Harris had pledged to revamp the educational system and Mike's year was the second to experience what was referred to as the "new curriculum." Basically, school got a lot harder. The workload was much heavier; the course content much more difficult and demanding, especially in mathematics (which, by the way, is Kryptonite to all the McKenzie boys, starting with me). Compounding the problem was that the teachers and their union were basically at war with the premier and the government. So at the time Mike was entering high school, his teachers were on a work-to-rule campaign with no after-school activities at all. There was also a huge overcrowding issue; there were more than 2,200 students at Austin, and a fleet of portables.

Mike got his midterm marks and we were thunderstruck to learn he had a forty-two in math. The other marks were much better, but not what we were used to. It was also plain to see that Mike wasn't really enjoying his first year of high school in any way, which was painful for us because he'd always loved everything about going to school, from the classes to the social and athletic aspects of it.

Cindy and I went to the parent-teacher meetings in the gym—which were more like a cattle call because of the overcrowding issue—with line after line of parents waiting to talk to their kids' teachers for no more than three or four minutes at a time before moving on to the next line. Our focus was obviously on seeing the math teacher and the exchange went something like this:

"Our son is Mike McKenzie and he has forty-two in math."

"Yes," the teacher said, looking down at her book of grades. "That's correct."

"Well, that's not so good, so what do you think we can do about that?"

"I don't know," she said. "Why don't you ask Mike Harris?"

I bit my tongue. Hard.

"Let's not bring politics into this. The issue is my son and what we're going to do about this mark of forty-two."

"I don't know," she said. "I didn't finish teaching the whole curriculum last year because I stopped to help the kids who were struggling with the concepts. Because I spent that time going back over the material to make sure they understood it, I wasn't able to finish teaching them everything I was supposed to. I got in trouble for that. I'm not going to do it again."

"So you're just going to forge ahead with the course and if kids don't understand the material, too bad, they get left behind and that's their problem?"

"Yes," she said.

Cindy and I were livid. Partisan politics aside, Mike was clearly caught in the crossfire between the teachers and the provincial government. He was basically on his own; that was this teacher's message.

This was unacceptable to us so we charted an immediate course of action. One, he would get what extra help was available from his math teacher (two mornings a week, twenty minutes at a time, before school started). Two, we would get him math tutoring from one of the many independent companies that had sprung up all over the place because of the obvious need. Three, we would start exploring the idea of enrolling Mike in a private school for Grade 10. We weren't going through this experience again.

So that was my mental state at the time—temporary insanity perhaps?—and all of these thoughts were bouncing around that night in North Oshawa Arena, when the substandard performance of Mike and his team made me see the light. On the way home, I broached the subject with Mike, told him that as much as we all loved hockey perhaps the time had come to broaden our horizons a little. I ran the idea of going to a private school by him and, surprisingly, he didn't reject it. He was intrigued. I was selling him on the fact that maybe it was time to get involved in more sports—play some football, run cross-country—and get an education that would really prepare him to be successful in whatever he chose to do with his life.

We are not the boarding school type of people—our attitude is the longer you can keep your kids under your roof, the better—so our options were fairly limited because of geography. We homed in on Trinity College School in Port Hope, a very fine private co-ed school with a population of about five hundred, including a couple of hundred day students who were bused in from surrounding areas. Port Hope is about twenty-five miles due east from Whitby, or a thirty-minute drive right along the 401. If he were to go there, Mike could catch a bus at the Whitby commuter train (GO) station each morning at 7:15 and it would drop him back there after the day's activities, including the many extracurriculars, around 5 or 6 p.m.

It wasn't cheap—in the $15,000 to $20,000 range for a year—but we thought it was a good investment in his future.

There was a wide variety of extracurriculars and students were not just encouraged but obliged to participate in them. I checked out the TCS hockey team—they had their own rink—and while the school was top-notch, there was no question the hockey was going to be a major step down from AAA for Mike. This was something of a concern for me. Sports are a big part of TCS life, but in a school with about only 250 boys, many of whom hail from foreign countries, it goes without saying their football and hockey teams, among others, didn't always stack up well in the wins and losses against all-boys' schools with powerhouse athletic programs such as Upper Canada College, St. Andrew's and St. Michael's College.

But if hockey and athletic results were the focal point of this exercise, we would just keep playing AAA, so the three of us—Mike, Cindy and I—decided this was the way to go, that education and a well-rounded experience were paramount. Mike was going to go to TCS for Grade 10, but he did have one request or condition—he wanted to finish his Whitby minor hockey career the next year in major bantam.

It was a reasonable request. He had played AAA hockey in Whitby every year from minor novice all the way up to minor bantam. There was just one more year to complete the eight-year cycle and he wanted to finish it with the four remaining kids he started it with—Kyle O'Brien, Kyle Clancy, Steven Seedhouse and Matt Snowden.

I talked to TCS headmaster Rodger Wright—brother of former Canadian Football League commissioner Tom Wright and one of the more impressive people I've ever met—about Mike's desire to finish this chapter of his life before he wholly committed to the TCS experience. Rodger was great, he said that Mike's AAA hockey would, for that one year, count as an extracurricular activity and so long as Mike made an effort to do what other extra activities he could, an exception could be made.

So that settled it. Mike would go to Trinity College the following school year; he would finish his major bantam season playing AAA hockey in Whitby and he would embark on a new journey with an emphasis on education and becoming a more multidimensional person than his father ever was.

Though I have to tell you, Dad was feeling pretty good about finally seeing the light and realizing there's more to life than hockey. What is it Cindy called it? Oh, yes, balance. Yes, that's it. Balance.

Well, that was the plan anyway.

THE DRAFT YEAR: Looking for Love in All the Wrong Places

"SCOUTS?"

It's just a one-word line from a movie, but if you're an aficionado of *Slap Shot*, you instantly get the picture. The thuggish Charlestown Chiefs have seen the light and decide to stop gooning it up to play real hockey—until team owner Joe McGrath barges into the dressing room and says: "You're blowin' it, boys! Every scout in the NHL is out there tonight with contracts in their pocket, and they're lookin' for talent, for winners!... They come here tonight—to scout the Chiefs! The toughest team in the Federal League! Not this bunch of...pussies!"

To which playing-coach Reg Dunlop (Paul Newman) raises an eyebrow and says: "Scouts?"

The next scene, of course, shows absolute mayhem on the ice as the Chiefs immediately revert to their old goony ways.

It's a classic illustration of how good intentions, honorable as they may be, just sometimes aren't meant to be, especially where hockey is concerned.

And so it was for the McKenzies in Mike's major bantam AAA season of 2001–02. It was supposed to be Mike's farewell season to high-level competitive hockey. Our newfound emphasis with Mike was going to be on education, Trinity College School in Port Hope, where it was time to start focusing on balance (football, cross-country, volleyball, culture, academics, personal growth) as opposed to living the one-dimensional minor hockey life.

Well, it was a nice thought while it lasted.

Actually, we didn't entirely abandon that quest. Mike was, in fact, enrolled at TCS for Grade 10. Education had become a higher priority for us. He would dutifully get up each day just after 6 a.m. and be on the bus to Port Hope by 7:15. That wasn't always easy either, especially if he had a weeknight game in Barrie at 9 p.m. and wouldn't get home until well after midnight. Mike found the academics to be much more challenging—they even had classes Saturday morning to make up for time lost playing sports on Wednesday afternoon. He made many great friends there, loved the teachers and was thriving in spite of the heavier workload and extra travel time.

The fly in the ointment was that the aliens had returned with the real Mike McKenzie who they took away when he was twelve years old.

I'm not saying Mike was an elite-level player as a fifteen-year-old, because he wasn't. But "old Mike" was back in a big way, with confidence and performance I hadn't seen since major atom. Still not the greatest skater in the world, he was competing consistently hard, showing no fear or hesitation, getting physically involved at every turn. He was putting up great numbers—I recall two games where he scored five goals in each game and he finished the season with close to fifty—and his feet never stopped moving. His work ethic was off the scale. While he had sort of settled in as an average to slightly below-average skater, all the other parts of his games were back at a high level.

Hockey people will tell you there comes a time in some players' lives where they just wake up one day and "get it," which is a euphemism for the player figuring out what it actually takes to play the game and play it well (feet always moving, competing hard every shift, winning more battles than they lose and just coming up with a consistency of effort that maximizes whatever talent they possess).

Mike, for reasons I still can't comprehend, "got it" in major bantam. Like many kids at that age, he started to attract interest from Ontario Hockey League teams and scouts.

What's now known as the minor midget AAA year (Mike's major bantam season) is unquestionably the most bizarre year of minor hockey because there's a whole new dynamic at work—the foreboding presence of the next level. The entire focus, unfortunately, changes for everyone—coaches, players and parents—because there are scouts and general managers and agents to deal with.

It changes everything. It shouldn't, but it does.

Sadly, the value system I've always maintained should exist in minor hockey (have fun; teach values; improve individual skating and skills; teach team concepts, strategies and tactics) goes out the window when the kids are fifteen years old and draft eligible for major junior hockey.

On Mike's team, we were fortunate to have a level-headed coaching staff. My pal Bucky Crouch, who was the goalie coach when I was Mike's peewee coach, was in his second year as the head coach of the Wildcats and he had experience with kids of this age. Mike's cousin Mat was on the AAA team and Cindy's brother John (Mat's dad) was an assistant coach with Bucky. Having been a star OHLer and pro player himself, John had been through all of this; he knew what it was all about.

And it's not like the Wildcats had a lot of hot commodities for the draft. Mike was probably considered the team's top OHL prospect and he was predicted to be a fifth- to- eighth-round candidate, strictly middle of the pack (he ended up being chosen 125th overall, in the seventh round, to the Saginaw Spirit). But even on a lower-level team like Whitby, "draft fever" occasionally made an appearance.

The big mistake coaches and parents inevitably make in the draft year is to repeatedly use the S word, thinking it's a catalyst to great performance, when, in fact, it's quite the opposite.

"Scouts."

It should never even be uttered in the presence of a fifteen-year-old player. I believe it is the cardinal sin to do so. If coaches and parents would just realize the impetus for a fifteen-year-old to play hockey, and play it well, should never be to do it for the scouts, the world would be a much happier place. Yet most minor hockey coaches say it without even thinking. "Lotsa scouts in the building tonight, boys," the coach will inevitably tell the lads in the pregame speech, thinking he's motivating them or pushing their buttons and the result will be a big win. Oh, he's pushing the kids' buttons all right, but not the ones that should be pushed.

If a player is playing to impress the scouts, that player first has to think what it is that will impress a scout. The first response from the kid, or his parents, is usually "score a lot of goals," which means that player is thinking that is the measure of success. He is not thinking about doing all the small things necessary to not only score a goal, but help his team win the game. Which is too bad because scouts, while statistics certainly aren't ignored, often do look for the little things and intangibles that make up a hockey player. But players, and their parents, often don't understand that. They think it's all about goals and, not surprisingly, this leads to unprecedented levels of selfishness.

Hockey is a team game. It is supposed to be seventeen players (two goalies and fifteen skaters) dedicated to a common cause, doing whatever it takes for the team to do its best.

Playing for scouts is simply playing the game for all the wrong reasons. If the players play for each other first, the scouts will go home happy and satisfied. Trust me on that, because ultimately that's what they're looking for. And if the coaches of minor hockey teams would only realize that, they and their players would be so much better off.

Yet the competition and jealousies within a team—and this involves mostly players and parents—can rip it apart.

If some players on the team get letters from the OHL clubs saying they're interested in them, the ones who don't get them feel slighted and out of sorts. When the mid-season OHL draft list—you have to be on the list to be drafted and it ranks players according to AA, A, B and C levels—inevitably makes its way into the public domain, imagine the furor when Johnny is on the list but Billy isn't; or Steve is a AA prospect and Bobby is a mere B; wait until Peter shows up at the rink with an agent and the other players and parents think if Peter has an agent, surely we need one, too.

Forget *Slap Shot*; this can be, in its most extreme form, the minor hockey equivalent of an X-rated flick, a depraved orgy of immoral excess and self-satisfaction.

The culmination of all of this, of course, is the OHL draft each May. I don't have any problem with the draft itself, or how the OHL does its business. It is a wholly necessary function to equitably distribute or assign players' playing rights to allow for the league to exist with a reasonably competitive playing field. My problem is how, for better or worse, kids and their parents perceive the draft as if it defines a kid at age fifteen.

This is true of all drafts in all sports. I often end up talking to friends' kids who either didn't get drafted or didn't get drafted as highly as they anticipated. I try to make them understand the draft is an artificial process of highly subjective evaluation. It assigns their rights to a team; it doesn't affect them in any appreciable way as a player.

Example: The OHL draft is held on a Saturday in May. No one is playing any games in May. I ask a player what kind of player he is on the Friday before the draft. I ask him what kind of player he is on the Saturday of the draft, and what kind of player he is on the Sunday after the draft. The answer, of course, is that he is the same player on Friday as he is on Saturday as he is on Sunday, because he hasn't done anything on the ice that could possibly change the way he's played the game or even alter the perception of himself and his ability. All that happened on Saturday is that some people (scouts) made a highly subjective evaluation of that player, which brands him a first-rounder or an eighth-rounder or a no-rounder. This would be fine if the people making this highly subjective evaluation were perfect, but they're not and they would be the first to tell you that.

There are some first-round picks in major junior who never develop into OHL stars and there are many mid-to-late-round picks who do. It's absurd to allow anyone to hang a brand or label on you as a fifteen-year-old and suggest you should embrace this as your standing in the hockey community.

Let's also try to keep the whole thing in perspective. In Mike's OHL draft year of 2002, exactly three hundred players were chosen. As of the middle of the 2008–09 season, seven— just seven of them—have gone on to become what I would define as NHL players—Wojtek Wolski (3rd overall in the OHL draft); David Bolland (8th); Tyler Kennedy (16th); Patrick Kaleta (31st); Kevin Porter (60th); Jared Boll (101st); and Benoit Pouliot (207th). That's it, although it must be noted the 1986 birth year in Ontario was not a particularly strong one (keep in mind, Kaleta, Porter and Boll are Americans, so only four Ontario kids from that '86 draft class were regular NHLers seven years after their OHL draft year). Still, it gives you some idea of the odds against your fifteen-year-old, even if he's an OHL first-round flavor of the day, becoming an NHL player.

The point is, at the age of fifteen, you don't let anyone define you. You are way too young to accept someone else's notion of who you should be or what you're going to be. You do all that yourself. There is plenty of time for self-determination.

The analogy I like to use is that once a kid goes through what is now known as his minor midget season, and if he has aspirations of playing at the next level, he gets on The Ladder. Every other player of any age, sixteen and older, who wants to keep playing hockey at the next level, is on it, too. The Ladder is crowded and it's frenetic, because there is only one rule on The Ladder—you're always moving, either up or down. You can be moving up fast or down fast; up slowly or down slowly; but whatever it is, you're either passing guys or getting passed; if you're standing still, you might as well be going backwards as there's no shortage of guys blowing by you. And for all the players there are who move up or down, there are others who simply fall or jump off for one reason or another.

My TV analyst pal Keith Jones, who had a good nine-year NHL career, puts it another way, in his usual funny fashion. "If you play long enough, all the really good players quit and then you make the NHL," Jonesy says. "That's what happened to me. I go home in the summer and have beers with the guys I played hockey with when I was a kid and they say to me, 'We were a lot better than you were, how did you make it to the NHL and we didn't?' I tell them, 'You quit, I didn't. You should have kept playing.'"

Now, that's funny. Jonesy is, of course, selling his talent and ability far short for the sake of a laugh—and that's why we love him—but his premise, to a point, has some validity. You play as hard as you can for as long as you can, you don't allow other people to define your limitations and you just never know how far you'll go up The Ladder and how many people you'll pass until you finally fall, jump or get knocked off.

And it doesn't hurt if along the way you make good friends with the Hard Work Fairy.

I know what you're saying. The Hard Work Fairy? Is this guy serious? I don't recall exactly when I started it, but I was driving home from one of Mike's games and he was lamenting his hard luck around the net and how a recent hot streak he had been on turned into the coldest of cold streaks. I told him he had obviously offended the Hard Work Fairy. Where I came up with that one I have no idea, but it just came out.

It got a laugh out of Mike, which was the idea. The notion of there being fairies in hockey is, well, it's pretty funny. Someone else might call the Hard Work Fairy the hockey gods. Whatever. I only know I have an unwavering faith that if an individual works hard enough long enough at anything, good things will happen and there will be a reward. But the problem with that philosophy is that every hockey player of any age or ability always thinks he's working hard, and most of them aren't. Not even close.

So I suppose I feel there needs to be this mythical figure—the Hard Work Fairy—who takes stock of who's actually working hard and who's not, and doles out rewards and/or punishment accordingly. You can't jive the Hard Work Fairy. He(?) knows. He always knows.

Laugh if you like, but you show me a hockey player who's on a roll, scoring goals in game after game after game, and I'll show you a player who somewhere along the line during that hot streak allows complacency and comfort to creep into his game. At some point, he forgets how hard he worked to be successful and even though he may still be filling the net, he's on borrowed time. There's a day of reckoning coming. At some point, the Hard Work Fairy says "enough is enough" and steps in and now that player is in big trouble. It may not be nice to mess with Mother Nature but you definitely don't want to screw around with the Hard Work Fairy.

Then the stick goes cold and even after the player realizes he has to work harder to get back into the good graces again, it's going to take some time to build up the account and for the player to find himself on the right side of the ledger again. That's when, and only when, the Hard Work Fairy will see fit to bestow a reward. I have seen it happen with individual players. I have seen it happen with whole teams. Complacency and comfort are the enemy. Hard work is the ally.

I'm not saying the Hard Work Fairy doesn't sometimes work in mysterious ways and I'll admit there have been a few occasions when I've wondered if the Hard Work Fairy has abandoned me and my kids in their time of need, but my faith remains resolute: You work hard enough for long enough and you'll be rewarded.

The point of all of this—for us anyway—was that Mike had, seemingly against all odds, played well enough in his major bantam year that there was no chance in the world he was prepared to close the door on playing hockey at the next level. He wanted to get on The Ladder; he wanted to please the Hard Work Fairy.

Football? Cross-country? Volleyball? High school hockey? Balance? You could have summed it up in just one word.

"Scouts?"

26 DISCRETION ISN'T ALWAYS THE BETTER PART OF VALOR

I WASN'T SURE where Mike's hockey renaissance was taking him, but it goes without saying, as a Crazy Hockey Dad, I was most certainly enjoying the rather unexpected ride.

What was supposed to be his farewell tour had seemingly become a launching pad. It was kind of surreal, to be honest, and I kept thinking this would be the day the clock would strike midnight and the party would be over.

For kids who are going to play at the next level, the days and weeks immediately following the minor midget season are like a whirlwind. First up, once the actual team's season is over, is the regional tryout camp for the provincial Under-17 program. For us, it was on an April weekend in Peterborough. They create six teams; play a round-robin type tournament; do a lot of physical and fitness testing; try to give the kids a sense of what it will take to continue playing at a higher level and then pick a dozen or so kids to move onto another camp. I kind of figured Mike was a long shot to advance, but that was fine. It was just fun to be there.

Mike played well enough over the course of the weekend, scored a few goals and didn't look out of place, but something happened in his next-to-last game that I thought sealed his fate. Mike was coming back through the neutral zone towards his own end when a defenseman on the other team turned and, out of nowhere, pitch-forked Mike with a major-league spear to the midsection. I was really worried that he might be seriously injured, it was that vicious. The attack was totally unprovoked in the context of that game, but it was a rival defenseman from another ETA team who Mike had a running battle with over the course of the season. This player definitely wasn't going to get to the next level so I suppose he decided to give Mike a going-away present in what was probably their last-ever on-ice meeting.

There have been times in Mike's hockey-playing days when I have perfectly understood opposing players' desire to annihilate him because there were occasions when he may have said or done something to justify it. But this attack was indefensible.

Mike was down on the ice for a bit and then the trainer took him in the hallway beside the bench in Peterborough's Memorial Centre. I made my way down to make sure he wasn't seriously injured, but aside from a big red welt across his stomach, he seemed to be okay. I could see by the look on his face he was furious. He never said a word to me, he didn't have to; I knew exactly what he was thinking and wondering: Should I forget about what had just happened and focus on trying to advance or should I seek some vigilante justice at the expense of moving on?

I knew what I was voting for and it wasn't detente.

"You do what you want," I said to Mike, "but if it was me, I'd give it to him. It's your call, though."

I went back up into the stands, but I knew what was coming next. On Mike's next shift there was a dump in for a line change and Mike was first onto the ice. The defenseman who had speared him was going back to retrieve the puck. Mike flew in there full steam and ran the defenseman hard into the end boards with a vicious, nasty and high hit into the glass. As they both rebounded off the boards, their gloves were off and they attempted to fight but with full cages on it wasn't much of a battle.

Afterwards, between that game and Mike's final game of the weekend, a lot of the other kids at the camp told Mike he was stupid for fighting because the rule was if you fight, you won't move on. After his final game of the day, we headed home and Mike was regretting what he had done, upset that he had no chance to move on.

I disagreed. I told him, in the grand scheme of things, moving on at the U-17 didn't matter as much as standing up for himself, that the chances of him actually making the provincial Under-17 team were nonexistent—it is almost exclusively the domain of first-round OHL draft picks. I told him I would much rather see him defend himself the way he did than allow some dirty bastard to try to seriously injure him and that if he had done nothing to respond to the spear, it would have sent a message to others that they could go after him any time they like without reprisals. I told him there are occasions when turning the other cheek is the smart thing to do—discretion is sometimes the better part of valor—but this wasn't one of them. I told him I was proud of him and there would be times in life when he had to stand up for himself, make sacrifices for the sake of principle and accept whatever consequences came his way. This, I said, was one of those times. I believed it then; I believe it now.

The funny thing is we got a call that night from the U-17 camp director, who informed us Mike was moving on to the next level of U-17 camp for the entire OMHA, in Guelph in May. I expressed surprise that they picked Mike after the fight and the camp director said: "I would have been disappointed if Mike hadn't responded."

Mike was ecstatic at the news he was moving on, but within the hockey circles we traveled, there was a lot of chatter about Mike's selection. Not much of it was kind. Other kids told Mike he only made it because "his dad was on TV," that he violated the rules by fighting and they still picked him. The message boards on internet sites that the kids and many parents frequented were full of stuff about the inequity of Mike McKenzie getting to the final OMHA camp at the expense of this good player or that good player.

None of this was new for Mike, or me, although it was a little more intense and personal than usual this time. Mike never said a word to me, but I could tell going into the second OMHA U-17 camp in Guelph that he was a man on a mission.

I try to say this without sounding like an Overbearing Hockey Dad, but Mike and Michael Haley from Oshawa, who Mike had played lacrosse with since they were Paperweights, dominated the entire weekend in Guelph. They were teammates and linemates. They were virtually unstoppable, although the camp administrators made them play on separate lines for a couple of games to see if it would slow them down. It didn't. They continued to score and lead the way.

Bear in mind that no one from that camp has made it as a regular in the NHL, and the OMHA crop of '86s was really quite weak compared to the GTHL players (who had their own U-17 camp), but this was nevertheless a stunning development for me. I could scarcely believe what I was seeing. I had never seen Mike play so well, skate so fast, compete so hard and elevate his play to that level. It was the first time I ever actually believed Mike might be able to play at a level as high as the OHL or perhaps U.S. college hockey.

I asked him on the way home, "What the hell got into you?"

"I wanted to prove to everyone I deserved to be there because of me, not because of you," he said. "All of that talk I didn't deserve to be there pissed me off."

Now, reality did strike at the final U-17 camp at York University in June, when all the best players from the GTHL, the Ottawa area, northern Ontario, southwestern Ontario and northwestern Ontario got together. Mike played reasonably well but he had hit his ceiling. His play there showed he still had a lot of work to do if he was going to play at the next level.

While this U-17 process was unfolding in April, May and June, lots of other things were happening as well.

In April, the Oshawa Legionaires Junior A team was holding its spring tryouts. For a sixteen-year-old Mike, that was the very definition of his next level at that point. He tried out and made the team that could take no more than six local sixteen-year-olds. Mike and Zack Greer made it from Whitby; Mike MacLean, Derrick Bagshaw, Andrew Gibbons and Daniel Larocque made it from Oshawa. The coach of the Legionaires was Wayne Marchment, the brother of NHL defenseman Bryan Marchment, and the GM was Peter Vipond, a local Brooklin,

Ont., lacrosse legend who once played NHL hockey with the California Golden Seals. They were terrific guys. Wayne Marchment was a very good coach with a great feel for the game. Mike was thrilled to be moving into Junior A hockey, where he would play against players as old as twenty-one.

In May, Mike was chosen in the seventh round of the OHL draft by Saginaw, a franchise that had just relocated from North Bay, Ont. Mike had thought he might go as high as the fifth round and was equal parts disappointed and relieved while sitting in front of the computer (the OHL draft is conducted on the internet) to see he had been chosen 125th overall.

All of this—the U-17 experience, making the Junior A Legionaires as a sixteen-year-old and getting drafted into the OHL—was really quite unexpected, especially for a kid who had, one year ago, been on the verge of giving up high-level competitive hockey.

Go figure.

27 MAKING THE BIG TIME
Shawn Steps It Up

LIFE WAS GOOD for Crazy Hockey Dad in 2002. Very good.

Mike had effectively been born again, in the hockey sense, and was looking forward to his first season in Junior A. Shawn, meanwhile, was playing AAA hockey for the very first time.

I've never gotten too hung up about the number of As attached to a team name. Shawn played AA for three years and I thought that was great because he thought that was great. Shawn played A for two years and I was cool with that because Shawn was cool with that. But Shawn was sincerely thrilled to be part of John Annis's AAA Whitby Wildcats for 2002–03 and, well, I don't need to tell you how I felt, especially since I was going to help out as an assistant coach.

I talk to a lot of people about their kids playing hockey and I often get dads of younger kids saying, with an overtone of disappointment or resignation, "My boy doesn't really care that much about hockey, he doesn't take it that seriously, he's not that good." I have two responses for that. One, there's nothing wrong with any of it, as long as the kids are happy and healthy and having fun playing the game. Two, you never know when a kid will suddenly develop a greater passion for the game or play it at a level you never would have imagined possible. Shawn would be a prime example of that.

The timing of all this for Shawn was especially exciting because this was supposed to be his major peewee (thirteen-year-old) season and that's the year of the Quebec Peewee Tourney. If I got Mike's hard-working-but-not-very-talented peewee team to Quebec, it would be a slam dunk to do it for this highly ranked team that Shawn was on.

But Hockey Canada had other ideas. This was the year Hockey Canada revamped the age groups to make them consistent across the country, so a thirteen-year-old player in Ontario became known as a minor bantam instead of a major peewee. Shawn's team was out of luck for Quebec on what amounted to an administrative technicality, a name change.

Shawn liked playing on the AAA team. He was good friends with a lot of the kids on the team. He was enjoying his new-found confidence at that level. He played a solid physical game and his puck skills were decent enough that he could make plays. He could keep up just fine as he was a much better natural skater than his brother. Shawn wasn't nearly in the same class as the top two players on the team—Patrick Daley, who would go on to have a good OHL career, and Louke Oakley, who would go on to get a scholarship at Clarkson University—but he often played on their line. Whether Shawn was alongside the two big guns or playing a role on the third line, he was happy and fitting in.

Shawn liked playing for John Annis, or Johnny A, as Shawn and the kids often called him. John is a guy who grew up in hardscrabble Regent Park, the tough, low-income, downtown Toronto housing projects (home of NHLer Glen Metropolit). He's a no-nonsense guy who can be a little rough around the edges, but also a lot of fun, too. As a minor hockey coach, John was very successful, winning some OMHA titles and icing competitive teams that played hard. He ran some of the best practices I've ever seen at any level, just for the players being able to skate, pass and shoot and work on their skills. He didn't tolerate slackers. If a kid was floating through practice or being a nuisance, John would just order him off the ice and send him home, and that was as true of his goaltender son Wes as it was any player on the team.

Some kids and parents no doubt ran hot and cold on John—depending on whose ox was getting gored at the time—but I always sensed that John had real affection for this group of kids and cared about them.

He definitely favored high-paced, offensive hockey with not a lot of time spent on systems or structure. He motivated the kids to play hard, demanded they compete, and as rough and tumble as he was in so many ways, his first priority was to get the kids playing the game fast and skilled and with the puck. Because he had a team with a fair bit of talent and skill, other weaker teams would try to rough them up, put the game in the gutter, and it used to drive John crazy. He called it "bullshit hockey," but rest assured that if the fertilizer did hit the fan in a game, it didn't take much to set off Johnny and his Regent Park side would come out. When that happened, uh, well, things could get interesting, to say the least.

The team had some tough kids and competitors so they could play it any way the opposition wanted. Shawn was becoming an interesting case study in this regard. As laid back and easygoing as he was off the ice, Shawn was starting to enjoy the physical part of it. Shawn wasn't tall—about five foot eight then (no more than five foot nine now)—but he was strong and didn't mind at all when the game would get edgy.

Mike's primary focus when he played was scoring goals and creating offense. If that wasn't happening to his satisfaction, Mike might get frustrated and let his emotions get the better of him. The next thing you know Mike would be in the middle of everything. Shawn also started to find himself in the middle of some "situations," but it was never because Shawn was frustrated or angry; it was more calculated on his part. Shawn loved to torment players like his brother because he had an advantage over them—he wasn't taking any of this too much to heart. It was all just good fun or sport for him.

But that didn't mean Shawn didn't need to be reeled in that season, perhaps feeling a little too full of himself as a new AAA player.

I wasn't at this particular regular-season game in November against the Clarington Toros because I had to work, but there was a Clarington defenseman who was engaging in some hit-and-run tactics, playing what John Annis would say was "bullshit hockey." It was only a matter of time until there was a response because that's how John's teams played. It was Shawn who took it upon himself, right off a face-off, to engage this opposing player. Shawn ran into him and when the guy pushed back, Shawn's gloves came off and it was on. This kid clearly didn't want to fight. He covered up and that was that. Shawn was ejected from the game and received an automatic one-game (regular season) suspension.

I wasn't too amused when Cindy related the story to me, but John Annis told me not to be too hard on Shawn, that

Shawn, left, as a paperweight house-league lacrosse player and Mike, below, as a novice house-league player.

Lacrosse teammates Mike, Kyle O'Brien, Kyle Clancy, Adam Berti and Steven Seedhouse (left to right) on their way to Wildcat basketball camp in summer of '96. Adam Berti was drafted by the Chicago Blackhawks.

The five players who started and finished every year of Whitby AAA hockey – Mike, Kyle O'Brien, Kyle Clancy, Matt Snowden and Steven Seedhouse. These are their "player cards" from the Quebec Peewee tourney.

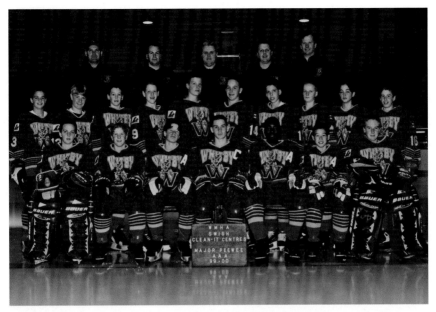

The 1999-2000 Wildcats AAA Major Peewees that went to Quebec – that's Bob Anderson, Steve Hedington, me, Kevin O'Brien and Stu Seedhouse in the back row, left to right. Manager Ron Balcom was missing.

After only coaching AAA hockey with Mike, I was pleased to find out the A level had a lot to offer too. My two years as Shawn's coach in major atom and minor peewee were terrific.

Left: Mike as a 16-year-old in his first year of Jr. A hockey with the Oshawa Legionaires.

Below: The captains of the 2005 OPJHL champion St. Mike's Buzzers, Mike, Andrew Cogliano, Kain Tisi, Mark Lozzi, Kevin Schmidt and Cory Wickett.

Above: Shawn struts his stuff as a AA rep player in minor novice.

Left: Shawn plays a little pond hockey during the fateful major bantam year.

Shawn and Mike flanked by Kid Rock, left, and Nickelback's Chad Kroeger at Game 5 of the 2008 Stanley Cup final at Joe Louis Arena in Detroit. The boys love hockey but they like to rock, too.

The McKenzie men take in the NHL Awards show in Toronto in 2008. Dad got chirped unmercifully by the boys for being a party pooper and us not going to the NHL Awards in 2009 in Las Vegas.

One of the highlights of Mike's freshman year at St. Lawrence University, for me and him, was playing against Michigan State at Munn Arena. Mike wore No. 27 for two years but switched back to his familiar No. 11.

Shawn and Mike are all smiles, and why not? They're chilling in their hotel room in Detroit for Game 5 of the 2008 Stanley Cup final between the Red Wings and Pittsburgh Penguins.

It's not easy to get all four McKenzies under the same roof at the same time, but Shawn, Cindy and Mike were all there for my 50th birthday party, which, of course, I threw for myself. Family times are the best times.

Shawn was standing up for his teammates. I did give Shawn a lecture about picking his spots—how there's a right time and a wrong time to send a message; that fighting and getting suspended in minor bantam hockey isn't always the best way to go about it. But you could tell he was pretty pleased with himself and he had the admiration and respect of his teammates for stepping up. Whether you happen to like it or not, that, in a nutshell, is the culture of hockey, even in minor bantam.

Fortunately for Shawn, the suspension wouldn't affect him for the coming weekend, when the team was competing in a tournament in London, where Whitby's first game was against the London Junior Knights. With future Los Angeles Kings star Drew Doughty and future San Jose first-round pick Logan Couture, the Junior Knights were one of the premier teams in the province.

Shawn and I were driving to London on the Thursday night—Cindy was staying home so it was a boys' weekend away—and we were both looking forward to a fun weekend road trip.

The first game turned out to be a huge dud for Shawn's team. They got steamrolled. The Wildcats lost by a considerable margin, seven or eight goals. It was just one of those games.

The next game, then, would be crucial. Lose it and the Wildcats would play out the string with one more round-robin game on Saturday. Win it and, if there was another win on Saturday, there was at least a chance of moving on. The afternoon game on Friday was against the Mississauga Reps, a GTHL team that wasn't considered very good. But whatever ailed the Wildcats in the London game, it was still with them against Mississauga.

It was a dreadful hockey game, the absolute worst of minor hockey on display. It went from being chippy to pretty much out of control. Some games are just like that. There was a lot of hacking and whacking, cheap shots all over the ice. Johnny A's combative Regent Park side had surfaced. At one point, he was looking at the other coach and putting his fists up in a John L. Sullivan boxing-style pose on the bench, checking to see if the other coach wanted to take this outside.

Normally, I would have found some level of amusement at that, but Shawn had become involved with some player on the other team who had run him. On this occasion, whatever the kid had done to him, Shawn was genuinely angry, which was rare. Shawn then blatantly and viciously cross-checked the other player in the head. Shawn was assessed a five-minute major, was ejected from that game, and would be suspended for the balance of that tournament plus his next two OMHA league games as well. Throw in his fighting suspension from the week before and he was going to be sitting down for three league (OMHA) games.

I was furious. As soon as Shawn came off the ice, I told him to get out of his gear because we were going home. He came out of the dressing room—the game was still going on—and we drove to the hotel, packed up our stuff, checked out and drove the two hours back to Whitby, with me pretty much going up one side of Shawn and down the other.

Shawn is the kind of kid who doesn't like being in trouble—Mike could have gone the two hours without saying a word—so it was an uncomfortable ride home for Shawn. And I wanted it to be uncomfortable because as happy as I was with him playing AAA, he damn well wasn't going to play like this all season long.

The good news was it was just one of those weeks for the Wildcats, and Shawn. The team rebounded to play better; Shawn served his suspensions totaling three games and came back to play hard and aggressively, but without any nonsense the rest of the season.

The Wildcats were playing host to the OMHA championship that year because they had won the title in the previous year. It's a good thing they were the host team, too, because they lost in the second round of the playoffs to Ajax-Pickering, who were led by Marcus Carroll, Bill's youngest son who went on to play for Owen Sound in the OHL. If not there as the host team, the Wildcats wouldn't have made it at all. Whitby did rebound to beat Ajax-Pickering in the semi-finals of the OMHA tournament, but lost a heartbreaker to the North Central Predators in the championship game. In Shawn's first year of AAA, he got somewhere his brother had never been— an OMHA championship game, albeit on the losing end.

It was John Annis's last game with that collection of kids. It really was quite a remarkable minor hockey run for that group, which had been together for a number of years. Shawn, meanwhile, was just happy and proud to have been a part of it and to have proven he was a AAA-caliber player. I could see no reason he wouldn't continue to play at that level for a good, long time.

Little did I know . . . .

28 TURN OUT THE LIGHTS, THE PARTY IS OVER

I WOULDN'T WISH the last seven months of 2003 on my worst enemy—and that's saying something, because I've been known to suffer from Irish Alzheimer's (where you forget everything but your enemies).

The year had started with such promise. Shawn had just finished his first full season of AAA, loved it and had already made the AAA team for the next season. Shawn was going into Grade 9 at Trinity College. Mike had just completed his first year of Junior A and had excelled—the Saginaw Spirit indicated they were prepared to sign him; a number of U.S. colleges had expressed some interest in him as a potential scholarship athlete. Mike was back for his second year, Grade 11, at TCS.

As I headed off to the '03 Cup final between the Mighty Ducks of Anaheim and New Jersey Devils, I was thinking life didn't get any better than this. And I was right, the part about life not getting any better, because it didn't.

While I was in Anaheim I got an urgent message from Cindy, who had received a panicky phone call from my dad, who called her up out of the blue one morning and said: "Tell Bobby [he always called me Bobby] to come home, I don't think I'm going to make it." My dad was seventy-five years old but in reasonably good health, enjoying life to the fullest—playing golf three or four times a week, driving his Sebring convertible, pumping the Andrea Bocelli tunes and holding court at his favorite pub, Paddy O'Farrell's. He woke up one morning with a piercing headache—he hadn't been feeling quite right for a couple of weeks—and whatever sixth sense humans possess to know something is seriously wrong, well, his alarm bell had gone off.

I rushed home from Anaheim and within a week or two of that, after a bunch of doctors' appointments and tests, he was diagnosed with an inoperable brain tumor. The doctor said he might, if he was lucky, have six months; he ended up with six weeks and lost most of his mental faculties within two weeks of the diagnosis. He played out the string in palliative care at the Salvation Army Toronto Grace Health Centre in downtown Toronto (which, as an aside, is the very definition of grace, kindness, compassion and dignity). He died on July 23, 2003.

———— ● ————

It was, obviously, a tough summer, but you know what? As painful as it is to lose a parent, it is the natural order of things. It's the cycle of life. It's when bad things happen to your kids that it really hits you hard, because you like to think, in a perfect world, kids are spared. We know only too well that's not the way it works and there are far too many sad and tragic stories as evidence. In the pantheon of bad things that can happen to your children, what befell the McKenzie boys in 2003 isn't what anyone would necessarily deem tragic, not when you compare it to what so many parents have to deal with. But if your kids are hurting, as a parent, you hurt, too.

Six games into Mike's second season with the Legionaires, in late September, he suffered a concussion. A doozy. He was back-checking through the neutral zone at full speed in a game at North York Centennial Arena (we don't like this arena very much). He was chasing down a North York Ranger forward when a Legionaire defenseman stepped up for the big hit at the blue line. At the last second, the Ranger player jumped out of the way and Mike took the full force of his defenseman's hit, right smack dab in the middle of his face. On impact, it sounded like a bomb going off.

He never lost consciousness, but that didn't mean anything really. We took him to hospital to make sure there were no complications and he checked out fine, but it was obvious he was concussed. His face hurt like hell and his head was pounding. The headaches didn't go away either. Not the next day or the day after that or, for that matter, the next week or the week after that.

This was Mike's first-ever concussion and it was quite clear he had significant post-concussion symptoms—headaches, difficulty concentrating, motion sickness—that weren't receding any time soon. If you have never experienced these symptoms, or aren't close to someone who has, you simply have no idea how dark, desperate and scary it can be. It is like a dark cloud consumes your entire being, affecting your mood and ability to function in everyday life.

A few weeks into Mike's recovery, he thought he was getting better and started skating again at practice. He thought he was symptom-free, but even after a couple of days of hard skating in practice without any ill effects, the minute he got into a drill where there was a little jostling, some bumping and grinding, he felt like he was right back to where he was, his head hurting and not feeling quite right.

Aside from the obvious physical and emotional effects of post-concussion syndrome, the worst part is the fear and uncertainty of wondering when, or if, it's ever going to be better. When is normal going to return? It's pretty fair to say, given Mike's passion for all things hockey, he was a basket case through much of this. When he had his setback at practice, I really started to get concerned. So did he.

If you haven't already figured this out about me, I tend not to be a patient person. I don't like doing nothing. My job gives me opportunities or connections that aren't necessarily available to other people. I'm not shy about utilizing them either, especially on health concerns relating to my kids. So if the best course of treatment for a concussed NHLer is to see noted concussion specialist and neurologist Dr. Karen Johnston in Montreal, then that's the treatment I wanted for Mike.

Mike and I made the trek to Montreal to see Dr. Johnston (she has since moved to Toronto). Dr. Johnston is a wonderfully reassuring woman, who eased Mike's mind immediately by telling him that he would get better. But she also said he should be aware he would be more susceptible to future concussions, the key being to make sure he was fully recovered from this one before returning to play. Buoyed by that prognosis, Mike weathered his recovery through the balance of November. By early December—about nine weeks after he was initially concussed—he was finally symptom-free.

Dr. Johnston provided us with a very good, but extremely gradual, return-to-play protocol that was in and of itself a couple of weeks long. Since that process would put Mike back on the ice for just a couple of games before Christmas, we opted to hold him out until after his team's Christmas break and buy him almost two additional weeks of recovery time. I appreciate the sense of urgency all concussed hockey players have to get back to playing as soon as possible—to say nothing of their coaches and parents. But if all concerned would only realize the benefit of taking a little extra time to fully recover, err a little on the side of caution, the hockey world at all levels would be a much better place.

I should probably take a moment here to tackle the issue of safety equipment as it relates to concussions.

In Mike's first year of Junior A, the Legionaires' team rule was that first-year players had to wear a full cage as opposed to the half visor that all Junior A players are permitted to wear. Naturally, once he became a second-year Legionaire and had the option of discarding the cage that is precisely what he did. I'm not sure whether a full cage as opposed to the half visor would have made a difference in protecting Mike from his first concussion, but it certainly wouldn't have hurt, given the point of contact was directly on his face.

You should know this, though. While hockey helmets most certainly go a long way to preventing skull fractures and help to minimize trauma directly to the head and may ultimately prevent some concussions from occurring, in many cases the hockey helmet is almost inconsequential to brain trauma. Most concussions are the result of a person travelling very fast and being stopped so suddenly and forcefully that the brain literally smashes into the inside of the skull. In many cases, no amount of outside protection will cushion the blow of the brain on the inside of the skull. This, by the way, is not true of some types of bicycle helmets, which do in fact absorb some of the shock in a crash. I'm not advocating anyone to not wear a protective helmet; I am just pointing out that hockey helmets are often powerless to prevent brain trauma.

It's the same thing with mouthguards. All players should wear mouthguards because they protect the teeth and gums and while there is a "sense" that wearing a mouthguard helps to absorb the shock in trauma that may cause concussions, the truth is that there is no scientific or medical data that proves mouthguards minimize or prevent concussions. In that vein, it is quite possible that Mike would have suffered a concussion even if he had been wearing a full cage instead of a half visor that day, but I still think he would have been far better off with the cage.

Hockey really is a macho game. Kids who choose to wear the most protective equipment—a full cage, for example—are branded "pussies" yet most of the players who play Junior A are doing so in order to get a scholarship to a U.S. college where full cages are mandatory. Go figure.

Mike and I had a battle royale when he was coming back from his concussion in January. He wanted to keep wearing the visor; I wanted him to wear the cage. I knew the abuse he would take for being a "cage" wearer, but I also knew that his season or maybe his hockey-playing career could be over because of an errant high stick or puck to the face. That first serious concussion he suffered had reduced his margin for error greatly, especially if he was intent on getting a scholarship. For me, it was a no brainer. I won out on that battle with Mike and only two games into his comeback, something happened to get Mike fully on board with my view

There was a scrum in the corner for a loose puck. Mike was on the periphery of it, bent over and trying to fish the puck out of a mass of skates and legs. The opposing defenceman was right behind Mike and just as Mike fished out the puck, the defender crosschecked Mike hard in the middle of his back. The force of it drove Mike's caged-face into the top edge of the dasher board. On the way home, Mike was looking at his cage that had been badly "shmushed" in and duly noted that could have been his face that got "shmushed" in and his season, maybe even his hockey-playing life, would have been over.

I don't know how much easier that incident made it for Mike to deal with million or so "cage-wearing pussy" comments he got over the next two-plus years of Junior A hockey, but I do know this: He never got another concussion in Junior A, despite being struck forcefully in his (caged) face numerous times with a puck or a stick or the boards, and he ultimately got a scholarship to play U.S. college hockey, where there is no choice but to wear a full cage anyway. I know there are no guarantees and that no amount of "protection" can keep a player safe because hockey is a dangerous game and stuff happens. I know it all too well.

But my attitude on this issue of protection is obvious—if you're not making your living at the game, why wouldn't you wear the maximum protection permitted to safeguard whatever opportunities exist? But that attitude flies in the face of hockey's macho code.

Oh, well, I guess that makes me a "pussy." That's okay, I've been called worse.

———— ● ————

The good news, if there was any of that in the fall of 2003, was that Shawn was thriving on the major bantam AAA team. The new coach was a fellow by the name of Louis Atkinson and while his style differed greatly from John Annis's, he seemed to like Shawn. The personality of the team had greatly changed, too, as the top two players from last season—Patrick Daley and Louke Oakley—left the Wildcats to play in the GTHL. So the team was no longer a powerhouse, but they still had a solid nucleus and were very competitive. Louis must have seen something in Shawn because he gave him an A as alternate captain and Shawn responded in a positive fashion. He played hard, physically, made some plays, scored some goals and was, generally speaking, behaving himself. No more suspensions anyway.

Shawn will never forget the game that season—a career game, for sure—when the Wildcats beat Oshawa to the tune of 10–2 or 12–2 or something like that. Whatever the score ended up, Shawn scored five goals and four assists that night. A nine-point outing. It was just one of those nights where everything he touched turned to goal—and it didn't even cost me so much as a chocolate bar. That was a very enjoyable ride home.

Shawn had a game on Saturday, December 13, 2003, at the Evinrude Centre in Peterborough. The only reason I know the exact date is because it turned out to be the last game of high-level, competitive hockey Shawn would ever play.

Peterborough, at the '89 level, was never a very good team, almost always finishing in last place. What they lacked in skill, they made up in aggression. They had a couple of players who, in my estimation, were just plain dirty, out there for no reason other than to hurt people. The games with Peterborough were not a very good advertisement for what minor hockey should be.

Anyway, tensions were running high—remember, we're talking fourteen-year-old boys in their first year of high school—and a melee broke out on the boards. One of the players on Shawn's team had done something to one of the Peterborough players. Several of the Petes were trying to get at the Whitby player. Shawn was on the ice at the time and he didn't need to be told what the protocol was. He went right into the pile of Petes and started pulling them off his teammate. One thing led to another and if it wasn't a line brawl, it was damn close to it, with everyone paired off.

Shawn happened to draw the biggest kid on the ice—he was easily six feet tall to Shawn's five foot nine—and milliseconds after the first fight broke out, this big kid from Peterborough dropped the gloves and went after Shawn.

The fight was happening about twenty feet from where I was standing at ice level. I don't know if you have ever had the occasion to witness your son in a hockey fight, but it is an emotional experience like few others. Your first instinct, like that of your son, is simply survival. While this may not be the sociologically correct thing to say, survival in a hockey fight means winning, and hoping your son is on the giving end of a lot more punches than the receiving end.

The other dominant emotion for a father watching his son fight is fear, because when two kids starting wildly throwing punches there is a very real chance someone is going to get hurt, and maybe badly. Don't believe that nonsense about no one ever gets hurt in a fight. I had additional reasons to be deeply concerned (more on that later).

· Shawn's fight was no little scuffle either. It was a major-league tilt. The gloves were off. The Peterborough kid got Shawn's helmet and cage off in no time and Shawn, at first, couldn't do the same to him. They started whaling away on each other. With his height and reach advantage, the bigger kid was landing some blows—three or four shots hit Shawn—and my fear was that Shawn was going to get overpowered and beaten up very badly if he didn't get the other kid's helmet and cage off. The on-ice officials were trying to break up the first fight that was going on at the same time, so Shawn was very much on his own.

What Shawn lacked in height, he made up for in strength and toughness—watching him, you could never conceive how easygoing and mild-mannered he is off the ice. He managed to get himself in tight with the big kid, finally got the other guy's helmet and cage off, and started to deliver uppercuts that hit the target. Suddenly, the Peterborough player was on the defensive. The tide had turned greatly and Shawn was really laying into the kid. Shawn came over the top and landed a hard blow right in the middle of the other boy's face. It buckled him big time, put him right down on his knees. At that point, thankfully, the officials got in and separated them. The fight was over.

I am not one of those hockey people who trumpets fighting as some great mythical part of the game, but I've spent my whole life in and around hockey, so I get it. I understand fighting and the culture of the game as well as anyone; I know what it's like to be in a hockey fight (mostly on the receiving end); I know what it's like to see my boys in fights; I don't turn my eyes away from a fight, but I don't go to the game hoping and expecting to see one either.

Fighting in the NHL is one thing, and this is not the forum to engage in that debate, because I believe, at the NHL level, it is a very complex issue, far more involved a discussion than the most vehement pro- or anti-fighting forces would have you believe. Besides, fighting in the NHL involves men who are making their living at the game.

So if there's going to be an anti-fighting crusade, I say identify the most appropriate target. And for me, that means all levels of hockey below professional—minor (kids), Junior A, major junior, college and university—should have much tougher anti-fighting rules. That's what is going to be needed to have any chance of putting a dent in fighting's place within the culture of the game.

Shawn's league had a rule that if you fight, you are out of the game. That rule was no deterrent to anybody in Shawn's game. Mike played four years of Junior A hockey with the same (fight and you're out of the game) rule and there were still lots of fights more nights than not. Don Sanderson's tragic death in an Ontario Senior A game—he hit his bare head on the ice when he fell during a fight—was in a league that punishes fighting with automatic ejection. And yet that didn't prevent that fight either. That automatic ejection rule doesn't "ban" fighting.

The penalties for fighting need to be far stiffer if you're going to modify the behavior and mindset of young hockey players. For me, any league where there are teenagers involved and the majority will never make their living at the game should adopt much more stringent anti-fighting measures.

You see, here's what you're up against. When a fight is over, even when it's involving fourteen-year-olds, the adrenaline and testosterone coursing through the arena are off the scale. It's absolutely tribal and raw. Shawn's teammates were beating their sticks on the boards as he skated to the dressing room. So were the Peterborough players for their teammate. The parents on both teams were up and cheering.

Shawn's game was happening immediately before a Junior A game between the Wellington Dukes and Peterborough, so the Junior A players from both teams were lined up at the glass watching the fight and cheering wildly when it was happening.

When Shawn skated off the ice to his dressing room, the Wellington Duke players mobbed him, welcomed him like a conquering hero, patting him on the back, telling him he'd won the fight and lauding him for dropping the bigger player. The Peterborough player who fought Shawn received the same hero's welcome from the Peterborough Junior A players.

A lot of players, even fourteen-year-old kids, will tell you that sort of adulation, respect and attention is well worth getting kicked out of a game for now and again.

By the time I got around to the dressing room to check on Shawn, he and the other player on his team who had been kicked out for fighting were still high-fiving each other and whooping it up, the adrenaline rush was still that great. I was only there to make sure Shawn was okay, that he wasn't going to go through what his brother had just experienced.

"How's your head?" I said.

"Great, it's fine, I'm okay," he said. He had a little mark at the corner of one eye but otherwise looked as though he had emerged unscathed.

When the game was over and his team was back in the dressing room, the coaching staff presented Shawn with the game puck and he received an ovation from his teammates, who seemed a little awestruck by the NHL-style fight they had witnessed.

Shawn's last game of competitive hockey was memorable, if nothing else.

29   INTO THE ABYSS AND THE LONG, HARD ROAD BACK

IT TOOK ONLY HOURS for my worst fears to be fully realized.

As soon as Shawn and I got home from Peterborough, the McKenzie family was off to a Christmas get-together at the home of some friends. As the night wore on, I noticed Shawn was quieter than usual.

"Your head is sore, isn't it?" I asked him.

"Yeah," he said. "A little."

Great. Now that the adrenaline had run its course, I wasn't at all surprised. But I was upset. Keep in mind, Mike had just gone through two months of hell with his post-concussion issues. Now that Mike was finally symptom-free and on the verge of playing again, we thought we had put the dark days behind us.

If ever there were a player who should *not* have been fighting and tempting fate with head trauma, it was Shawn. And that's because Shawn already had a long history with knocks to the head.

When Shawn was four years old and hanging on monkey bars at a playground outside a rink where Mike was playing lacrosse in Hamilton, one of Shawn's pals grabbed his feet and pulled on them while Shawn was about four or five feet off the ground. Shawn lost his grip and fell, the back of his head hitting the ground hard. He was briefly unconscious and taken by ambulance to a local hospital, where he appeared none the worse for wear, other than the fact he had obviously just suffered concussion No. 1 of his young life.

No. 2 came a couple of years later when I was away at the Stanley Cup final. Mike was chasing Shawn around our backyard pool. Shawn tripped and banged his noggin off the concrete deck. He wasn't knocked out and appeared to be fine. He didn't even cry. (In fact, I must say I have never seen Shawn shed a single tear or cry out, ever, because of physical pain; this kid's pain threshold is legendary.) But when Shawn woke up in the middle of the night somewhat disoriented, saying his name was Brandon, Cindy and her dad took him to the hospital emergency room to be on the safe side.

No. 3, at least we awarded it No. 3 status, happened one winter when Shawn and some schoolmates were playing at recess. He ended up at the bottom of a pile of kids and someone must have pushed his head into the frozen ground. Shawn came home from school and told us about it, saying he thought he saw Dave Thomas of Wendy's Hamburgers fame sitting in a tree in the schoolyard. That was good enough for us to call it No. 3.

No. 4 was in the fall of 1999—six years after No. 1—and was spectacular in its sheer ghastliness. Shawn was Rollerblading home from school and was no doubt flying right along. He went to make the turn onto our street and clipped someone's front lawn trying to cut the corner. He apparently did a full-speed face-plant into the concrete sidewalk. One of the neighbors on the street found Shawn face down and semiconscious with his entire face scraped and badly bloodied.

No. 5 was three years after that, in the summer of 2002, when Shawn was cross-checked in the head in a lacrosse game in Peterborough.

No. 6 was on September 14, 2003, exactly two weeks to the day before Mike suffered his concussion at North York Centennial Arena. This one came in the semi-finals of the Ajax-Pickering Early Bird tournament. Shawn took an elbow to the jaw, but never lost consciousness. In fact, Cindy and I didn't even realize he had suffered an injury of any kind because he didn't tell us about it and it wasn't obvious. His head was sore after that game—he never said a word to us while we were getting lunch before the final—but he played quite poorly in the championship game. He seemed totally out of it on the ice. I was all set to give him grief for a lack of effort until he told me why he had been so out of it—his head was sore and he felt nauseous throughout. He never should have played.

The fight in Peterborough, not-so-lucky No. 7, was obviously the bad news. The good news, if there is such a thing with concussions, is that in each of the first six Shawn suffered, he never had a single symptom beyond the day on which the injury occurred. In other words, once he got rid of the initial headache or confusion or whatever he suffered that day, he woke up feeling perfectly fine the next day and reported no further problems. Also, because I was familiar with concussion protocols, we always erred on the side of extreme caution in protecting Shawn. Seven days is the recommended shutdown period—that's seven days from the first day of *no* symptoms; not seven days from when contact to the head was first made— and we often kept Shawn out of any potentially hazardous activities longer than that. The other noteworthy point is that Shawn's concussions all came on significant blows to the head. This was only good news insofar as some who suffer multiple concussions get to the point where even the slightest contact will produce a concussion and symptoms (see retired NHL player Pat LaFontaine's final concussion, which was caused by the most minor of contact). While Shawn was concussed often, he was not concussed easily and he had never experienced true post-concussion syndrome in terms of lingering effects.

So as fearful as we were because of Mike's recent experience, there was still a hopeful part of me thinking Shawn would wake up Sunday morning feeling perfectly fine. That, after all, was his history.

But that didn't happen and, to be perfectly honest, it still hasn't happened. I mean, as I write this book in 2009, coming up on six years after the fight, Shawn still has headaches.

———— ● ————

Shawn's headaches were dull and constant. They carried on right through Christmas and into the New Year. They would occasionally—probably a time or two a week—spike up into something more intense and painful. By early January, I figured it was time for Shawn, like his brother, to visit Dr. Karen Johnston in Montreal. She was still somewhat reassuring. She said the determining factor(s) in the severity of concussions in children was not necessarily how many had been suffered as it was how symptomatic they were.

The frustrating part about concussions is there's really not a lot that can be done to treat them. Doctors will tell you the basic prescription is rest. Shut it down completely. Little or no physical exertion that elevates the heart rate and blood pressure. Try to give the brain as much of a holiday from any activity as is humanly possible.

Many of these things are easier said than done, especially for a fourteen-year-old boy who felt like he was really starting to take off in minor hockey at the time he was forced to shut it down. It's fair to say Shawn woke up every day hoping it would be the day the headaches would be gone and he could get back to playing again. This was a time I maybe wished Shawn was more like he had been when he was six or seven and didn't seem to care so much about the game. But he was unquestionably smitten with it now that he had emerged as a pretty fair AAA player (he was one of his team's leading scorers at the time he was injured).

The beastly part of brain trauma is how the after-effects can pile up on you, layer on top of layer on top of layer. Think about it. Shawn had a constant headache, every minute of every day. That, and that alone, is more than enough to wear on anyone. But he also wasn't permitted to do any physical activity so he rapidly lost his fitness level. On doctor's orders, he spent an inordinate amount of time lying on the couch. He didn't have a lot to look forward to. No hockey practices or games. He couldn't even read a book or play a video game because he wasn't supposed to stimulate his brain.

The sense of loss was huge. Shawn was a kid who had played hockey in the winter and lacrosse in the summer, and being part of those teams was his social life and peer group. Really, Shawn lost his identity.

Day after day after day, and keep in mind we're talking weeks and months here, it was like we were all slipping into an abyss. We felt powerless to really do anything. It was a dark time for us. As a parent, there is no worse feeling than that. Nothing.

Now try to factor school on top of all of this. Shawn, unlike Mike, was never entirely sold on going to Trinity. He was doing it as a one-year trial and even before he suffered concussion No. 7, I wasn't convinced he was going to stay at TCS beyond Grade 9. Which was fine, we just wanted him to give it a one-year shot to see if he liked it.

What had started out with the best of intentions—giving him the best educational opportunity—was now problematic. He had to get up far earlier than he otherwise would to get to Port Hope for school in the morning. Shawn's life at TCS was, generally speaking, more challenging and difficult than it would have been if he'd stayed at school in Whitby. And while he was doing quite well with his marks at TCS before the injury, the headaches were an obvious impediment. Factor in the anxiety over whether he would play hockey again and it was indeed a dark, difficult time for all of us.

Shawn had to be medically excused from writing his Grade 9 exams because his ability to concentrate well enough to study, never mind write the exams, wasn't where it needed to be. Summer vacation came and that helped because Shawn's brain would get some downtime. But the physical limitations placed on Shawn were still an issue.

He, of course, wasn't able to play lacrosse and this was a year where he would have played on the Whitby Warriors' Midget A team, even though he was only a first-year midget. He had played extremely well on the Bantam A team the summer before—he led the team in goals, points and penalty

minutes and by a fairly significant amount in each category—
and the Midget A coach was eager to have him as one of only
three or four first-year midgets. Shawn had finally arrived on
center stage athletically and now he wasn't allowed to compete. As it turned out, that underdog Whitby midget team
won the provincial championships that summer and Shawn
would have, if he'd been able to play, finally won a championship of some kind.

Shawn would try to keep busy and engaged in whatever
social activities his friends were involved in—playing golf, for
example, used to make his headaches much worse—but it was
often something that he either couldn't do or shouldn't do.

But that didn't mean he wouldn't try sometimes. What I
gleaned from that was there were occasions when Shawn would
get his heart rate elevated and it wouldn't exacerbate his headache or any other post-concussive symptoms. He would ride
his bike with his friends and tell me he felt no different during
or after the ride than he did before. That, generally speaking,
is not consistent with post-concussion syndrome. After we
consulted with Dr. Johnston, she raised the possibility Shawn
might be suffering from a headache or migraine condition as
opposed to actual brain trauma or post-concussion syndrome.
What became readily apparent to me was that it was time to
start healing his heart and soul more than his brain.

So we did two things. One, we started to encourage him
to be much more physically active, as best he could with the
headaches. Play tennis; ride his bike; work out; just try to be
as normally active (minus contact sports) as he would have
been. We even hooked him up with a personal trainer to get
his fitness level back. Two, we decided to pursue medical treatments on the premise this was a headache/migraine problem
as opposed to a concussion.

In September of 2004—a full nine months after the fight in Peterborough—Shawn saw a headache specialist who indicated it was entirely possible that Shawn's initial brain trauma had at some point morphed into a migraine-headache condition. This was somewhat encouraging for us insofar as there were many medications and other treatments that could be used to break the cycle of constant headaches.

I have neither the time, the space nor the inclination to detail all that went on in our efforts to help Shawn, but trust me when I tell you that starting in September of 2004, Cindy and I spent the better part of the next two years dedicated to finding something or someone to give Shawn relief. He had MRIs; CT scans; blood work. He tried homeopathic treatments; acupuncture; massage therapy; active release therapy; pain management; chiropractic treatment. He had balloons blown up into his sinus cavities; he had Botox injections—sixty needles in one sitting, from his eyebrows, up his forehead, into his scalp and skull and right down to the back of his neck. He took more vitamins, supplements, remedies and prescription drugs than you could possibly imagine. He was treated by some of the best doctors in the world and foremost medical/health care authorities in their respective fields and travelled near and far to see them.

Still, the headaches remained. Over the course of our undying quest for a solution, Shawn's outlook on life—his fitness level and spirits—improved substantially and some degree of normalcy—if you can call it that with the headaches—returned.

If we were unable to find an absolute solution to what ailed Shawn, at least we found a name for it. In August of 2005, Shawn and I paid a visit to the world-famous Mayo Clinic in Rochester, Minn. It allowed a shopaholic like Shawn a chance to savor the giant Mall of the Americas in the Twin Cities and it gave me peace of mind we had tried absolutely everything humanly possible to find a remedy.

The doctors at the Mayo Clinic weren't able to provide us with anything to break Shawn's headache cycle, but they identified his condition as Chronic Daily Headache Syndrome. It wasn't altogether different from what Dr. Johnston and Sunnybrook Hospital headache specialist Dr. John Edmeads had initially hypothesized, but now it had a real name, and superficial as that may be, it made us feel a little better.

The Mayo Clinic information sheets say Chronic Daily Headache Syndrome can afflict up to four per cent of North American young women and two per cent of young men and it is migraine-related. It is often triggered by minor head trauma or an infection such as mononucleosis. In addition to the headaches, other symptoms can include dizziness, sleep disturbance, pain at other sites of the body, fatigue, difficulty in concentration, decreased mood and increased anxiety and Shawn has experienced a number of them. It can last from months to years and some teenagers simply grow out of it in time.

At least that's what we were hoping for. I suppose we still are.

30 ON THE COMEBACK TRAIL; THIS IS NO-CONTACT HOCKEY?

THERE WAS NEVER A DEFINING MOMENT in time when a doctor ever directly told Shawn he would never again play high-level competitive contact sports such as hockey or box lacrosse. It was certainly implied, though, and as long as Shawn was suffering from headaches, it was really kind of a moot point. With his concussion history, the absolute given was that he would suffer another if he continued to play contact sports. As bad as the headache condition was, we all knew it could be much worse in terms of acquiring other post-concussive symptoms that could further jeopardize his quality of life.

So for the 2004–05 season, or what would have been Shawn's minor midget "draft year," while Cindy and I were on our quest to find a remedy for what ailed our boy, Shawn was still a member of the Wildcats AAA team, in a manner of speaking. We thought it was important for him to maintain his ties to his team, and his friends. Louie Atkinson and the coaching staff/management were terrific in that regard. Shawn was treated as a full-fledged member of the team in every way.

He just couldn't play in any games or take any contact drills in practice. But he attended a lot of practices, did the skating and flow drills, took stats during the games and took part in a lot of team functions. If Shawn had something better to do, he wasn't obliged to attend anything but more often than not he did.

On one hand, it was great. Shawn desperately needed to be part of a team and stay busy and physically active. On the other hand, it was obviously difficult. Being that close to game action and not being able to play was torture for Shawn. But it was either that or totally divorce himself from the minor hockey lifestyle and neither Shawn nor I could see any huge upside to that. And I am sure Shawn was still holding out hope he might one day play again.

I would have been thrilled if Shawn had come to me and said he didn't want to do this any more in order to go in a completely different direction, say, take up skiing or whatever. But if Shawn were ever going to do a snow sport, it wouldn't be skiing; it would be snowboarding. Anyone who knows any-thing about that activity understands his chances of getting concussed would be as great on the slopes as on the ice in a hockey game.

Shawn always had recreational interests outside of hockey. He played volleyball. He liked to golf. He loved playing ten-nis. He enjoyed riding his mountain bike. He dabbled with road biking. He liked all of them and did them, from time to time, but was never as passionate about any of them as he was hockey and lacrosse, especially hockey. He just wasn't going to do those others things consistently or competitively.

I wanted to protect Shawn from anything that might worsen his condition so I was pretty vigilant in what he could or couldn't do, but I also recognized we couldn't put the poor kid in a bubble either.

So when I saw an advertising brochure for a *noncontact* three-on-three summer hockey league at Oshawa Ice Sports, I asked Shawn if he would be interested in giving it a shot. He was all for it and was able to recruit enough of his former teammates and friends to put in a team entry. He was making a comeback of sorts and I was going back behind the bench, too.

I wasn't about to ask any of Shawn's doctors if it was okay to do this because, quite honestly, I didn't want them saying he couldn't. Some might think that makes me negligent, running that type of risk. I think it's all about what I, for lack of a better term, call "acceptable/manageable risk." Sure, Shawn could lose an edge and slide into the boards or collide at high speed with another player, but he was probably as likely to bang heads with his brother when they played "hall ball" at home (it was a game they created, using the palms of their hands like hockey sticks to try to shoot a small spongy ball through their facing bedroom-door openings as they tried to make like a goalie). And getting to play this type of hockey would do wonders for his heart and soul and that was important, too.

I have never been a big believer in kids playing summer hockey. My personal philosophy is that kids, even those who are intensely passionate about the game, need a break from it. That's why we always put the skates away as soon as the hockey season ended.

But my first experience with three-on-three summer hockey made me understand how easy it would have been to be seduced by it. It was terrific. The lack of structure was refreshing. As the name implies, it's three skaters versus three skaters. The only face-off that takes place is to start the game or the period. There are no offsides. It's played wide open and when a goal is scored, the team that is scored on fishes the puck out of the net and begins attacking immediately. There's no time to even celebrate a goal or you're likely to get burned for one against. There are no penalties, only penalty shots. There are no whistles of any kind for line changes, so everything is done on the fly. No one overstays their shift because it's too damn tiring. Shawn loved it and so did I.

Incidentally, I don't understand why all minor hockey organizations in Canada don't use this as a developmental blueprint for any leagues involving kids aged five to seven. They could play it four-on-four—go with four units of four skaters per team—but the key is getting rid of all face-offs, offsides, penalties and just letting the kids air it out in a less structured environment. It would make better use of the limited ice time and the kids would have more fun, become more creative. There would still be plenty of time to teach kids eight and older how to play the five-on-five game and the rules/structure that go with it.

Of course, the noncontact part of Shawn's three-on-three experience was an issue sometimes. And that's just hockey, isn't it? You can have all the noncontact rules in the world, but if one player, and this is true of any level from little kids to old-timers, does a little something to another player, it can set off a chain reaction that goes like nuclear fission. Which is another way of saying things can get stupid in a hurry.

There was one game where I was going to be late. Mike said he would fill in as coach. I got there halfway through the game and had fully intended to just watch from the stands, let Mike coach his first full game, but it was all-out war by the time I arrived. The kids on both teams were hitting each other all over the ice. The threat of fights, and a brawl, was very real. I was absolutely mortified because of Shawn's situation.

I could see one of the reasons things were as they were—the guy coaching the other team was a capital-A A-hole, who was up on the bench, yelling and screaming and swearing at everybody, including his own players, my players and the referees.

Once I got a quick sense of it, I immediately went to the bench and took over for Mike, who was trying his best to keep a lid on things. I walked onto the bench and the other coach instantly recognized me. He stopped going nuts for a moment, put on a big smile and said, "Hey, Bob McKenzie, the Hockey Insider, awesome, nice to meet you." I thought he was going to ask me for my autograph, so you can only imagine how crushed he appeared when I said: "Shut the %$#& up, don't talk to me, don't talk to my players, quit being such an asshole."

Somehow we got through the game—I briefly considered pulling the team off the ice and forfeiting to avoid any serious injuries. If I came back from Shawn's *noncontact* hockey game and he'd been in a fight, Cindy would have been playing *full-contact* divorce with me and there would have been injuries for sure.

If only that were the end of the story.

One of the fathers from the other team had been well over-served in the arena bar during the game. As we came off the ice and were headed to our dressing room, he came down to ice level and accosted me, swearing and going on about the Hockey Insider this and the Hockey Insider that. I was trying to ignore him but Mike was getting incensed with this guy. I couldn't have that. I told Mike to go to the dressing room with the team. Then, I lit into this guy—verbally.

Understand one thing—I knew this was a fight I couldn't even start, never mind win. No matter what he said or did, I couldn't get physically involved with him in any way, as tempting as that was. Regardless of how it started or who was at fault, two things would happen and neither of them was good. One, I would end up as a front-page headline in the Toronto *Sun* (HOCKEY INSIDER IN RINK RAGE EPISODE). Two, I would likely lose my job at TSN. That, unfortunately, is what it means to be a public figure. You can't always act like other people, which maybe isn't such a bad thing because it forces you to engage in a little common sense when emotion may otherwise take over (although I must add, on at least one occasion you will soon hear about, I forgot to apply this logic).

So even when this SOB faked like he was going to punch me in the face, I didn't flinch or react, other than to explain how foolish he was acting and that if he really wanted to hit me, I would be happy to call the police, my lawyer and anyone else I could think of to help me ruin his life. I mean, I charged Phil Esposito with assault; I would not think twice about taking down this lout.

Common sense ultimately prevailed—in fact, the guy apologized to me a week later when he was sober—but it was a reminder, as if I needed it, of how hockey can really make people lose their minds. Leave it to Shawn, of course, to put a great big bow on the day on the way home.

"That," he said, laughing, "was wild."

———— ● ————

Shawn and I were encouraged by how his return to somewhat competitive (supposed noncontact) sports had gone. Other than that one game, the three-on-three hockey was outstanding. It had allowed Shawn to experience competition again and to be part of a team, playing a sport he loved. Now, Shawn and I were prepared to consider something else.

Shawn wanted to play for the Oshawa Blue Knights in the Ontario U-19 field lacrosse league. Technically, field lacrosse is a contact sport—when the ball ends up on the ground there can be some very big hits—but if a player plays the attack position, contact can be fairly limited. Was there risk involved? Absolutely. But Shawn was well aware of his unique situation and confident he could play field lacrosse and play it well without exposing himself to a great degree of risk. He was right on that count. He played in the fall of 2005 and 2006, winning his first-ever provincial championship in '06, and he also played high school field lacrosse for those years.

I was thrilled Shawn was playing (field) lacrosse again, but I was a little conflicted heading into an October weekend when Shawn and Mike both had big-time events on their respective 2006 calendars. Shawn's provincial tournament was in Hamilton on Saturday and Sunday. Mike, in his freshman season at St. Lawrence, was playing Michigan State at Munn Ice Arena on Friday night in East Lansing, Mich.

Hmmm, what's a man to do?

Easy. Everything.

Crazy Hockey Dad drove on Friday afternoon to Detroit, checked into a hotel there. Shortly after that, I drove to East Lansing for Mike's game against the Spartans, drove back to Detroit and stayed there Friday night.

Meanwhile, Cindy got Shawn to Hamilton on Saturday morning for the beginning of his tourney.

I got up very early on Saturday morning in Detroit, made the three-hour drive to Hamilton and watched two of Shawn's three games that day. As soon as the second was over, I drove back to Detroit to watch Mike's game that night against Wayne State University. Immediately after that game ended, I drove as far as Sarnia, Ont., grabbed a motel room and five or six hours of sleep. I got up early Sunday morning, drove the two plus hours to Hamilton and watched Shawn's team win two more games to capture the provincial field lacrosse championship.

In all, I think I put about 1,000 miles on my truck that weekend. But I was able to watch both my boys do something they loved.

It doesn't get any better than that (although if you want to know the truth, the time Cindy and I watched Mike play at Harvard in Boston on a Saturday night and got up at 4 a.m. to drive to Ithaca, N.Y., to watch Shawn play a full day of field lacrosse and finally make our way home to Whitby at midnight on Sunday evening, well, that was a lot more challenging).

On the driving stuff, you either get it or you don't. Some will read this and deliver the insanity verdict. Others, and I know a lot of them, would say, "Pffft, you call that driving?"

———— ● ————

Shawn could have played U-19 lacrosse in 2007, but chose not to because he was busy with his high school co-op program, interning as a sports reporter at Rogers Community Television in Oshawa before being accepted into Fanshawe College's broadcast journalism program for the fall of 2008. The way I saw it, it was nice that Shawn chose to not play lacrosse that year. He got to dictate his terms and conditions for not play-ing. I liked that he made the call, not someone else telling him he couldn't play.

Thanks to a decision by the Whitby Minor Hockey Association in the summer of 2006 to make all age levels of house-league hockey non-contact, Shawn was able to mount a winter hockey comeback of sorts for the 2006–07 season.

To be honest, Shawn's personal situation aside, I believe all house-league hockey should be non-contact. For kids who are interested in a game with truly equal ice time and no pres-sure or preoccupation with wins and losses, I'm not sure what purpose contact serves in house league. For anyone who wants the real hockey deal, there's contact in Select, A, AA and AAA. And when the WMHA went to non-contact, they saw their reg-istration numbers for Midget-Juvenile house league skyrocket. There's an obvious message there.

I was quite surprised at the caliber of play. The hockey was pretty fast and quite competitive; the referees did a good job of making sure there was no flagrant contact or nonsense. There was the odd incident here or there, but violators were suspended and, overall, it was a hugely positive experience.

Because Shawn was still an AAA-caliber player, who just couldn't take contact, he excelled in the house league. He scored lots of goals and after a rough start for his team, they started to win a lot.

Shawn's team made it all the way to the championship final, a two-game playoff series against a team with which they had quite a heated rivalry. Shawn was a bit of a marked man. He was unbelievably stoked at the challenge of trying to score and win, knowing the other team was really keying on him. It was quite intense and Shawn's competitive juices were really flowing again. For most of the first game, the other team did a nice job on Shawn. It looked like they were going to take the opener, but Shawn scored a goal with five seconds left in the game to get the tie.

That would make the second game of the series a winner-take-all contest. Even though it was Midget-Juvenile house league, there was an air of electricity at Iroquois Park Arena for the finale. It had the feel of something special. It felt so good to be driving Shawn to the rink again for a hockey game that mattered to him. And it felt even better when Shawn scored a couple of goals to help lead his team to the championship that day. After all he had been through, it warmed my heart to see him so happy and engaged again, doing what he loved to do.

There was never any doubt Shawn was coming back for his final season of the Midget-Juvenile house league in 2007–08. This time around, though, he was on the worst team in the league, which is how it goes in house league. Shawn's team won a game now and again, but most nights they lost and lost badly. Shawn handled the losing part of it fine, but I noticed a big drop-off in the overall caliber of play in the league. Shawn was an easy target on a team with a weaker supporting cast. The referees were also letting a lot more go; it was a lot chippier than it had been the season before. Shawn was getting run at, hard sometimes, and if no penalties were being called, and on many nights they weren't, he was getting angry and frustrated. He started to retaliate and it was beginning to get dangerous, for him and others. I didn't like where it was going.

There were a couple of times that season when I thought Shawn was going to quit, and I wouldn't have blamed him. But he hung in to the end, stayed clear of any nonsense and got through it. As wonderful as the first house-league season was, his second year was a huge letdown and, truthfully, it couldn't end soon enough for either of us. Which, really, was too bad.

I was working at TSN on the night of Shawn's last-ever game of minor hockey, but I still got there in time to catch the last half of it. Thankfully, it was a tame affair, the two worst teams in the league. Shawn scored a bunch of goals, his team won and he went out on a high note. He skated off Pad Two at Iroquois Park Arena and gave me a nice, big smile as he came off the ice.

After all he'd been through in the past three years, it was nice to see him skate off the ice for the final time still smiling.

He's a special kid that way.

31 MAJOR JUNIOR VERSUS COLLEGE
Making the Right Call

MUCH IS OFTEN MADE OF SIXTEEN-YEAR-OLDS having to make difficult decisions on their hockey future at such a young age. And I suppose for some players—a distinct minority, mind you—that is true.

But it wasn't for Mike. Not really.

When OHL teams were thinking about drafting Mike and asking if we were prepared to commit to major junior hockey, our answer was honest and straightforward.

It's too soon to say.

Mike wasn't nearly good enough to play in the OHL as a sixteen-year-old. And based on where he was taken in the draft (seventh round), the rules wouldn't have allowed him to play in the OHL that year anyway. So why would we feel obliged to make a commitment, especially if they're not in a position to make a full-fledged commitment back?

A seventh-round pick of the Saginaw Spirit, Mike attended their training camp in the fall of 2002 for forty-eight hours, so as to not lose college eligibility. It was just a taste test, for them and for us, and it was clear he had a long way to go if he was going to play at that level. At just barely six feet tall, and a shade over 150 pounds, he was way out of his weight class.

I am a big believer that a lot of decisions, not just in hockey but in life, tend to get made for us. Or at least if we wait until the proper time to make the decision, the choice becomes a lot more obvious than if we try to force it too soon.

There are, of course, two options for young players wanting to go to the "next level." One is the Canadian Hockey League (the CHL; it includes the Western, Ontario and Quebec leagues). The other is U.S. college hockey in the NCAA. There is this perceived battle between them for the services of the players.

In Ontario, it's not much of a fight. With the odd exception, the OHL crushes the NCAA in terms of getting the high-end talent, the players who are chosen in the first few rounds of the OHL draft.

There are a number of reasons.

The first is practical. A high-end player can graduate out of minor midget and go directly to the OHL. If that same high-end player decides he wants to play U.S. college hockey, he first has to graduate from high school, or wait another two years, or two full hockey seasons. Not many players are willing to be that patient.

The other reason the OHL crushes the NCAA in competition for elite players is that it's such a well-run league. OHL commissioner Dave Branch, a fellow Whitby resident and a longtime friend, is one of the most progressive hockey minds in the game. Some old-school hockey people bristle at Branch's safety and antiviolence initiatives, but he does what he thinks is right and parents like that.

Plus, the primary attraction of playing U.S. college hockey is getting a free education. Well, CHL teams pay all educational costs while a player is in the league and high-end OHL grads get all their postsecondary education paid for (as long as they don't sign a pro contract). If a high-end OHLer wants it, he can get a free education. It's really up to him.

The farther down the food chain you go—or the draft list, actually—the more interesting and complicated the decisions become on this whole junior versus college thing. So it was for Mike.

Mike had a good first Junior A season with the Oshawa Legionaires. He scored nineteen goals (second on the team), thirty-nine points (third) and was plus-thirteen (fourth), which was one of the better rookie seasons in the league.

Maybe it was his new contact lenses. Mike had discarded his glasses for athletic competition long ago, when he was 13, but it wasn't until he was 16 that he started wearing contacts. I'm not quite sure how he saw anything in those intervening years, but it didn't seem to hurt him.

Saginaw, which owned his OHL rights, was encouraged with Mike's first Junior A season. But Mike was also attracting some interest from U.S. colleges.

So, upon completion of that first Junior A season, it was decision time. Sort of.

The Spirit said they would sign Mike to a contract but, of course, he would have to make the team. They offered an educational package of $5,000 (Canadian) a year. That is, for every year Mike played in the OHL, he would get $5,000 towards his postsecondary education. They would, of course, cover all educational costs while he was actually playing in the league. The $5,000 per year was a far cry from the $15,000 to $25,000 it can cost (all in) for one year at a Canadian university, but it was something. And I'm sure we could have negotiated for a a little more.

But I still didn't think it was the right time to make a decision. Mike was scheduled to go into Grade 12 at TCS that fall. We agreed it was a good idea to finish what he started at TCS before potentially moving away from home to play hockey. Mike was also still working hard to put on weight and get stronger and I told him he likely still wasn't strong enough to play regularly in the OHL at that point.

Whatever level of hockey you play, the indisputable truth is that if you are not physically strong enough or fast enough to compete, the coach isn't going to put you on the ice. It's that simple. Now, if it's an elite-level prospect, the coach will sometimes force himself to live with the growing pains, knowing there is a pot of gold at the end of the rainbow. But if you're a small fish, and seventh-rounder Mike was a minnow, it can be a killer.

Plus, while Mike had played well in his first year of Junior A, it's not like he dominated. It wouldn't hurt him to spend another year with the Legionaires. A number of U.S. colleges—Bowling Green, St. Lawrence, Clarkson, Mercyhurst, Rensselaer Polytechnic Institute, Western Michigan, Michigan State and UMass Lowell—had expressed varying degrees of interest. We agreed we would let this play out for one more year.

It seemed like a plan.

But six games into Mike's second Junior A season, he suffered that nasty concussion that would keep him out of action for three months. All those schools that had shown interest quickly fell by the wayside. Who knew if they were ever coming back?

I was concerned for another reason. Wayne Marchment, who had done such an outstanding job of coaching the Legionaires, had stepped down in the off-season. A lot of the good young players who came in with Mike a year earlier had gone off to the OHL.

The Legionaires, struggling badly on the ice, were either going to miss the playoffs or be one and done in the first round. With Mike missing much of the regular season, he desperately needed a good, long playoff run to reestablish interest from the colleges. And he wasn't going to get that in Oshawa.

I was always a big believer that once a player graduates out of minor hockey, he's basically his own man. If he has issues with the coach or the team, my advice is to handle it himself, speak to the coach or the manager one on one. Parents, for the most part, should not be seen or heard beyond minor hockey.

But this development with the Legionaires caught me by surprise. I had to make a philosophical change on the fly. Mike needed to be traded out of Oshawa and I wasn't convinced a seventeen-year-old kid would be able to get that done as cleanly or efficiently as I could. I felt sick about the prospect of asking for a trade. When Mike signed there, I assumed he would play there until he went off to college or the OHL. I really liked and respected GM Peter Vipond, but Mike's concussion and the collapse of the Legionaires, and Marchment's departure, changed everything.

I very quietly made two overtures—one to St. Michael's Buzzers' GM/coach Chris DePiero and the other to Bowmanville Eagles' GM Perry Bowles—to see if they would be interested in Mike once he was healthy. Those were the two best Junior A franchises within commuting distance of our home and I figured they would both have a chance of going deep into the

playoffs. DePiero had some interest but could make no guarantees. Bowles said they would love to have Mike. Bowmanville
was a much better fit because of geography—it's on the way
home from TCS in Port Hope.

I'll never forget going into Pete Vipond's office that night
in December. I was shaking, not enjoying this at all. I laid it
out honestly to Pete, who handled it like the gentleman that
he is. The trade to Bowmanville went through.

It turned out to be a great move. Mike played with some
fantastic players in Bowmanville—James Neal of the Dallas
Stars, among others—and was reunited with his longtime
minor hockey linemate Steven Seedhouse. And the Eagles
had a long, deep run into the playoffs. They won the Eastern
Division championship, knocking off the Wellington Dukes
in the Dukedome, which is the OPJHL equivalent of beating
the Montreal Canadiens for the Stanley Cup at the Forum.
Bowmanville subsequently lost a hard-fought OPJHL semi-
final against St. Mike's, but the trade had served its purpose.
Mike had a good playoff; the U.S. colleges started showing
some interest again.

As far as the OHL was concerned, it was time to fish or
cut bait. I told Mike the final decision rested with him. He
had graduated from TCS, if he really wanted to go to Saginaw
to play two years (or three, with an overage season), that was
fine with Cindy and me. But I also gave him my considered
opinion of him as a hockey player. I told him he had a lot
of great qualities that would serve him well—hockey sense,
playmaking ability, goal-scoring ability, work ethic and competitive fire—but that his skating and physical strength were
still going to be liabilities. I told him I thought he was a classic
late bloomer; he would most likely be at his best when he was

into his twenties and more physically mature. But I also told him there was no guarantee he would even get a scholarship.

Mike decided to take a chance on the scholarship route, which I personally thought made sense for him. That, to me, is the real essence of the major junior versus college decision-making process. It's very much a personal thing, tailored to the needs and circumstances of the individual, not a blanket endorsement or widespread vilification of one system or the other.

Then, once the season was over, I had to figure out how to tell the Eagles Mike was requesting a trade to St. Mike's, the team that had just beaten them in the playoffs. That was tough, because Bowmanville was a first-rate organization. But Mike was enrolled at the University of Toronto part-time (to maintain his U.S. college eligibility). He got a part-time job working at TSN in Toronto. The geography made more sense for St. Mike's in Toronto than it did for Bowmanville, which is east of Oshawa. It didn't hurt that St. Mike's was expected to have a strong team.

So Mike became a Buzzer. I'd done all I was going to do; the rest was up to Mike.

———— ● ————

The quest to get an NCAA scholarship seems to me to be an incredibly random exercise. There's no real rhyme or reason to it, as near as I can tell. Well, I suppose there is if your kid is a blue-chip prospect. But for a kid like Mike, it was really a bizarre dance.

It's the exact opposite of the OHL draft, which is both comprehensive and finite. OHL scouts come out in droves in the minor midget season to watch all the prospects. They evaluate them and on one Saturday in May, they render judgment. The kids get drafted, or not, but everybody knows where they stand.

The trying-to-get-a-scholarship process is a lot less defined. If schools have interest, they make contact. But there are myriad rules and regulations on when they can contact, how much they can contact and even how many times they can watch a player play.

The college recruiters come and go like apparitions. Sometimes they're there; sometimes they're not. Sometimes they talk to your kid after the game; sometimes not.

By my count, there were at least half a dozen schools that I thought were seriously interested in Mike as he prepared for his third year of Junior A. We were pulling out all the stops, too. Mike went off to a two-week power-skating school in North Dakota to address the No. 1 weakness in his game. He was working out at Gary Roberts's Station 7 gym in Toronto.

There was one college in particular that had maintained fairly regular contact over the summer—letters, phone calls— with both Mike and me, leaving us with the distinct impression they were perhaps on the verge of offering Mike a scholarship.

Mike came back from the power-skating school and went immediately into training camp with St. Mike's, which was a grueling experience. The Buzzers took pride in being the best-conditioned team in the league; training camp was like boot camp. There was also an ambitious schedule of preseason games, with a string of five in seven days. Because the team had a bunch of kids away at OHL camps and their star player, Andrew Cogliano, was taking a little time off after playing for Team Canada at the U-18 tournament in the Czech Republic, Mike found himself playing in all these preseason games.

I could immediately see he was fatigued even before the preseason games. Maybe power-skating school right before training camp wasn't such a great idea. Oops. After the third game in three nights, the college recruiter who maintained contact with us all summer walked by me in the arena lobby. When I said, "Hey, how you doing?" he nodded at me and just kept on walking. Strange, I thought. Oh, well, maybe he's busy.

A few days later at another game, he was there again. It was the same deal. This guy was blowing me off! I couldn't believe it. He had done a complete one-eighty from the summer. I could only guess it was because he'd seen a very weary Mike playing those preseason games and determined he wasn't what they were looking for. Two things really ticked me off about that. One, all he had to do was tell me that to my face. Two, it's the %$#&*!% preseason. They make decisions on scholarships based on a few preseason games? You gotta be kidding me.

Mike was playing decently for the Buzzers, but not as well as he needed to. Instead of the list of prospective schools getting longer, it was getting shorter by the day. Our last two hopes were down to St. Lawrence University and Clarkson University—upstate New York rivals separated by only ten miles. Clarkson decided it wasn't sold on Mike's skating but were honest and up front about that, which I greatly appreciated.

So now it was down to only St. Lawrence. If Mike didn't get an offer from SLU, Plan B was to play the following season in Division III at Oswego University on the southeast corner of Lake Ontario, northwest of Syracuse and northeast of Rochester. St. Lawrence had been watching Mike since he was a sixteen-year-old with the Legionaires. While they seemed fairly interested over those three seasons, and maintained cordial contact, they were totally noncommittal through the entire process.

SLU associate coach Chris Wells was at back-to-back Buzzer games in late November/early December. Call it fate or whatever, but almost any time SLU was in the building, Mike scored a goal and played well. So it was on a Friday night in early December Chris Wells told Mike, and then me, they were prepared to make Mike a scholarship offer.

Hallelujah!

But standing in the lobby of St. Mike's Arena that night, Chris Wells told me that it was for two years. I quickly did the math. Two years of scholarship would mean two years of paying for school. And, at $40,000 (U.S.) per year (tuition, room and board), that was way out of my snack bracket. I told him that's a lot of money for us, at which point he indicated he wasn't talking money; he was talking about when he wanted Mike to attend the school; in two years, or the fall of 2006. He was trying to say he wanted Mike to play one more season of Junior A before going to college.

That was no problem. I actually preferred Mike go into college as a twenty-year-old freshman because his skating and strength still weren't where they needed to be.

As it turned out, the St. Lawrence scholarship offer was for three years, meaning I would have to pay for one year. The amount, $40,000 (U.S.), was not insignificant, but if you calculated the cost of Canadian university for four years, minus what Saginaw would have paid, it was pretty much a wash.

The three-year scholarship, or three-for-four as it's called, is not uncommon in the world of college hockey. It allows the schools that do it to divvy up more scholarship money among more players. Plus, if the player turns out to be a bust in the first year and quits, there's no expense to the school. A lot of scholarship players do get full rides, all four years paid for, but those kids have real competition for their services.

Beggars can't be choosers, they say, so Mike and I were thrilled to take what was offered.

Mission accomplished.

32 BADA BING, BADA BOOM
Once a Buzzer, Always a Buzzer

ONE OF CINDY'S FAVORITE QUESTIONS to me is: "Do you ever get tired of being wrong?"

No, dear, apparently not.

When we orchestrated Mike's move from Bowmanville to St. Mike's, I warned Mike about what he might be getting into. As good as we expected the Buzzers to be and for as much as they promoted players to the NCAA, I thought Mike might experience a little culture shock. The Buzzers were composed of primarily two types—Italian-Canadians and graduates of the Greater Toronto Hockey League (GTHL). Actually, it was mostly Italian-Canadian graduates of the GTHL.

I try not to fall into the stereotype trap, but our OMHA community-hockey sensibilities were that a lot of GTHL people, generally speaking, emphasized a different value system, one where self-interest was dominant. As for Italian-Canadians, well, without getting myself into any more trouble than I already am, let's just say the stereotype is they tend to be emotional and excitable (not like my Irish kin...yeah, right).

The I.Q. (Italian Quotient) on St. Mike's was extremely high. The management/coaching staff consisted of two DePieros and a Ricci. The trainers were Frescura and Coccimiglio. The opening night lineup was Tisi in net, with Lozzi and Potacco flanking Cogliano up front. On defense, it was Zamparo with Schmidt. Schmidt? Okay, so there was a token German-Canadian (just kidding, Horst). We mustn't forget Cassiani and, thanks to a few mid-season trades, Forgione, Dileo and Sgro.

I thought I had found my kindred spirit in Buzzer owner Mike (Ace) McCarron, only to discover he's as Sicilian as he is Irish. Well, there was always Father Mike (Lehman), the popular team chaplain.

Anyway, here I was telling Mike how he could be walking into this dressing room of self-centered extras from *The Sopranos* and, what was it Cindy said, do I ever get tired of being wrong?

Mike's two seasons at St. Mike's with the Buzzers were the two best years of his hockey life. Mine, too. That is saying something, because Mike led a charmed life growing up in Whitby, and playing for and with great people in Oshawa and Bowmanville, too. But there was something special about St. Mike's, especially those two Buzzer teams that won back-to-back OPJHL championships in 2005 and 2006. There is obviously a rich tradition at St. Mike's, but it was the people—the management and staff, the players, the parents, the families—who made it something special. It was as if all of us who were there at that time knew we were in the midst of something quite special, on and off the ice; just as we all still know it today. The value system with this group was extraordinary. The St. Michael's College School motto is "Teach me goodness, discipline and knowledge." GM/coach Chris DePiero created one for the Buzzers—"Commitment, belief, trust." It was all of that, and then some, fostering a special feeling that is best summed up in another slogan: "Once a Buzzer, always a Buzzer."

So, after our two years there, even I became a full-fledged, honorary *paisan*. If Bert or Carm or Sam say the word, I'm there, baby, and I'm bringing the *porchetta* and *spiducci*.

———— ● ————

Of all the dumb things I've ever done, and you know there have been several, this was easily the dumbest, and potentially most hazardous.

It was a Sunday afternoon game in Ajax, a month or two into Mike's first season with the Buzzers. The Axemen were, by far, the worst team in the league. This one was over early; the Buzzers were up by five or six after the first period. Midway through the second period, Mike beat a guy one-on-one at center ice and went in on a breakaway but failed to score. The guy who got beat raced back and drilled Mike in the head from behind and received a five-minute major and game ejection.

A minute or so into the power play, Chris DePiero put Mike back on the ice. While the play was going on, and St. Mike's was setting up in the offensive zone, whichever Ajax player was closest to Mike tried to get him to fight. They would spear him or whack him. It wasn't just one player; it was every Ajax player on the ice who came within ten feet of Mike. I'd never seen anything like it when a team is killing a penalty.

Now, I will be the first to admit there were some nights when entire teams wanted to rip Mike limb from limb. Some of those nights, I would even say he brought it on himself, for bumping a goalie or trash-talking or hacking someone. But in this game, I couldn't for the life of me see how he had done anything to provoke that level of response. I was convinced the Ajax players were acting on the direct orders of their owner/ GM/coach Larry Labelle.

Carolina Hurricane scout Tony McDonald was at the game and walked by me as the second period was winding down.

"Bob, is it always like this for your son?" he said.

"No," I replied, "not usually this bad."

"Well, it's ridiculous," he said. "It's sick, actually, sickening. I don't know how you put up with it."

I thought about what he said. He was right. This, I said to myself, is bullshit; I'm not going to put up with it.

The period ended. I made my way to the opposite end of the stands that hang over ice level. The Ajax coaches were walking towards the dressing rooms directly beneath me. As Larry Labelle walked under me, I leaned over and said: "Hey, Larry, if you want to fight McKenzie so badly, why don't you come on up here?"

"Why don't you come down here?" he replied.

I don't know what possessed me to do it—I rarely say boo when I'm in a rink watching a game—but I accepted the offer. I located the staircase to ice level and as I got halfway down, if anyone had been able to see it, the thought bubble coming out of my head would have said: "What the hell am I doing? I can't fight this guy. I will lose my job at TSN if that happens."

A reasonable man would have turned around. A smart man never would have gone down in the first place. But since I am sometimes neither, I just kept on trucking.

Larry and I had a rather spirited verbal exchange. He questioned Mike's manhood and said Mike should drop his gloves and fight. I said something to the effect none of the players on the Ajax team were worth fighting; that he and his team were an embarrassment. What turned out to be my parting shot was that Larry, of all people, should realize any coach whose own son plays on his team should know better than to send players out to fight someone; that maybe someone might decide to send someone out to do harm to his son. How would he like that?

He didn't. Larry had to be restrained by his assistant coaches. I sensed an opportunity to escape with a little honor, and my career still intact. On the way back up the stairs, Larry's wife and daughter, who ran every aspect of the game-day operation in Ajax, were coming down. They hurled a few choice obscenities at me as we passed. I returned the favor, rather emphatically, only to see that Father Mike, the Buzzers' chaplain, was right behind them.

"Sorry about that, Father," I said.

If only that was where the story ended.

At the start of the third period, someone told me they overheard Larry's wife telling people she just called the police because "Bob McKenzie from TSN assaulted my husband."

Great, sure enough, ten minutes later, two of Durham Region's finest arrived in the stands. I walked up and said hello and started laughing. One of them recognized me, but the other one wasn't as friendly.

"You think something is funny?" he said.

"Yeah, the fact you are even here," I said. "That's funny."

"You think assault is funny?" he said.

"Buddy, the only assault here is what's happening on the ice right now," I said and at that precise moment the head coaches for both teams, Larry Labelle and Chris DePiero, were being physically restrained from going after each other behind the penalty box and fighting. "You want to arrest someone, start down there."

I went outside with the officers. They asked me what happened.

Did you touch Mr. Labelle?

No.

Did you threaten him?

No.

Did he touch you?

No.

Did he threaten you?

No.

At that point, they said they were going to ask Larry Labelle the same questions. I told them the game was still going on. They said they didn't care; they would take him off the bench in the middle of the game. And they did.

Ten minutes later they were back outside and told me the matter was closed, they were convinced no assault of any kind had taken place.

Whew, baby.

On the way home, Cindy asked me if I learned anything from that day.

"I'm a badass?" I said.

She wasn't amused.

Actually, I did learn a valuable lesson that day. I hope the Labelles did, too, although I suspect their enlightenment, if it occurred, took place a little after the fact. The kicker to my story is their story.

A matter of weeks after that game, a visiting player in Ajax who had once played for Labelle took a vicious run from behind at Larry's son. Lucas Labelle was laid out and it was, by all accounts, a terribly frightening situation, where he was down on the ice for five minutes and had to be taken off the ice on a stretcher. There was speculation that the hit by this player may have been aimed as much at Larry as his son. As the player who made the illegal hit was escorted off the ice towards the dressing room, he was confronted by two women. He had coffee thrown at him and there was an attempt to hit him with the metal bar that was used to secure the door to and from the ice surface.

Larry's wife was charged with two counts of assault and assault with a weapon. His daughter was charged with assault with a weapon and uttering threats. It was a front-page story on the Toronto *Sun*. When it went to trial about a year later, Larry's wife was found guilty of one charge of assault, but she and her daughter were acquitted of all other charges. Larry's wife was sentenced to one hundred hours of community service.

I don't take pleasure from any of that, because at the core of it was what could have been a potentially catastrophic injury to a young man, and no parents—not Larry, not me, not anybody—should ever have to deal with that, especially if it's initiated because of the player's surname or who his dad happens to be. I would like to think we could all learn some valuable lessons here. Every kid on the ice is someone's son and we're all responsible for our own actions, on and off the ice.

Just remember, you never know when someone is going to call the police and you never know when someone puts in a call to the karma police either.

———— ● ————

There are times you can just sense when a hockey team is coming together and something special is brewing. So it was with the '04–05 Buzzers as they headed into the playoffs. They beat their arch rival, the (now defunct) Wexford Raiders, to win the OPJHL South Division title. St. Mike's–Wexford series were something special, hard and intense, and no love lost. Junior A hockey in Ontario just hasn't been the same since Wexford departed the scene.

Mike was finally stepping up his game in the playoffs, playing on a line with future NHLer Andrew Cogliano and six-teen-year-old Matt Halischuk, who would go on to be Team Canada's game-winning-goal hero in overtime of the 2008 World Junior Championship. Mike could play hockey a long time and not get two better line mates than he had that play-off year.

The Buzzers played the Port Hope Predators in the OPJHL semi-final and although Port Hope was much older and big-ger than St. Mike's, the Buzzers won that series in Port Hope in Game 7.

That put the Buzzers into the OPJHL championship against the favored Georgetown Raiders. Again, the Raiders were an older, more experienced team; bigger and physically stron-ger, too. It really looked like the Buzzers might be in trouble when Andrew Cogliano went down early in the series with a separated shoulder. But as so often happens, other players stepped up. Mike was one of many who elevated their play. He was finally, for the first time that season, playing for St. Mike's the way I had envisioned he would. He scored better than a goal a game in the final against Georgetown, includ-ing Game 4 where, down 2–0 in the third period, he scored a natural hat trick, including the OT winner, to give St. Mike's a 3–1 series lead. St. Mike's ended up winning the series in OT of Game 6 at St. Mike's and the Buzzers were crowned OPJHL champions. For us, it was a momentous occasion. Neither of the boys—Mike or Shawn—had ever won a legitimate playoff championship in hockey.

———— ● ————

After winning the OPJHL championship, the next level of play-offs was the Dudley-Hewitt Cup, the Central Canadian Junior A Championship, which brought together a predetermined host team (Georgetown), plus champions from the Northern Ontario Hockey League (North Bay), Superior International Hockey League (Fort William) and the OPJHL (St. Mike's). The winner of that four-team tourney would advance to the national championship RBC Cup.

Andrew Cogliano returned to the Buzzer lineup for the Dudley and even though he was playing hurt, he was dynamic. The Buzzers, though, were running out of gas and injuries were mounting. But they got themselves into the one-game, winner-take-all finale against Georgetown.

Georgetown's Alcott Arena was jammed; the atmosphere was charged. I was watching the game at ice level, right up against the glass, in the corner. There was a large group of friends and TSN colleagues with me, including (at the time) out-of-work NHL GM Brian Burke, who was spending the lockout year doing television work.

Mike's line started. Right off the opening face-off, he came in hard on the forecheck and got tangled up with a Georgetown defenseman, who put him down on the ice behind the net. The whistle had gone; the defenseman was more or less draped over Mike while he was down; they were giving each other the business. It got to the point where Mike was flat on his back and the defenseman was still standing right over him. From a totally prone position, Mike put the bottom of the blade of his stick on the defenseman's chest and was trying to push him away when the blade quickly slid up, right into the defenseman's face. It didn't do a bit of damage—no cut, no scrape, no mark, nothing—but the optics and audio weren't good. Mike's stick clipped the other player's visor and pushed the helmet up; it made quite a noise on the plastic.

The referee wasn't more than five feet away. His reaction was instantaneous. He pointed. Out of the game. A five-minute major for high-sticking.

I'm not going to say it was a bad call. That doesn't mean I'm prepared to say it was a good one either. The truth is it didn't matter. Mike had, on the very first shift, just been kicked out of the most important hockey game of his life.

I felt like I could be physically ill. I couldn't say or do anything. It was like I was paralyzed. The Raiders fans were roaring in the stands above me. Brian Burke was standing beside me. He just muttered, "Sorry, Bobby." I had so many friends and work colleagues there with me, but I couldn't even turn around to face them. I felt anger, embarrassment, humiliation and confusion. I continued to watch the game but it was really just a blur.

I allowed myself to be a totally self-absorbed ass for, say, about five or ten minutes before I realized it was time to start being a father and a husband. Cindy and Shawn were up in the stands. I knew, once the period ended, I better get up there to make sure they were okay. Georgetown fans are passionate; some were more than that. When the first period ended, I walked around the rink at ice level and by Buzzer owner Mike McCarron, who was with head coach Chris DePiero.

"I'm sorry, guys," I said to them. "I don't know what else to say."

Mike McCarron tried to make me feel better by saying it was a "horseshit call." Chris DePiero pulled me aside.

"Bob, what's done is done, but Mike has to get changed out of his equipment and the guys have to see him back out here," he said. "He's a mess and I understand that. But do me a favor, get him out here. We still have a hockey game to play. Our guys need to see him cheering us on, supporting us. It will be good for them. It will be good for him."

I went into the little room where the players hung up their street clothes and Mike was sitting there alone on a folding chair, still in full equipment, with his head buried in a towel between his knees.

It wasn't the end of the world, I suppose, but, at that moment, it sure had that feel to it. I went into the room feeling angry, bitter and disappointed that Mike would do something to get himself kicked out and hurt his team when it needed him the most. But the second I saw him sitting there, my heart ached for him. He knew what he had done was wrong. He didn't need me or anyone else to tell him. There are times when, within a family, you simply circle the wagons and offer unconditional love and support. This was one of those times.

I told Mike to stand up and gave him a great big hug. I told him his team still needed him; he had to get changed, showered and show his face; that he needed to walk out of that room with his head held high; that he should be proud of what he accomplished this season and he had nothing to be ashamed of. I told him, win or lose, to make sure he was in the handshake line on the ice when the game was over; that shit happens; it was over and done with, time to move on and that he had a chance to play many more games, something his brother Shawn couldn't say.

I left Mike, who was peeling off his equipment, to check on Cindy and Shawn in the stands. They were fine, as fine as we all could be under those circumstances. The advice I gave to Mike I took for myself as I walked through the crowd. I tried to ignore a lot of the wisecracks and smart-ass remarks, just smiled at them all. I wasn't about to give anybody the satisfaction of a reaction. It wasn't easy. There aren't many days in my life when I wish I wasn't on TV, but this was definitely one of them, when a little anonymity would have been nice.

Georgetown won the game and moved on to the RBC Cup. Mike was out there on the ice at the end, in the handshake line. That's hockey for you. There's never any place to hide. Oh, well, what is it they say, if it doesn't kill you, it makes you stronger?

I can laugh about it now.

A little.

33 PLAY EVERY GAME LIKE IT'S THE LAST; IT JUST MIGHT BE

YOU LIVE AND LEARN. If you do it properly, you become older and wiser and get some much-needed perspective on what's important, what's not and how to tell the difference.

I would say there were only two things that happened in my Hockey Dad years that had a truly profound impact on me, that really rocked me to my core.

One was obvious—Shawn's situation, with the constant headaches, having to quit playing the game competitively at age fourteen and everything that went with that. If that didn't provide perspective on what's important and what's not, nothing will.

The other came in the summer of 2006, just a few months after what I refer to as the Dudley Disaster. It was a bright, sunny August morning and Mike decided to drive to a casino in Port Perry for a poker tournament. He hadn't been gone ten minutes when our phone rang.

"Dad, I've been in an accident," he said shakily. "It's bad, really bad."

"Is anybody dead?" I asked.

"Just come now," he replied.

Cindy and I raced the few miles to the scene of the accident. There are no words to explain how you feel when you pull up to a car-crash scene involving one of your children—flashing lights from the ambulances, fire trucks and police cars. Had someone been killed? Was Mike okay?

Fortunately, the answers were no and yes, in that order.

Mike had been driving eastbound on a single-lane road behind a very slow-moving cement truck when the truck moved into a right-turn-only lane at an intersection. With the truck no longer directly in front of him, Mike began to accelerate slowly, not realizing the cement truck was effectively blocking Mike's view of a stop sign at the corner. Mike went through the intersection totally unaware he should have stopped. Mike's car was broadsided by another car, traveling northbound.

He was quite fortunate. The contact was on the passenger-side rear quarter panel. The driver of the other vehicle, an elderly gentleman, wasn't driving too fast. It could have been so much worse. Large gravel trucks traveling at sixty miles an hour routinely roar up and down that road. He easily could have been killed; he easily could have killed someone. As it was, Mike's car spun wildly out of control, sheered off a large signpost on the corner, and ended up thirty feet into a field northeast of the intersection.

Miraculously, there were no serious injuries—Mike had bruised ribs—but he was in a total state of shock when we arrived. His car was totalled.

It could have been tragic. If ever there were an incident that provided perspective on what's important, this was it.

Whatever the reason, Mike played every game that season like it was his last. He took his game to a new level. He became a dominant player in the OPJHL.

I can think of a lot of reasons it happened. In some ways, he was just picking up where he left off from his great run in the OPJHL championship final against Georgetown. But there had been a lot of talk that Mike's playoff success had more to do with his line mates, Andrew Cogliano and Matt Halischuk, than it did with him. Mike was highly motivated to prove his critics wrong.

A lot of people also said the Buzzers would never be able to repeat as champions without Cogliano and some of the other fine players who had graduated, so as a co-captain (the first time Mike wore the C since Select 7), Mike figured the whole team had a lot to prove.

Also, after St. Lawrence had committed a scholarship to him, a lot of people had said Mike wasn't worthy; that he wasn't Division One material. He heard a lot of "if it wasn't for his dad" talk, which had fired him up to play so well at the U-17 camps a few years earlier. Mike also wanted to show St. Lawrence he wasn't about to get complacent or coast now that he had a scholarship in his back pocket.

I also think Shawn's situation, his inability to play competitive hockey, had a profound influence on Mike, too. Mike took to writing Shawn's initials—S.M.—on all his sticks. Or maybe Mike just realized, between his brother's situation and his car accident, there were no guarantees in life; one should make the most of whatever opportunities one was granted.

I know that's how I felt. Whatever it was that motivated Mike, it worked.

A month into the season in a game at Oshawa against his old team, the Legionaires, Mike was credited with scoring three shorthanded goals in thirty-two seconds. That's what the game summary said, but it wasn't really accurate. St. Mike's was leading Oshawa 3–2 in the third period, but not playing very well. Mike scored a shorthanded goal to make it 4–2 at 6:18 of the third period. Nine seconds after that, he scored another shorthanded goal to make it 5–2. Four seconds after that, though, Oshawa took a minor penalty to nullify the Legionaire power play. Twenty-three seconds after he had last scored, Mike got the natural hat trick—two shorthanded goals and one four-on-four goal in thirty-two seconds.

It was still pretty remarkable, any way you look at it.

When the game was over and Mike came out to the lobby, he received hearty congratulations from all the other parents. "Great game," they told him.

He looked at me, knowing I'm a tough marker. "Great shift," I said, with a smirk and then cracked up laughing. It was true he only played one good shift that game, but what a shift it was. Even Crazy Hockey Dad had to give him a free pass.

Mike played so well that season a lot of the colleges that had shunned him in the past came back to make sure he was fully committed to St. Lawrence. Other schools that had never shown serious interest in him suddenly checked into his availability, suggesting a full four-year scholarship could be had. But St. Lawrence was the only school that believed in Mike enough to offer him a scholarship the season before. We were totally committed to SLU. I believe a person's word has to be worth something; the value on our word was more than $40,000 (U.S.), which was how much money we could have saved if we reneged on the commitment to SLU and took an offer from another school.

Mike finished the 2005–06 regular season with 39 goals, 77 points and 110 penalty minutes (PIMs) in 40 games, including 8 shorthanded goals (SHG) and 8 game-winning goals (GWG). He was named South Division MVP and was the division's leading scorer. He finished the playoffs with 13 goals, 32 points and 60 PIMs in 25 games, including 6 GWGs. He helped lead the Buzzers to their second consecutive OPJHL championship; beating the Markham Waxers for the South Division title; the Bowmanville Eagles for the South-East Conference title; and the Stouffville Spirit for the OPJHL championship. The Buzzers came up short, once again, at the Dudley-Hewitt Cup in Thunder Bay, but at least Mike finished his last Junior A game on the ice.

Mike would have certainly set a Buzzer franchise record for goals that season—he came up one short—if he hadn't been injured in early December and missed nine games. One of his own players hit him in the ankle with a power play dump-in. X-rays were initially negative. He played five games badly hobbled and it was obvious he wasn't right, but he had been named to play in the Canadian Junior A Hockey League Top Prospects' game in Yorkton, Sask. Nothing was going to stop him from getting to that game in front of the NHL scouts.

But the day before he was scheduled to fly to Yorkton, in a Sunday afternoon game at North York Centennial Arena (yes, that same cursed arena), Mike separated his shoulder on a hit when he couldn't properly brace himself because of the weakness in his ankle.

So there he was, sitting in the hospital with his arm in a sling, getting confirmation his ankle was indeed broken, looking about as glum as glum can be. There would be no trip to Yorkton the next morning, no game to impress the NHL scouts. He was crushed.

If ever there were a time when perspective was required, this was it. In the grand scheme of things, weighed against what Shawn had been through and Mike's car wreck a few months earlier, this little setback wasn't such a big deal. But that doesn't mean it wasn't still a bitter disappointment. For Mike and his Crazy Hockey Dad.

———— ● ————

It's not like Mike or I were ever focused in on the NHL draft as some sort of goal for him. That's simply not how we operate. Remember, you don't play hockey for the scouts. That said, based on how well Mike had played that season, it wouldn't have been outrageous for him to be considered a late-round candidate, a project of sorts. Other college-bound players from the OPJHL were taken in the later rounds of the draft that year, and Mike was in the same universe as them. And yet I, better than anyone, knew his ugly-duckling skating style would be a huge impediment. As a hockey player, my kid is definitely an acquired taste. Scouts will quickly determine what a player can't do, but sometimes have difficulty seeing the possibilities for a player like Mike. And that's fine, whatever Mike gets from hockey, he will have earned every bit of it.

The week before the NHL entry draft, my player-agent friend Rick Curran told me an NHL team was thinking of drafting Mike in one of the late rounds. I assumed, correctly, it was the Carolina Hurricanes because I know GM Jim Rutherford pretty well. I talked to Jim a few days before the draft and told him if he was thinking of drafting Mike to please *not* do it. I told him people would say Mike only got drafted because Jim and I were friends; that he wouldn't be doing Mike or me any favors; that Mike was far better off going into his first year of college under the radar. Jim confirmed his scouts were thinking of drafting Mike; said that Mike deserved to be a consideration based on how well he played at St. Mike's and knowing he would have another four years of development time at college. Jim said he would think about my request to not take Mike, but he challenged me to name a prospect who I thought would be a better pick than Mike in the sixth or seventh round.

I told him Nick Dodge, an '86 from Oakville, Ont., who had just completed his sophomore year at Clarkson, was a better player and prospect at that point than Mike. Dodge was always one of the better '86s in Ontario and went to college as an eighteen-year-old freshman. He was, as far as I was concerned, more deserving to be drafted at that point than Mike. And that, as it turned out, is what the Hurricanes did, taking him 183rd overall in the 2006 draft. When Dodge graduated from Clarkson in 2008, Carolina signed him to a contract and he played the 2008–09 season with Albany of the American Hockey League.

After the draft, I told Mike about the Carolina possibility and how I had lobbied against it. He said he was happy with it, that he was looking forward to making his own way at college without any expectations beyond his own. He was just happy to still be on The Ladder—moving up, too—and if his own experiences had taught him, or me, anything, it was that he moves a lot faster when he's hungry and trying to prove people wrong.

34 CRAZY HOCKEY DAD'S MAGICAL MYSTERY TOUR

AS WELL AS MIKE played at various times in his life, whether he was seven or nineteen, I was never one of those Hockey Dads who took anything for granted. I always wondered, and worried a little, how he would fare at the "next level."

He and I developed a little routine. When he was fifteen, and a year away from perhaps playing junior, I took him to a Junior A playoff game between Wexford and Pickering to get a sense of what it was like.

"Think you can play this next year?" I asked him.

"I don't know," Mike said. "I think so. I'm not sure."

Neither was I, to be honest.

When Mike was seventeen, and desperately seeking a scholarship, we used the downtime during the dark days of his concussion to visit Clarkson and St. Lawrence. It was probably as much to keep up Mike's spirits because he wasn't sure when he would play hockey again, but it also gave us both a chance to see our first ever U.S. college hockey game. Mike saw Cornell play at Clarkson on Friday night (I was working).

I joined him to see Cornell play SLU on Saturday night. Cornell, as is Big Red tradition, was huge. The hockey was fast, unbelievably so. Many of the players were as old as twenty-four and twenty-five. I was totally blown away by the whole experience.

So there I was looking at Mike—seventeen years old; a little pencil neck, all of 160-odd pounds; not quite sure when he would play again because of the concussion; a bit of a tough skater to begin with—sitting there, him looking at me through his glasses. (That, by the way, was the only time I've ever seen Mike angry with Cindy—she accidentally threw out his last set of contact lenses, forcing him to wear his glasses for his one and only U.S. college "official visit.")

Then I was looking out onto the ice at SLU and the behemoths from Cornell and then back again at Mike. I am not going to lie; he was looking very much like a boy in the presence of men.

"Think you can play this in a couple of years?" I said.

"I don't know," he said. "I think so. I'm not sure."

Neither was I.

But a little less than three years later, a twenty-year-old freshman, wearing No. 27 in the scarlet and brown of St. Lawrence University, stepped onto the ice at Appleton Arena against the Rochester Institute of Technology for his first-ever NCAA Division One college hockey game. I didn't shed a tear at that moment but it wouldn't have been difficult to work one up. After all Mike had been through in his hockey-playing days—the ups, the downs, all that time and effort—to say nothing of the trials and tribulations of his brother—I truly thought it was all quite remarkable Mike had made it to the "next level."

That night kicked off Crazy Hockey Dad's version of a four-year Magical Mystery Tour.

Thanks to some very understanding folks at TSN—a big shout out to my very good friends and colleagues Steve Dryden and Darren Dreger, among many others—to say nothing of some really inspired juggling on my part, as well as ridiculous amounts of driving, expense and Aeroplan reward miles, not to mention an all-world wife and son, I haven't missed much.

If Joe Marsh's St. Lawrence University Skating Saints were playing a game between the fall of 2006 to the spring of 2010—pretty much anywhere, anytime—chances are I was there. So, on many occasions, were Cindy and Shawn, because hockey has always been nothing if not a family affair for the McKenzies. Shawn, for all he has been through, has never begrudged his brother's success and has supported him every step of the way. For all the sacrifices everyone in our family had to make because of the demands of my career, sneaking away on so many weekends with Cindy and/or Shawn to watch Mike play was a terrific payback for the many times and opportunities missed in the past.

Personally, I love college hockey. It's fast and entertaining, played at an incredibly high level most nights. The games are usually finished in a shade over two hours. There's little or no nonsense or goofiness, virtually no fighting but lots of contact. I had been warned the college game was chippy and dirty with rampant stickwork and hits from behind because the players wear full cages and can't self-police the game due to the anti-fighting measures (fight and you're out of that game, plus two more). But I saw little or none of that most nights. All levels of hockey, college included, have incidents or problems at times, but I would submit college hockey has fewer than most. The vast majority of nights I walked out of Mike's games thinking what a terrific athletic spectacle I had just witnessed.

For a Crazy Hockey Dad living in southern Ontario, there's no better place to have a son playing than at St. Lawrence, because it's so easy to get to. It is thirty minutes off Highway 401 and the Prescott-Ogdensburg international bridge crossing. SLU is a small but quite lovely liberal arts college that reminded Mike very much of Trinity College School. When he was seventeen and we drove onto St. Lawrence campus for the first time, and visited Appleton Arena, with its traditional wooden church-style pew seating, Mike said: "This is where I want to play; this is where I want to go to school."

It would be a toss-up to say who enjoyed it more—me or Mike.

To visit campuses like Cornell and Colgate, Yale and Brown, Dartmouth and Harvard and Princeton—well, that was the only way I was ever going to get to any of those Ivy League schools. I don't know that there's a better college hockey experience anywhere than watching the Cornell Big Red at the Lynah Skating Rink. To get to places like Boston University, Yost Arena at the University of Michigan (and slip in a visit, tailgating and all, to the Big House to watch the University of Toledo upset the Wolverines in football), Munn Ice Arena at Michigan State, the Whittemore Center at the University of New Hampshire or The Gut at the University of Vermont...I tried hard not to take a single minute of it for granted.

I marveled every time I went into Princeton's Hobey Baker Arena, a hockey rink that used to be a church; I was always awed by the unique design of the Whale at Yale, from the same architect who gave us the famous St. Louis Arch and managed to incorporate an element of that into a hockey arena. There was always something a little special about walking by an empty and frigid Harvard Stadium en route to Bright Arena;

getting to know the lovely little town of Hanover, N.H., home of Dartmouth College; or feeling the air of hostility on any visit to Cheel Arena and that "other" school just down Route 11 from SLU and Canton, N.Y.

Mostly, though, I will never forget the special feeling of walking into Appleton Arena, my hockey home away from home for four years, so bright and inviting and traditional with its small-town, North Country charm and sensibilities.

It certainly didn't hurt that Mike demonstrated, in spite of my fears, he could actually play the game at this level, and play it quite well. He scored the game-winning goal in his very first college game against Rochester Institute of Technology though he would be the first to tell you he didn't even realize he had tipped the puck in and played like he was in a fog most of that night. He finished his freshman season with very good numbers—twelve goals, including seven game-winners (tied for second in the country), and twenty-five points in thirty-one games.

The only two freshmen games he played that I missed—damn the World Junior Championships—were in the Dartmouth tournament at Christmas, when he scored on a penalty shot in overtime to beat Boston University. I was back at TSN working, watching the SLU-BU game on TV. Mike was interviewed after scoring the winning goal and was asked why he chose to attend St. Lawrence. I could see him pause and think about how he was going to answer and I mouthed it just as he said it.

"Well, actually, it was the only school that offered me a scholarship," he said.

That's my boy.

But as idyllic as a lot of it was, it's still hockey; you're still subjected to the volatile ups and downs of the game.

Mike missed the final eight games of the regular season his freshman year with a sports hernia, but when the doctors told him he was going to need off-season surgery whether he continued to play or not, he took a cortisone shot, got taped up and gutted out the playoffs with his groin all torn up.

The Saints were predicted to be a middle-of-the-pack team in the regular season, but finished in first place in Mike's freshman season. Though they lost in the ECAC tournament semi-finals against Quinnipiac, Mike scored two goals, including the game winner, in a come-from-behind win over Dartmouth in the ECAC consolation final. That win propelled SLU into the NCAA tournament (final sixteen teams in the country) only to lose to Frozen Four finalist Boston College in the first round. That first year was fantastic.

Mike's sophomore season was as difficult as his freshman year was wonderful. Coming off his sports hernia surgery, Mike went fourteen games to start the season without a goal, managed only seven goals and twenty points in thirty games. He lost his confidence; he lost his focus; he didn't get as much ice time and there were occasions when he was just plain miserable. Ditto for me. And the Saints finished a disappointing ninth before meekly bowing out in the first round of the playoffs.

Mike did, however, bounce back to have a terrific junior season. The Saints played well and finished in fourth place, earning a first-round playoff bye. For the second time in three years, SLU made it to Albany, home of the ECAC tournament, but lost a heartbreaker in the semi-final to Yale. The Saints just missed qualifying for the 16-team NCAA tournament, but all in all it was a good year of hockey for the team and Mike, who scored a team-leading 16 goals and 34 points in 38 games.

I wrote this book before Mike's senior year. So who knows what's in store for Mike and his team, but I feel safe in saying Mike's four years at St. Lawrence will be something that stays with both of us for the rest of our lives. I have no doubt he'll come out of it a better player and a better man, with a degree to boot, and it's hard to beat that.

I am well aware not every parent of a college hockey player feels as positive about the experience as me. It's not some sort of Utopian paradise. It's the next level, after all. There's not enough games for my sensibilities (if you play forty, that's a big year), but that, I suppose, is why they call them student-athletes.

I am not here to tell anyone how much better the college hockey experience is than major junior. There are OHL organizations to which I would never entrust the care of my son, but there are some college coaches or programs I would put in the same category.

Not every freshman has the kind of year Mike had at SLU. Too many of them don't see enough action for no reason other than they're freshmen. I have friends whose kids' college hockey experiences have been a complete and utter nightmare; players who went to a school only to get there and be told their scholarship would be honored but they wouldn't be part of the team. I have friends whose kids' experiences in major junior have been nothing but a bitter disappointment and rejection.

But that, I'm afraid, is what hockey is all about at the next level.

No system has the market cornered on anything, good or bad. At the end of the day, when your kid arrives at the next level, anything and everything could happen. It may not always seem fair, but then, as I loved to tell my boys, life isn't always fair. In fact, I've always maintained every league above minor hockey—Junior A, B, C; major junior; college; and ultimately the pros—should have only one slogan because this is the absolute truth once you get out of minor hockey: "We will love your kid so long as he's playing well; we'll treat him like gold...unless someone better comes along."

I hope that doesn't come across as too cynical or crass, because it's not meant to be. In fact, that reality check should reinforce to everyone to try to enjoy the journey, not get too hung up on the destination. There are just so many ups and downs for the vast majority of kids who play hockey at any level above minor hockey. If you permit yourself, you can get eaten alive by them.

For Cindy and me, the hockey has always been the bedrock on which we try to build relationships and friendships. For as much as we have loved watching Mike play college hockey, the enduring payoff for our time in Canton, N.Y., has been becoming such good friends with Tim and Teri Phalon, having their family open their home to our family; getting to know the Cunninghams and the Flanagans; sharing time and stories with the other Crazy Hockey Parents/road warriors like the Bogosians or Fensels, the Generouses, amongst many others; getting to the Hoot Owl—"Scary, isn't it?"—for a night of One Mo's. (It's a long story.) Or trading text messages with my Colgate friend Don McIntyre or my Cornell pal Dan Whitney or my cattle-ranching SLU alum Tom Giffin.

Oh, the hockey is important—I would never suggest otherwise and anyone who knows me would call B.S. if I did. But if as a parent that's all you're taking from it, I have to tell you something—you're missing the boat.

Nevertheless, maybe at some point before Mike graduates, we'll go on a little father-son excursion, maybe see an East Coast Hockey League or American Hockey League game.

Maybe I'll ask him: "Do you think you can play this?"

And he'll say: "I don't know. I think so, I'm not sure."

And I'll say: "Neither am I."

And then, all things being equal, we'll find out.

Mind you, one day—who knows when?—there'll be no more next level, it will all be over.

And you know what? That's just fine, too, because it's been quite a ride, a lot longer and more thrilling than either of us ever could have imagined.

And hey, it's not over just yet.

BLOWING THE WHISTLE AND DOCTOR, DOCTOR

I COULDN'T LET AN ENTIRE BOOK GO by without some mention of my "friends" who wear the striped shirt.

There is, of course, no more thankless job in minor hockey than that of the on-ice official. They take far too much abuse—sadly, some of it is physical—and I have been guilty, on occasion, of dispensing some of the verbal variety. I can admit that. But I'm also not shy about suggesting Mike, Shawn and I, between the three of us, have been on the receiving end of some mistreatment, too.

There was the ref in Barrie who started a tournament game by saying to me: "I hope you're a better coach than you are a broadcaster." I started laughing, thinking it was a pretty funny line, until I realized he wasn't kidding. This particular referee, who I had never met before, could not have been more blatant in his disdain for me and clearly took it out on the kids I coached. Which is kind of pathetic.

Most of the zebras are good guys trying to do a good job. But it was quite obvious when we would get one who would take great delight in making my life difficult. This was much more likely to happen at home in Whitby than on the road. What is it they say, familiarity breeds contempt?

I know this to be true because a guy I know started working as an OMHA linesman. He told me after the fact that there were a couple of local Whitby refs who, prior to a game, would sit in the referees' room and brag to their colleagues about how they were planning to get a reaction from me or the other local Whitby coaches who had some profile. "Watch me get [fill in the blank] going crazy," one of these refs would say *before* the game. My buddy couldn't help himself one time. "Aren't we just supposed to call the game?" he said. "I didn't realize our job is to plan on getting the coaches upset."

There may be some who would suggest I actually got favorable treatment from some refs because they were intimidated by my TV persona. I never saw it that way, but that's just me.

In all the years I coached minor hockey or lacrosse, I only ever got one bench minor penalty for verbally abusing an official.

Honestly, though, I could handle the back and forth between me and the refs; it's all part of the game. It was when I thought they were targeting my sons for extra attention that it really upset me. It still does.

I can't count how many times over the years a referee would make a much more flamboyant penalty call—the demonstrative/theatrical pointing of the finger towards the penalty box is a dead giveaway—or loudly use my kids' surname for dramatic effect when he banished one of them to the box: "Let's go, McKenzie, two for roughing, McKenzie." I'm not arguing my kids didn't deserve penalties—far from it—but I am saying there were refs who visibly enjoyed assessing those penalties a lot more than they should have.

But there is one Hall of Shame officiating story I will leave you with because it so far crossed the line that I still can't quite believe it happened.

It was the sixth and deciding game of the first round of the playoffs in Mike's major bantam AAA season. The winner of the game between Oshawa and Whitby would move on. I was away at the Salt Lake City Winter Olympics. I was on pins and needles awaiting the result.

Oshawa beat Whitby that night; Mike's season was over and that was Mike's last game of minor hockey. When I came home from Salt Lake City a couple of days later, I was told by Mike's coaches, including my brother-in-law John, that the referee had more or less verbally abused Mike from the beginning of the game to the very end.

I asked Mike about it. He confessed that in all the years he'd played hockey or lacrosse, he had never experienced anything quite like this. He said if he missed a shot on goal, the referee would skate by and say, "Ah, did you miss the net? Do you miss your daddy at the Olympics, too, poor baby?" This torrent of abusive dialogue was, I was told, pretty much constant. By the time the game was over, Mike was overwrought.

I was going to let it slide. I mean, it was over and done with, what could I do now? The more I thought about it, though, the angrier I got. So, just for the hell of it, I called the OMHA and talked to the referee-in-chief. I told him the story. He said he would get back to me, but I wasn't holding my breath. A week or two later, though, he called. He said he had concluded an investigation—I was waiting for the "lack of evidence" line—and after conferring with the linesmen who worked the game with that referee, he determined the ref had indeed acted inappropriately. This referee's behavior was so reprehensible that his own linesmen in that game ratted him out. That tells you how bad it was right there. The referee-in-chief said the ref would be disciplined—he was scheduled to work the all-Ontario midget championships in Peterborough and was subsequently taken off that assignment.

The kicker to the story is that the next season in a Junior A game in Oshawa, Mike was in an altercation and down on the ice. A linesman jumped on top of him to restrain him and rather zealously, I thought, put what amounted to a choke hold around Mike's neck. The altercation was over as far as I could see, but the linesman still was on top of Mike and had his arm locked around Mike's neck. Mike was kicking his feet because he was getting choked. I started to yell from the stands, it was that obvious to me. Finally, the linesman let up. It was a day or two after the fact, when I happened to look at the game summary, I realized the overly aggressive linesman and the ref who had verbally abused Mike were one and the same.

At the end of the day, officiating hockey is not an easy job. I get that. I also know the vast majority of guys who do it are doing it for all the right reasons—because they like hockey; they want to stay involved; get a little exercise; they want to contribute something to the community; and maybe make a buck or two. To all those guys, if I ever offended you, I am sorry. But there are also a few bad apples who are raging egomaniacs and power-hungry control freaks with an ax to grind.

Hey, maybe I should apply.

Actually, I've occasionally thought I might like to get my referee's card one day, although I acknowledge it's probably just a flight of fancy. (Mike and Shawn both officiated minor lacrosse briefly, but didn't like the responsibility and abuse that went with it.) But I think it would be a fascinating experience and a tremendous challenge. I would love to see if I have any feel for the game in that capacity. Now, wouldn't that be fun for the coaches, players and parents to see me skate out in the stripes with a whistle in my hand?

The final word on officiating, though, goes to my buddy Kevin O'Brien, who came up with the best "chirp" of an official I've ever seen or heard. This one was so good that even the ref who was being chirped burst out laughing. Just one warning, though, your timing has to be impeccable.

"Everyone here who thinks the ref is doing a lousy job," Kevin would yell from the stands, "put up your hand."

If the line is delivered in a dead-quiet rink just as the ref makes the signal to say the visiting team can't make a line change, tell me you can't see the sheepish smile on the ref's face as he slowly lifts his arm above his head.

Priceless. Just priceless.

———— ● ————

As difficult as it is to deal with some referees, the hardest part of having kids playing minor hockey is the whole injury experience.

Injuries are, unfortunately, unavoidable. If your child plays sports, he or she will get hurt at some point. What you come to realize very quickly—or at least you should—is that a bad game or a game where Junior misses a shift or gets into the coach's doghouse pales in comparison to the child getting hurt and not being able to play at all, whether it's for a game, a week, a month, a year or forever.

Shawn had the obvious problem with multiple concussions/headaches, though most of them weren't experienced in organized sports. But Shawn also had a whack of other injuries from hockey and lacrosse. We have a collection of crutches and splints and braces around our house. Most of them were for Shawn, who banged up his knee almost as often as he did his head. He has had tears of the anterior cruciate ligament (ACL) and medial cruciate ligament (MCL) and even the lesser-known lateral cruciate ligament (LCL)—no knee surgery was ever required—and when he skates now, he wears a brace for support.

Even in a noncontact sport like volleyball, Shawn managed to get injured. When he was in Grade 7, he jumped up to spike a ball at the same time as his teammate. The teammate's karate chop spike got more of Shawn's baby finger than the ball. The result was a broken finger, with the portion above the knuckle jutting out at an almost ninety-degree angle from the base. It was really quite horrendous. He nearly passed out from the pain but never cried, not even when at the hospital they repeatedly gave him needles to freeze it before setting it. Finally, Shawn got fed up with the needles—the freezing wasn't taking—and he stoically told them to "just set it."

Mike battled his way through a lot of injuries, too, but let's just say he was a tad more verbal than Shawn in expressing pain and suffering. Mike was much more likely to cry or scream or yell or curse, but like his brother, he would never want to let an injury keep him down.

In addition to his broken arm in lacrosse and his one notable concussion, Mike has had separated shoulders (one in lacrosse; one in hockey), a fractured ankle, a sports hernia that required surgery—not to mention a painful cortisone shot with a really big needle that was inserted near the pubic bone (I break out in a sweat just thinking about it)—and too many soft-tissue injuries to count.

Like many who are so deeply embedded in the minor hockey culture, the McKenzies subscribe to the age-old, macho philosophy that you don't lie on the ice when you're hurt; you do everything possible to get to the bench on your own. Within reason, you play hurt and battle through injuries, but that does not, of course, include trying to play through a concussion, which is simply not possible.

But of all the things that qualify me as a Crazy Hockey Dad, my obsession with and fanaticism about getting my kids the best possible medical/injury treatment is probably right up there at the top of the list.

If your child is injured playing sports and all you do is visit the local hospital emergency room or your GP or family doctor—all due respect to all of them—there is a pretty good chance your child may be on the sidelines longer than they might otherwise be.

I believe it is paramount to seek out specialized medical treatment from those who live and work within the sports medicine community. It's just a matter of finding these people. Once you do, you are on your way because they generally operate within a network of other health-care experts (medical specialists, chiropractors/active release therapists, physiotherapists, massage therapists, nutritionists, strength and conditioning trainers, homeopaths) who can also be a huge help in healing and getting the injured athlete back playing.

A good sports chiropractor/active release/soft tissue therapist, for example, is worth his or her weight in gold to treat or even help prevent injuries.

I obviously have an advantage over most Hockey Dads, but I like to think that even if I weren't the Hockey Insider I could still track down good people to treat my kids. My boys like to give me a hard time about my medical "hookups" because I have this team of experts, depending upon what is required.

I am sure these "experts" all go running for the hills when they see my name and number pop up on their call display, but I don't know where I would be without this network of health-care professionals. They all know who they are—K.J.; Dr. Tim; Mark the chiro/ART/soft tissue wizard and Duane, too; Dr. M for imaging; Jeremy the massage therapist; Matt for strength and conditioning; and so many others too numerous to mention.

In another lifetime—the one where I'm born with a brain—I would love to do what they do. They all take such great pride in helping and healing and going out of their way; it really is quite extraordinary what they offer and accomplish. I am often awestruck, to tell you the truth, not just at their expertise, but their willingness to share it and go to such great lengths to help and heal as best they can. So while I can't do what they do, I try to make an effort as much as possible to help other Hockey Dads, and Moms, navigate their way through the difficult world of injuries and the like.

So many wonderful people have been so giving of their time, expertise and experience to me and my boys, I feel like I should do the same whenever and wherever possible. I can't count how many people I've referred to doctors or therapists; I only want to do whatever I can to help others.

Because if I've learned one thing as a Crazy Hockey Dad, it is this: It's no fun when your kids are hurting and not playing.

36 YOU TRY CUTTING THE GRASS OF A QUALITY CONTROL INSPECTOR

I WILL LEAVE it to far greater minds than mine—do you think Sigmund Freud is available?—to make sense of who I am and how I've behaved, or misbehaved, over the years. But if there's one thing I know, it's this: I am what I am largely because of my parents. And for that, I'm actually eternally grateful and proud, even though they're no longer around to see how their life's work has turned out. I would hope they're not disappointed. I am certainly not blaming them for any of my shortcomings.

It's just that everything in my life, including my wacky obsession with hockey, is pretty much viewed through the prism of how I was raised by Bob and Maureen McKenzie in Scarborough, Ont.

I was an only child, which some might say explains a lot, but that was only because my mom was afflicted with severe rheumatoid arthritis when I was one year old. Having any more children for her was out of the question. I don't know how much you know about rheumatoid arthritis, but it's a vicious, debilitating, crippling, incredibly painful disease that attacks the joints and causes swelling, intense pain and often disfigurement. I would estimate my mom had surgery on at least fifteen to twenty occasions and pretty much every joint in her body was red, swollen and/or severely disfigured. She was, every minute of every day I knew her, racked with pain. Yet for a good many years she still managed to drive herself to a full-time job. She eventually ended up in a wheelchair for the last fourteen years of her life and, quite suddenly really, died of complications from this dreaded disease at the age of fifty-nine in 1992.

My mom loved hockey, too. Her brother, George Rowan, was a decent player back in the day. She used to watch it as a young girl and I was home with my mom watching it when Paul Henderson scored The Goal on Sept. 28, 1972.

My mom was sharp, smart and well-organized. She did not suffer fools and was never afraid to speak her mind. She had enough experience with doctors to know there are good ones and there are bad ones and you better figure out which one is treating you; that you don't automatically accept what they say without at least questioning or challenging them. As tough as she was on so many levels, she was an incredibly loving mother who always put her only son first. She never complained about her lot in life; never had any pity parties, and if anyone ever had a right or reason to feel like they got a raw deal, it was her. What I learned from her, aside from everything, was this: You don't waste time feeling sorry for yourself because everyone has a sad story.

My dad was born in Windsor, Ont., but only months after that moved to Northern Ireland and was raised in the east end of Belfast. He had the Irish accent to prove it, too, although he was always quick, and extremely proud, to point out he was

a Canadian. As a kid who grew up not too far from the ship-
yards of Belfast, he survived the German blitz of World War
Two, though he once returned from the bomb shelters to find
not only his family home was gone, but so, too, was his entire
block. He was a rarity, I'm sure, in that he actually played ice
hockey in Belfast as a young man, as well as soccer, and he
would show you his vintage Kangaroo leather Tacks and tell
you he wasn't too shabby at either.

He came to Canada in the 1950s and proudly worked forty-
three years at DeHavilland Aircraft in Downsview, Ont., first
as a production worker on the assembly line, then as a quality
control inspector and finally as a production supervisor. You
would have thought he was personally responsible for every
Beaver, Otter, Buffalo, Dash 7 and Dash 8 that came off the
line there, that's how proud he was of his work. He wore a
tie to work every day of his life, even when he worked on the
line, and as a quality control inspector drove everyone there
crazy with his ridiculously high standards and expectations of
perfection. He had a voracious work ethic—when the roads
to DeHavilland were impassable because of a snowstorm, he
once got out of his stuck car and walked the rest of the many
miles through the snow to get there—and he always had two
jobs to help make ends meet. Between his job(s) and countless hours as a caregiver to my mom, I'm not sure how he
had any time for anything else. But he still loved to wash and
wax his cars—the 1963 Impala Super Sport; a 1966 Impala SS;
his big boat, the white 1968 Buick Wildcat convertible with
the black roof and the 430 four-barrel; the 1971 Monte Carlo;
and the 1973 Grand Prix—and he would take care of his front
lawn like it was a fairway at Augusta. Like a lot of Irishmen—I
mean, Canadians—my dad was a little quirky. He used to say

"Whether you're rich or poor, it's nice to have a buck," and he was a terrific singer, an Irish tenor who could bring down the house and a tear to anyone's eye with "Danny Boy." There's a New York City hotel where they still talk about the crazy Irishman who sang it so well in the packed lobby just before Ireland played Italy in the 1994 World Cup soccer game at the Meadowlands. That was my dad, the exasperated Toronto Maple Leaf fan who never hesitated to call them "a bunch of bums," the same guy who had a fine wardrobe (including the always stylish fedora, suit and tie) and a sparkling gold jewelry collection that would have been the envy of Don Cherry. He loved golf and holding court over a pint in the pub, right up to when brain cancer claimed him in the summer of 2003.

Like my mom, my dad didn't believe in complaining or feeling sorry for himself. He got up in the morning, did what had to be done and then did it all over again the next day.

Through all of that, though, my parents always made sure I didn't lack for anything, especially when it came to hockey. In spite of the fact we were a decidedly middle-class, blue-collar family, I always had the best of everything—the best skates, the best equipment; my dad believed you buy quality. And they always managed to get me to my practices and games. It would be fair to say I was the apple of their eye, but for anyone who might think that or being an only child equates to a life of privilege, think again. It wasn't always easy living in the home of two perfectionists, each of whom was either blessed or cursed with an extreme case of the old Protestant work ethic. You try cutting the grass of a quality control inspector.

Growing up, I was absolutely crazy about hockey, not that my passion for the game ever amounted to excellence playing it. My first year of organized hockey was when I was eight years old in the Dorset Park house league, although I recall playing it long before that for hours at a time on the outdoor rink at Bendale Public School. Of course, my friends and I played road hockey every free minute of every day. I played two years of Dorset Park house league on the outdoor pads at McGregor Park Arena. Then I moved up to play two years with the Agincourt Lions rep team in the old Scarborough Hockey Association. I played my peewee season with the Scarborough Lions of the old Metro Toronto Hockey League (Scarborough, Leaside, Ted Reeve, East York and Wexford) and Frank Mahovlich's dad used to sharpen my skates at Leaside Arena.

I tried to play at the highest level possible in minor bantam but was cut from the Agincourt Canadians partway through the season. I licked my wounds and went back to house league for two seasons before giving the lower levels of MTHL rep hockey another try, playing with a bunch of my buddies for independent minor midget and midget teams. I fancied myself a bit of a late bloomer. I played two years of juvenile hockey for the West Toronto Hawks and they were the two best seasons of my hockey-playing life. I tried out for Wilfrid Laurier University's varsity team but I lasted a lot longer at the school as a student (six weeks) than I did in the tryouts (about sixty minutes).

It was a decidedly unremarkable minor hockey career but I loved every minute of it. I knew that whatever I was going to do with my life, it was going to be connected to hockey in some way.

Even my romantic interests as a teenager were influenced, to some degree, by hockey. Before Cindy and I started dating in high school, I was already taking her little brother John, five years younger than me, to shinny. When Cindy asked him what kind of player I was, John said: "Really good, I think he's good enough to play Junior. B." John's scouting prowess most certainly could be questioned—I was actually cut from Sherwood Bassin's Pickering Panthers' Junior. B team when I was seventeen—but there was no doubting John's ability to play the game.

As much as I learned about life from my parents and about hockey from my own experiences as a player, and as much as I've learned of both from being a journalist who covers nothing but hockey, I learned so much from being around my brother-in-law in his formative hockey years and his time in the professional ranks.

When Toronto *Telegram* reporter John Iaboni wrote on Oct. 28, 1971, what is considered the first major newspaper article about (ten-year-old) Wayne Gretzky, after watching him score five goals and two assists in a 7–4 win over the MTHL's Toronto Kings, my future brother-in-law got a mention in the article. Iaboni wrote:

"[Gretzky's] Steelers were in front after the second period, but center John Goodwin, by far the Kings' best player, tied the score after 32 seconds of the final period. But Gretzky won the game with goals at 9:08, 12:28 and 14:59."

John played the game at a high level, but he wasn't a prototypical minor hockey star. He was as skinny as they come and he certainly wasn't the fastest skater, but he had vision and smarts and skills and could always score and create offense.

I first watched him play minor bantam with the Don Mills Flyers and saw his teammate, a young Larry Murphy, prepare to embark on a Hall of Fame career. I watched him play bantam and midget with Wexford, playing against Paul Coffey, Steve Ludzik, Daryl Evans, Greg Gilbert and others.

It seemed to me that life in the Goodwin household—father Tom and mother Mary, the baby Johnny and his three sisters, Joanne, Susie and Cindy—pretty much revolved around John's hockey. My father-in-law Tom was a (Crazy?) Hockey Dad. John can still hear him yelling, "Skate," and threatening to tape John's gloves to his stick if John insisted on skating with one hand on it all the time. My mother-in-law, Mary, may suggest otherwise—sorry, Mrs. G—but she can still tell you which coaches cut John from which team.

John's minor hockey even impacted on my career path. I ultimately ended up at the Sault *Star*, in large part because I was in Sault Ste. Marie with John's Wexford team for the Air Canada Cup midget championship playoffs. John was taken in the sixth round of the OHL draft by the Soo Greyhounds and he made the team just as that Gretzky kid left to play in the WHA.

For a kid who couldn't skate, John did all right, and then some. He beat out Sudbury goalie Don Beaupre for OHL rookie-of-the-year honors in 1978–79, scoring 43 goals and 125 points to finish top five in OHL scoring for the last-place Greyhounds.

It turned out to be the best of times and the worst of times. In John's final year of junior, he won the OHL scoring championship with 56 goals and 166 points and the Greyhounds came within a hair of taking the OHL championship, losing to the Kitchener Rangers of Brian Bellows and Al MacInnis vintage. In spite of his impressive accomplishments, John wasn't selected in the 1981 NHL entry draft. The scouts said he couldn't skate well enough; he wasn't strong enough. He was devastated. So was I. He wasn't at the draft in Montreal, but I was. I imagine there may be worse hockey-related kicks in the teeth than that one, but I'm not sure I can come up with one, to be honest.

That day had a large impact on me. I realized then what a hard life or business hockey can be. I learned a lot by covering junior hockey for the Sault *Star*, but not half as much as being intimately involved in the ups and downs of a family member who was trying to make his way in the game. Over the ensuing years—John signed as a free agent with the Montreal Canadiens and had a six-year minor pro career that included time in Nova Scotia, New Haven, St. Catharines and Peoria—I had a front-row seat to the good, the bad and the ugly of the true minor-league experience.

John never made it to the NHL, although he played with many who would. The other centers in his first year in Nova Scotia were Guy Carbonneau and Dan Daoust. They were replaced by Brian Skrudland and John Chabot. John only ever played in one NHL preseason game for the Canadiens, in Halifax, and that was after he'd already been sent down, but he evolved into a responsible, hardworking, two-way checking center who could still put up good numbers and satisfy the many demands of legendary tough-guy coach John Brophy, for whom John played in four of his six pro seasons. John won a Turner Cup championship playing for the Peoria Rivermen in 1985, playing through the playoffs with a broken orbital bone.

John finally decided to give it up in 1987 and start at a career at Ontario Hydro, where he still works today (although he did put up some very good numbers as both an assistant coach—first to Stan Butler and then Bill Stewart—and head coach of the Oshawa Generals).

I'm sometimes asked by people who I consider to be the best player who never played a game in the NHL. The answer for me is too easy—it's my brother-in-law, John Goodwin.

I've made his story—the abridged version anyway—part of my story here for the very simple reason that it is. I mean, between how my parents raised me, my own less-than-stellar experiences as a player, witnessing John's life in the game, to say nothing of my career path and my involvement with Mike's and Shawn's hockey, well, I never really had a chance to be anything but…

You know…Crazy Hockey Dad.

EPILOGUE

NOW THAT THE STORY is all down here in black and white—hopefully, as promised, an unvarnished look at the good, the bad and the ugly of multiple lifetimes in minor hockey—I am not quite sure what to make of it. I look back at all of it and ask myself, what would I change?

Honestly, probably not a lot.

Hey, if I could snap my fingers right now and Shawn's headaches were gone, you know I would do it in a heartbeat. He wouldn't have had to stop playing hockey and lacrosse at age fourteen and he wouldn't feel like he was cheated out of a lot of really good times in what should have been the best and most carefree years of his life.

I don't blame hockey for what happened to Shawn. I blame plain old dumb bad luck. Lots of people get a cross to bear in life; Shawn's was concussions and a migraine-related condition that was triggered by one of them. It could be a lot better; it could be a lot worse. I'm not pleased with how it ended for

Shawn—in a stupid minor hockey fight that didn't mean a damn thing—but if it hadn't happened in a hockey game, I really do believe it would have, given Shawn's propensity for hitting his head even outside of organized sports, happened while he was doing something else—riding a bike, snowboarding, wakeboarding, whatever....

If I were able to do it all over again, I would like to think I'm wise enough now to not pick up Mike by his hockey sweater on the bench in Kitchener that day, to not send him crying into the house by threatening to cut him and that I would not run down those stairs to foolishly get into it with Larry Labelle. But, truthfully, I couldn't guarantee you I wouldn't. You do what you think is right at the time, by you and your family, and hope like hell it all turns out for the best. That's the hard part of being a parent. Besides, in real life, you don't get do-overs.

But here's what I do know to be true. Cindy and I love our kids more than anything in this world. I'm confident they feel the same way about us. Our family unit is amazing, the bond between all of us is so strong.

The best times in life are when the four of us are all together as a family and, whatever it says about us, those times have often been set against the backdrop of something hockey-related.

My only fear in writing the book—and telling the crazy stories that entertain, amuse or irritate you—is you may not fully realize how many wonderful occasions there were when we were all just together having a terrific time. No conflict. No morality plays. No metaphors for life. Those stories aren't going to sell a book or keep you interested for long, but most of what our family experienced in sporting endeavors, and in everything else we did for that matter, were warm and tender family moments, the memories of which will last a lifetime.

I will tell you this—for all the specific errors in judgment I may have made, I feel no need to apologize for giving our kids a lifestyle that revolved primarily around minor sports, especially hockey. For the longest time, there were only two seasons in our house—hockey and lacrosse—and we embraced them both, highly anticipating the shift from one to another. It really is a way of life—you either get it or you don't—and I believe with all my heart the boys have no regrets in that regard. Neither do I.

For us, it was never meant to be only about hockey as much as it was the whole value system and the virtues by which we wanted our kids to live their lives. Whatever foul-ups, bleeps and blunders I committed, when I think of the lifetime of friendships and relationships Mike, Shawn, Cindy and I have experienced directly as a result of the boys playing hockey and lacrosse, I can't imagine trading any of that for anything. And neither can they, I'm sure, to say nothing of so many others who have willingly and passionately embraced the same so-very-Canadian lifestyle that we tend to wear like a badge of honor.

As for the judgment of whether I'm capital-C Crazy, it's not so difficult to make that call. If you are someone who is not immersed in the minor hockey culture, it's a no-brainer—you will say, "Dial 9-1-1, this guy is certifiable." But if you've spent any amount of time in the rinks over the years, you will have read the stories I've written here and say, "Pffft, that's nuthin', I know a hundred guys crazier than him."

In the end, it doesn't really matter. I'm comfortable with it either way.

Besides, it's probably fair to say I'm in the twilight of being a Crazy Hockey Dad. There's a part of me that is actually looking forward to spending more time with Cindy, and the boys, at our beautiful second home on Balsam Lake, far away from the din of the lacrosse and hockey arenas.

As long as Mike plays, though, I won't be relinquishing my title, trust me on that. And if, after Mike is finished playing, I still need my fix, I can always live vicariously through a new generation of Hockey Dads. My near and dear friend and TSN colleague Pierre McGuire is just getting started on his own magical ride with his son Ryan. They have much to look forward to as they author their own father and son story.

I used to think when our boys were all done, Stu Seedhouse, Kevin O'Brien and I might go back and do the whole minor hockey coaching thing all over again with a new crop of kids. You know, the Three Amigos ride again. But I don't honestly see that happening. Been there, done that; our time has come and almost gone.

We're much more likely to get together over a few cocktails at the lake and reflect on the good old days and what turned out to be quite the odyssey for all us.

Where the boys are concerned, I would like to believe Mike will be able to take what he's learned from playing the game as long as he has and apply it to his life in such a way he'll be successful in whatever he chooses to do. I would also like to think Shawn will be able to take all the adversity he has had to overcome and use that experience to make him stronger and better in his pursuits.

There are no words and not enough of them if there were to say how proud I am of my family: Mike, for having a passion and work ethic that do not allow him to give up on being the best he can be; Shawn, for picking himself up time after time because of physical ailments and emotional scars no teenage kid should have to deal with; and, last but not least, Cindy, for being an incredibly supportive mother and wife, who is always there for everyone in the family.

As for me and what I've learned? Oh, that's easy.

Don't let your foot get in the way of the coin toss....

Seriously, though....

When the game is over, regardless of what has transpired on the ice or whatever emotions may be welling up inside you, be sure to give your kid a hug and make sure he's okay, make sure he's healthy. As long as that is the case, it's all good, really good, because he's going to get another chance to go out and do it all over again.

You can't ask for any more than that. At the end of each day, it's all that really matters, in hockey as in life. I know that now.

And, believe me, there is nothing crazy about that.